Managing Complexity and Change in SMEs

Managing Complexity and Change in SMEs

Frontiers in European Research

Edited by

Poul Rind Christensen

Aarhus School of Business, Denmark

Flemming Poulfelt

Copenhagen Business School, Denmark

Edward Elgar

Cheltenham, UK • Northampton, MA, USA

Published by
Edward Elgar Publishing Limited
Glensanda House
Montpellier Parade
Cheltenham
Glos GL50 1UA
UK

Edward Elgar Publishing, Inc.
136 West Street
Suite 202
Northampton
Massachusetts 01060
USA

A catalogue record for this book
is available from the British Library

Library of Congress Cataloguing-in-Publication Data

Managing complexity and change in SMEs: frontiers in European research/
edited by Poul Rind Christensen, Flemming Poulfelt.
p. cm.
Includes bibliographical references and index.
1. Small business—Management. 2. Small business—Europe—
Management. I. Christensen, Poul Rind. II. Poulfelt, Flemming.
HD62.7.M3473 2006
658.02'2—dc22

2006012797

ISBN-13: 978 1 84542 908 9
ISBN-10: 1 84542 908 7

Printed and bound in Great Britain by MPG Books Ltd, Bodmin, Cornwall

Contents

List of contributors vii
Acknowledgements xi

Introduction 1
Poul Rind Christensen and Flemming Poulfelt

1 One decade later: following up the 'Gröna Kvisten' prize-winning growth firms 10
Leona Achtenhagen, Jenny Helin, Leif Melin and Lucia Naldi

2 New business early performance: differences between firms started by novice, serial and portfolio entrepreneurs 35
Gry Agnete Alsos, Lars Kolvereid and Espen John Isaksen

3 Small firms' relationships and knowledge acquisition: an empirical investigation 50
Mariachiara Colucci and Manuela Presutti

4 The evolution of firms created by the Swedish science and technology labour force, 1990–2000 69
Frédéric Delmar, Karin Hellerstedt and Karl Wennberg

5 Innovation and the characteristics of cooperating and non-cooperating small firms 103
Mark Freel

6 Complex explanations of order creation, emergence and sustainability as situated entrepreneurship 136
Ted Fuller and Lorraine Warren

7 Extreme entrepreneurs: challenging the institutional framework 156
Bengt Johannisson and Caroline Wigren

8 Debriefing and motivating knowledge workers in small IT firms: challenges to leadership 180
Mette Mønsted

9 Business angels investing at early stages: are they different? 198
Nils Månsson and Hans Landström

10 Internationalization of new ventures: mediating role of entrepreneur and top management team experience 220
Johanna Pulkkinen

Index 259

Contributors

Leona Achtenhagen is Associate Professor of Strategy and Organization at the departments of Entrepreneurship, Marketing and Management as well as the Media Management and Transformation Center at Jönköping International Business School. Her research interests include organizing and strategizing in SMEs, especially media firms, as well as different issues related to processes of continuous growth.

Gry Agnete Alsos is Senior Researcher at Nordland Research Institute, Bodø, Norway. She is also a doctoral candidate at Bodø Graduate School of Business, from where she received her Master of Science in Business in 1992 and her Master of Research in 2002. Her current research interests include processes of entrepreneurship, entrepreneurial experience and gender aspects of entrepreneurship.

Poul Rind Christensen is Professor of Small Business Management and Entrepreneurship at the Aarhus School of Business, Denmark. He is Vice-Chairman at the International Danish Entrepreneurship Academy (IDEA) and also a board member of the European Council for Small Business and Entrepreneurship (ECSB). Current research themes are around global entrepreneurship and relationship management in SMEs.

Mariachiara Colucci is Assistant Professor at the Department of Management of the University of Bologna (Italy), where she earned her PhD in Business Administration. Her current research interests focus on make-or-buy decisions and interfirm relationships, using quantitative methods.

Frédéric Delmar is a Professor at the Strategy and Organization Department at EM Lyon, France. He is also affiliated to the Center for Entrepreneurship and Business Creation, Stockholm School of Economics in Sweden where he also took his PhD. His main research interest lies in the early development of new ventures as well as organizational growth. His work has been published in a number of journals such as *Strategic Management Journal*, *Journal of Business Venturing*, *Entrepreneurship Theory and Practice*, and *Entrepreneurship and Regional Development*, and in books.

Mark Freel is an Associate Professor in Innovation and Entrepreneurship at the School of Management at the University of Ottawa. His current research interests are concerned with various aspects of the small firms – innovation nexus and with issues of economic development more generally.

Ted Fuller is Professor of Entrepreneurship and Strategic Foresight. He is Head of the Centre for Entrepreneurship and Small Business Development at Teesside University Business School, UK. His current research and consulting interests include enterprise development, sustainability and education, and theoretical work on complexity, social capital and foresight.

Jenny Helin is a PhD candidate in Business Administration at the Entrepreneurship, Marketing and Management Department at Jönköping International Business School. Her research interests focus on the role of communication in organizations in general, and related to growth processes of SMEs, and especially family firms, more specifically.

Karin Hellerstedt is a PhD candidate at the Entrepreneurship, Marketing and Management Department at Jönköping International Business School. Her main research interest lies within the area of knowledge-intensive entrepreneurship and entrepreneurial teams.

Espen John Isaksen is currently an Associate Professor at Bodø Graduate School of Business, Norway. He received his PhD from Bodø Graduate School of Business in 2006. His current research interests focus on entrepreneurial intentions and new small business performance.

Bengt Johannisson is Professor of Entrepreneurship and Business Development at Växjö University in Sweden. Since 1998 he has been the editor-in-chief of *Entrepreneurship and Regional Development*. He has published several books (mainly in Swedish) and a number of articles on entrepreneurship and family business in general, and from a territorial perspective in particular. Until recently Bengt Johannisson was the Head of the Entrepreneurship Programme at Växjö University. Since 1995 he has co-organized the European Doctoral Programme in Entrepreneurship and Small Business Management, and in 2001 he initiated a national doctoral network.

Lars Kolvereid is a Professor of Entrepreneurship at Bodø Graduate School of Business, Norway. He received his PhD from Henley Management College, UK. Current research interests include studies of entrepreneurial intentions, nascent entrepreneurs and new businesses.

Hans Landström is Professor of Entrepreneurship and Venture Finance at the Institute of Economic Research, Lund University School of Economics and Management, Sweden. He received his Doctorate in Industrial Economics from Lund Institute of Technology. He is a founding member of the Executive Group of the Center for Innovation, Research and Competence in the Learning Economy (CIRCLE), and responsible for programmes and courses in innovation and entrepreneurship at Lund University. His research interests include venture capital, young technology-based firms, and the development of entrepreneurship as a research field.

Nils Månsson is a PhD student of Entrepreneurship at the Department of Business Administration at the School of Economics and Management, Lund University, Sweden. He is currently writing his PhD thesis on business angels and how their investments are influenced by networks.

Leif Melin is Professor of Strategy and Organization at the Department of Entrepreneurship, Marketing and Management, and Director of the Center for Family Enterprise and Ownership at Jönköping International Business School, Sweden. His current research interests are strategizing and strategy as practice, continuously growing business firms, family business ownership and strategic change in family businesses.

Mette Mønsted is Professor of Knowledge Management at the Department of Management, Politics and Philosophy at Copenhagen Business School, Denmark. She is Director of the Doctoral School on Knowledge and Management. Her research interests include networking strategies of small firms, management of innovation processes in small high-tech firms, and innovation and research management under high levels of uncertainty. Her empirical research in recent years has been in small IT, biotech and multimedia firms, as well as research-based large firms.

Lucia Naldi is taking her PhD in Business Administration at Jönköping International Business School. Her PhD thesis focuses on growth of international SMEs. She is also a Lecturer in Strategic Management and Marketing at Jönköping International Business School and at Stockholm School of Economics in Riga.

Flemming Poulfelt is Professor of Management and Strategy, Vice-Dean of Research Communication and Director of the LOK Research Centre at the Copenhagen Business School, Denmark. His current research and consulting interests focus on managing professional service firms, knowledge management, strategic management, change management and management consulting.

Manuela Presutti obtained a PhD in Business Administration at the University of Bologna, Italy. At the moment she is Assistant Professor at the Department of Management of Bologna. She teaches Management and Strategy at the University of Rimini. Her main research interests include social capital, entrepreneurship, industrial clusters and internationalization of firms.

Johanna Pulkkinen is a Researcher in the Department of Marketing at the University of Vaasa, Finland. She has also earned her MSc (Econ.) and is finishing her doctoral degree in Marketing and International Business at the University of Vaasa. Her main research interests include entrepreneurship, internationalization and small firms. In these fields special focus areas are experience, entrepreneurial orientation, international orientation and new venture internationalization.

Lorraine Warren is a Senior Lecturer in Entrepreneurship at the University of Southampton in the UK. Her current research interests include the histories of emergent technologies and knowledge networks, and theoretical work on innovation, complex systems and entrepreneurial identity.

Karl Wennberg is a PhD candidate at the Center for Entrepreneurship and Business Creation, Stockholm School of Economics. His research interests include entrepreneurial performance and failure, as well as real options theory in strategic management and entrepreneurship.

Caroline Wigren received her PhD from Jönköping International Business School in Sweden, where she holds a position as a research fellow. Her main research interests are entrepreneurship and regional development, and she has a genuine interest in methodological issues, with a focus on qualitative methods and interactive research.

Acknowledgements

We wish to thank the European Council for Small Business and Entrepreneurship (ECSB) and all the reviewers who helped us with selecting the chapters and taking them through a thorough review process, in this way guaranteeing a high level of professionalism in the volume.

Introduction

Poul Rind Christensen and Flemming Poulfelt

Entrepreneurs and small businesses of today are living in a world marked by major transitions.

However, the current transitions in society are viewed though different lenses and thus a diversified and complex puzzle of images of the changing world are delivered to the research community, to entrepreneurs and to the small business community. In fact, major transitions are brought to life by entrepreneurs themselves, since they play a major role as agents of change.

The globalizing society is a stream of created images. The knowledge society is another, and yet others emphasize the digital revolution with the many images of what is to come.

While entrepreneurs are to be seen as vehicles of change, they are also caged by these transitional changes. The process of setting up new enterprises and making them grow and prosper is a far more complex undertaking today than just a few decades ago.

In Europe, as well as in other parts of the world, the sluggish economic perspectives have, at the same time, turned public awareness towards small businesses as vehicles of growth. The same wishful thinking is associated with the potentialities of entrepreneurial ventures.

Research in entrepreneurship and small business management has therefore received increased attention in order to understand better the role played by entrepreneurs and new businesses in bringing about growth and – not least – in order to gain improved insight into the logic of small business management in times of high complexity and turbulence. What can a wider community learn from their ways of organizing and managing new ventures and growing enterprises?

The increased focus on and importance of small and medium-sized enterprises (SMEs) for the renewal of the industrial structure have influenced entrepreneurial research. The field of entrepreneurship and small business studies has prospered and grown considerably during the past few years in all European countries. Remarkable developments have taken place in research frameworks and methodologies. The fundamental scientific discussion continues to unfold new theoretical perspectives as well as new aspects of the discipline. Simultaneously we have witnessed entrepreneurship research enter into new emerging fields. The field of globalization and the corresponding theme of Born Global entrepreneurs, and also the field of institutional entrepreneurship, are cases at hand illustrating important fields of expansion.

Progress in the field of entrepreneurship is not only triggered by the exchange of ideas and new analyses inside the research community. It is also triggered by the growing emphasis on entrepreneurship in policy agendas and business communities all over Europe. It has stimulated dialogue between the research community and communities of practice.

RENT XVIII in Copenhagen in November 2004 was organized to stimulate dialogue and reflections on progress in the field of entrepreneurship. The RENT conference in Copenhagen presented a programme comprising 161 papers organized in 38 sessions within the 17 RENT streams. Through a thorough review process of all contributions ten papers were selected and revised to be included as chapters in the present volume.

INTRODUCTION TO THE THEMES AND THE CONTRIBUTIONS

The chapters included in this volume explore three themes, representing different dimensions and images of the overall theme of complexity and change.

The first theme is institutional boundaries. A major emphasis in this theme is on how entrepreneurs cope with the institutional setting in which they are embedded, and also how entrepreneurs play the role of change agents in a wider societal meaning of the concept, thus fostering changes in institutional boundaries.

In the second theme – evolutionary perspectives on performance – studies on entrepreneurial performance are in focus. Different factors influencing performance – experience, ownership status, initial size and line of industry, for example – are analysed in a time perspective.

In the third and final theme – managerial complexity – the contributions analyse several dimensions of managerial complexity. All contributions, in one way or another, reflect on themes highlighting managerial and organizational complexity in a changing context. Focus is put on the theme of managing internationalization in new businesses, the challenge of innovation management, knowledge acquisition and knowledge management in small firms.

INSTITUTIONAL BOUNDARIES

Chapter 6 by Ted Fuller and Lorraine Warren – 'Complex explanations of order creation, emergence and sustainability as situated entrepreneurship' – has the aim of improving our understanding of the dynamics of entrepreneurship and those mechanisms leading to the formation of new ventures in specific contexts.

A model of the situated processes of emergence is proposed, based on the theoretical framework of complexity analyses. This model is grounded in the two case studies included and the theoretical framework outlined. The chapter illustrates how the entrepreneurs' engagement in reflexive interactions with actors in their network of relations, as well as inside the enterprise, shape emergent structures and images of the 'enterprise in context'.

A significant outcome of this contribution is a new and more faceted explanation of entrepreneurial emergence, emphasizing the situated dynamics of entrepreneurial processes. It is demonstrated that the results of entrepreneurial activities are complex (non-deterministic) and pre-equilibrium.

The authors conclude their chapter with reflections on limitations in their empirical foundation and suggestions for further research.

The ambition in chapter 7 – 'Extreme entrepreneurs: challenging the institutional framework', by Bengt Johannisson and Caroline Wigren – is to reconstruct the entrepreneurial subject with the help of institutional theory.

Johannisson and Wigren argue that, while institutions are seen to provide the rules of the game and also, in the mainstream of research contributions, are seen to define the appearance of entrepreneurial activities in society, rule breaking is a fundamental characteristic of entrepreneurship. However, although rules may be broken, at the same time they also cage or limit entrepreneurial action.

However, a few entrepreneurs act as agents of institutional change and thus do challenge fundamental established institutions by their creative way of organizing activities and actions. In this contribution four change agents from different arenas in society are introduced and portrayed. They are all living examples of what the authors call 'extreme entrepreneurs'. Extreme entrepreneurs are conceptualized as public persons, visible in the media and in public settings far beyond their professional community.

Based on the portraits of the four extreme entrepreneurs, the authors search for the phenomenon that constitutes the extreme entrepreneur *per se*. A list of six different characteristics are outlined, reflected on and discussed.

In the concluding section of the contribution, the agenda for studying extreme entrepreneurs is briefly outlined. It is argued that this stream of research has importance, since the study of extreme entrepreneurs may highlight mainstream understanding, theorize on entrepreneurial action and make us better understand the lack of entrepreneurship in specific markets or national and local cultural spheres and contexts.

Nils Månsson and Hans Landström develop a typology of business angels in chapter 9, 'Business angels investing at early stages: are they different?' The authors have based their study on a large database in order to find an empirical foundation for the typology.

In the typology outlined, the authors make a distinction between early-stage and late-stage investors. They find that early-stage investors believe that knowledge of the entrepreneurial process is most important, and late-stage investors believe that personal experience of the specific industry or technology is the most important.

Based on their empirical data material the authors conclude that early-stage investors are relatively more entrepreneurial and also less passive in providing managerial knowledge to the enterprises they invest in, than is the case for late-stage investors. The latter are, on their side, more adverse to risks than early-stage investors. Early-stage investors, on the other hand, seem to be more oriented to investments in ventures on their local scene.

Based on their study the two authors discuss institutional differences between Sweden – also representing several continental European countries – and the institutional framework in the US and the UK.

However, the basic theoretical contribution from the study is that it is established that there are two distinct groups of business angels. They find differences in motives, in their way of handling risk and also in their target ventures for their investments.

EVOLUTIONARY PERSPECTIVES ON PERFORMANCE

In chapter 2 by Gry Agnete Alsos, Lars Kolvereid and Espen John Isaksen – 'New business early performance: differences between firms started by novice, serial and portfolio entrepreneurs' – differences in performance of new enterprises started by three types of entrepreneurs are analysed. The three types of entrepreneurs are novice, serial and portfolio entrepreneurs.

The aim of the study is to explore whether firms owned by the more experienced entrepreneurs – the serial and portfolio business founders – perform better than those founded by novice and inexperienced entrepreneurs.

The underlying proposition is that experienced entrepreneurs have gained learning from former ventures. Therefore they may be better off in identifying and judging viable business opportunities, acquiring resources and utilizing available resources, for example.

The authors specifically focus on the acquisition of resources for the new venture and also on the impact on business performance.

The study is based on an imperial investigation. Data were collected from founders of new businesses shortly after they were established. Data were again collected 19 months after the first survey.

The authors' conclusions from their analyses indicate that experienced founders are superior in the acquisition of resources *vis-à-vis* novice entrepreneurs and that this is also the case for their relatively higher performance in relation to novice entrepreneurs.

As indicated in the title of chapter 4 – 'The evolution of firms created by the Swedish science and technology labour force, 1990–2000' – Frédéric Delmar, Karin Hellerstedt and Karl Wennberg investigate evolutionary traits among firms started and owned by people from the science and technology labour force in Sweden in the 1990s.

It is suggested that the science and technology labour force is in a position of high access to new technological knowledge. The economic behaviour of the science and technology labour force – not least the entrepreneurial activity among members of the group – is seen as an important link in the explanation of how new technological knowledge is exploited and converted into growth.

Therefore this study takes interest in understanding the magnitude of the entrepreneurial activities among members of the science and technology labour force and how these activities are related indicators of growth.

The study is based on register data from Statistics Sweden and comprises more than 7700 *de novo* enterprises started in the period of time in focus. The main focus of the study is on entry, survival (and exit) and growth in employment among *de novo* firms included in the data material.

Main results from the study show that industry affiliations, the legal form of the enterprise and its size at the start of the venture have long-lasting effects on survival and growth. However, it is also concluded that the economic impact of the new enterprises is limited.

The chapter is concluded with theoretical as well as practical implications of the study. It is emphasized that the study has led to new insights in relation to endogenous growth theory, entrepreneurship theory and industrial organization theory.

Practical implications outlined include such issues as the need for entrepreneurial activity among members of the science and technology labour force, the role of career patterns among science and technology personnel and the role of incentives to promote entrepreneurial activities. Finally, policy perspectives are discussed.

Chapter 1 by Leona Achtenhagen, Jenny Helin, Leif Melin and Lucia Naldi entitled 'One decade later: following up the "Gröna Kvisten" prize-winning growth firms' is based on the ambition to expand the knowledge of continuous growth processes.

Quantitative studies have undoubtedly added to our understanding of growth in SMEs. However, there is a lack of more qualitative studies to expand our understanding of what happens in companies during growth processes. This study is a qualitative investigation in growth processes.

The empirical foundation of the study consists of the enterprises who received the 'Gröna Kvisten' prize in the years 1993–96 – a prize given to fast-growing SMEs. The study thus follows the growth patterns and processes of all 30 award-winning enterprises from that period.

The aim of the chapter is to trace different patterns of growth, to analyse these patterns of growth processes, and to enhance the understanding of the interplay of growth processes and internal organization – thus going a step beyond studies that investigate the impact of determinants on growth and outcome.

The study makes four interesting contributions. Firstly, it fills a gap in the current body of literature on growth, which largely neglects internal growth processes. Various growth processes in companies are mapped, illustrating changes over time.

Secondly, the study adds rich empirical data to the understanding of different growth processes by providing insights into continuously growing companies across different industries.

Thirdly, it employs a method – the inverse or Q-type factor analysis – which is seldom used but seems to have potential in detecting growth patterns across firms.

And fourthly, the study reframes some common assumptions about growth.

MANAGERIAL COMPLEXITY

In chapter 8 by Mette Mønsted: 'Debriefing and motivating knowledge workers in small IT-firms: challenges to leadership', the focus is on the conditions for managing in complex organizational contexts.

The perspective of the chapter is to illustrate the complexity of management and leadership as a negotiated relationship in complex small IT firms. The conditions are demanding and complex and the knowledge workers are determined to be self-managing. This creates a high level of complexity with challenges to existing management roles.

The empirical part of the study is based on a case study of a small multimedia firm, which was studied longitudinally for 2.5 years. During this period the method of video interviewing was used.

The chapter focuses on managing knowledge workers. This is a delicate balance between motivation and coordination, between playfulness and efficiency. Therefore the chapter outlines and discusses some of the dilemmas to which the manager is exposed.

The chapter also discusses the issue of leadership, as the manager is responsible for division of labour, but lacks insight as he is not highly competent when it comes to the content of the professional issues. He is dependent on the knowledge worker's insight to assure the replicability and the explicitation of knowledge.

The knowledge workers such as 'nerds' and 'stars' among programmers are the highly valued knowledge workers, and probably very efficient at solving certain tasks and creating commitment. However, it is difficult to control them to make it economically feasible when projects have to meet deadlines and be sold. Thus this type of relationship sharpens the attention to different roles of leadership and the need for management and economic control.

The chapter focuses on the managerial implications of asymmetric knowledge, and handling complex knowledge. It therefore emphasizes that the role of the management in knowledge-intensive firms could be seen as a negotiation and social construction of power in communication with subordinates.

Mariachiara Colucci and Manuela Presutti discuss the role of social capital as a resource in SMEs in chapter 3, 'Small firms' relationships and knowledge acquisition: an empirical investigation'.

The purpose of the chapter is to illustrate the value of social capital and how social capital can facilitate external knowledge acquisition in the customer relationships of small firms.

Based upon a sample of 212 vertical dyadic relationships based in Italy, the chapter examines the effects on knowledge acquisition of social capital in small firms' business relationships. Building on social capital and network theories, the chapter proposes that social capital enhances external knowledge acquisition in customer relationships, and that such knowledge improves the value of these business networks.

According to an embeddedness perspective, the study has chosen the vertical dyadic relationships between a small firm and its customers as the level of analysis, considering social capital to be a source of value inherent in social structural arrangements.

The direction of the empirical findings supports the hypothesis that small firms consider external networks as a resource to get access to external resources and knowledge in order to compensate for their restricted internal portfolio of both tangible and intangible resources.

The results suggest that the structural dimension of social capital is positively associated with knowledge acquisition, while high levels of relational dimension limit the process of diffusion and spread of valuable information among partners, with a negative impact on knowledge acquisition.

The study also indicates that the third dimension of social capital, the cognitive one, is highly correlated with the relational dimension, showing the redundancy of information of the two constructs.

In chapter 10 by Johanna Pulkkinen – 'Internationalization of new ventures: mediating role of entrepreneur and top management team experience' (awarded the Best Paper at the conference) – the focus is on internationalization of new ventures and managerial experiences.

The aim of the study is to explore the link between international experience of the entrepreneur and the top management team, and the internationalization of these new ventures. Experience is regarded as a mediator of international new venture (INV) development through its influence on specific decisions and the use of strategies that might explain these firms' development.

The empirical findings of the study are based on survey data of 211 exporting Finnish SMEs and qualitative case studies of eight Finnish INVs from different fields of industry.

The theoretical base of the chapter is developed through combining approaches in international business, management and entrepreneurship fields, with special focus on SME research as INVs are regarded as a special type of SME. This leads to four hypotheses for the relationship between experience and internationalization, all suggesting that higher, prior, international experiences will have a positive impact on the internationalization processes of the firm.

The results give at least partial support to all hypotheses, indicating that the experience level in itself is directly related to the internationalization degree of the venture. It also reveals that in firms where the management has gained prior, international experience, this capital has been used in decision-making concerning the initiation of international operations of the current venture, as such being an important driver.

Mark Freel's chapter 5, 'Innovation and the characteristics of cooperating and non-cooperating small firms', focuses on the 'who' and 'why' of innovation networking.

The aim of the study is to contribute to an improved awareness of the characteristics of cooperative innovators in terms of both their resources and their strategic intent.

The study draws upon data from a large-scale survey of northern British SMEs including 1345 small firms.

The chapter identifies the characteristics of firms engaged in innovation-related cooperation with a variety of partners. The definition of innovation-related cooperation is broader than in similar motivated studies This means that the interest is in 'innovation-related activity including marketing and training and/or technology transfer' and not, narrowly, in R&D. To this end, innovation-related cooperation appears to be a far more widely distributed phenomenon than one might suppose.

The study points to considerable variation in the characteristics associated with cooperation by innovation partners. Whilst firm-size, R&D intensity and 'high-techedness' are generally thought to positively influence the propensity to engage in R&D cooperation, their influence over innovation-related cooperation is far more restricted.

1. One decade later: following up the 'Gröna Kvisten' prize-winning growth firms

Leona Achtenhagen, Jenny Helin, Leif Melin and Lucia Naldi

INTRODUCTION

The extensive public debate on how to foster growth is mirrored in the number of academic studies investigating determinants driving or limiting firm growth. These studies vary in their degree of comprehensiveness – from those testing the impact of just one or several isolated factors on growth, to more comprehensive multilevel models of growth, which also take into consideration indirect influences of factors (for example Baum et al., 2001). A number of studies also focus on the phenomenon that most companies do not grow (Barth, 2001; Wiklund et al., 2001).

In her seminal study, Penrose characterizes the phenomenon of growth as follows (1959, p. 1):

> The term 'growth' is used in ordinary discourse with two different connotations. It sometimes denotes merely increase in amount; for example, when one speaks of 'growth' in output, export, sales. At other times, however, it is used in its primary meaning implying an increase in size or improvement in quality as a result of a *process* of development, akin to natural biological processes in which an interacting series of internal changes leads to increases in size accompanied by changes in the characteristics of the growing object . . . 'Growth' in this second sense often also has the connotation of 'natural' or 'normal' – a process that will occur whenever conditions are favourable because of the nature of the 'organism'; size becomes a more or less incidental result of a continuous on-going or 'unfolding' process.

She criticizes the fact that in traditional economics growth would only be seen as an adjustment to the size appropriate to given conditions, while neglecting the internal processes leading to growth.

This is not only true for traditional economics. Rather, it is an inherent problem of many of the studies analysing determinants of growth, and largely due to their purely quantitative nature – for a quantitative study, data has to be assessed at one (or several) specific point(s) of time and operationalized into variables. However, explanatory qualitative information on these data is largely missing. As we will demonstrate below, neglecting qualitative information on organizations' growth processes can lead to a distortion of findings. For example, investing in a company's future might temporarily reduce its profitability. In a quantitative study, this company could end up being considered a failure, as the variable often used to measure growth – profitability – is not pointing upward. Wiklund (1998, p. 87) discusses the difficulty of assessing growth determinants as follows: 'we really do not know how much variables change over the studied time period, and whether or not this is a major problem. Growth, as such, is a change process and it could be that explanatory variables change quite substantially during this process. Until we do know, it must remain an unwise oversimplification to assume that nothing else but size changes'.

While the existing body of largely quantitative studies on growth is undeniably important, we still remain with a very limited understanding of what actually happens in companies during their growth processes. We clearly need a better understanding of the processes and patterns of growth. The aim of our chapter is to trace different patterns of growth and to analyse these patterns of growth processes. Each organization is unique – nonetheless, different typical patterns of growth can be identified. With this study, we aim to enhance the understanding of the interplay of growth processes and the internal organization, and thus go one step beyond studies investigating the impact of determinants on growth as an outcome.

The remainder of this chapter is structured as follows. We will first review the body of literature discussing processes and patterns of growth. Building on our criticism of that literature, we will present our empirical study of 30 companies that have received prizes for their successful growth between 1993 and 1996. We will map, categorize and analyse the growth processes and patterns of these companies. Thereby, we make the following contributions: (1) we fill a gap in the current body of literature on growth, which largely neglects internal growth processes; we map different growth processes of companies, and illustrate how these change over time; (2) we add rich empirical data to the understanding of different growth processes by providing insights into continuously growing companies across different industries; (3) for detecting growth patterns across firms, we employ a method which has strong potential but has so far rarely been utilized; (4) we question some common assumptions about growth companies.

PROCESSES AND PATTERNS OF GROWTH

Different bodies of literature exist which are concerned with the processes and patterns of growth (see discussion in Aldrich, 1999, p. 196–201). As pointed out by Van de Ven and Poole (1995), much of this growth literature is presented in the form of life-cycle or stage models (for example Greiner, 1972; Galbraith, 1982; Churchill and Lewis, 1983; Quinn and Cameron, 1983; Scott and Bruce, 1987; Kazanjian, 1988). Although the idea of sequential phases of growth has been questioned by different authors, these models continue to be predominant in the growth literature. A second body of literature discusses patterns of growth following a configurational approach (Miller, 1986; Miller and Friesen, 1984; Wiklund, 1998, p. 29). Here, attention is devoted to the emergence of configurations of structures, processes and strategies, which do not necessarily follow a determined pattern during growth. The review of these bodies of literature allows for a critical discussion of the shortcomings inherent in the existing concepts of processes and patterns of growth and, thus, illustrates the need for the study presented in this chapter.

Life-Cycle and Stage Models

Many different authors have conceptualized organizational growth processes based on the metaphor of organizational development as a biological life-cycle (Van de Ven and Poole, 1995; Aldrich, 1999). It is assumed that organizational growth would occur in a sequence of stages: just like the body of human beings changes over time in a certain pattern, also organizational activities, systems, structures and leadership would evolve through different stages. Concepts referring to this metaphor share certain (implicit or explicit) assumptions. First, the growth of firms is 'imminent', 'that is the developing entity has within it an underlining form, logic, program or code . . . that moves the entity from a given point of departure towards a subsequent and it is prefigured in the present state' (Van de Ven and Poole, 1995, p. 515). Expressed differently, what is elementary at the embryo stage becomes more and more obvious and realized in the following stages. A clear example of this can be found in Adizes's (1988) life-cycle model. Here, the progressive realization of the original business ideas is the imminent logic governing the development of the firm. In addition, firms grow following a unidirectional and cumulative sequence (Van de Ven and Poole, 1995). Growth is unidirectional as the sequence of stages allows a movement in one direction only: from a smaller to a bigger size. With very few exceptions (for example Garnsey, 1998), authors do not discuss periods of 'ungrowth' or reversal of growth as an option for survival. Furthermore, growth is cumulative as the characteristics acquired in previous stages are maintained and built on in later stages. Greiner (1972), for example, argues that the behaviour of organizations (just like the behaviour of individuals) is determined by past events and experiences. In these terms, each stage is the progenitor of the following ones.

A number of models follow through the analogy between organizational development and the 'seasons of a man's life' (Levinson, 1978) from birth to death and, therefore, are often referred to as life-cycle models. Whetten's (1987) work on organizational growth and decline is an example of this type of research, as well as Adizes's (1988) model which distinguishes between the growing and the ageing sides of the life-cycle curve.

However, the decline and death of organizations have received somewhat less attention in the literature than birth and early development (Neumair, 1998). The vast majority of biological models, indeed, focus mainly on the firm's development process up to the maturity stage. These have been referred to as stage or developmental models. The number of stages and sub-stages identified by different scholars varies significantly (O'Farrell and Hitchens, 1988). All models start with an initial stage which is typically characterized by a simple organizational structure and direct supervision, and particular importance is attributed to the founder or entrepreneur. In the following stage, a first division of managerial tasks occurs, but control is still achieved through personal supervision. The subsequent stages are characterized by an increased bureaucratization of the organizational structure and the separation between management and control. Though the authors of different concepts try to differentiate their contributions by stressing one or several factors, a number of structural and contextual characteristics are generally included in life-cycle and stage models (cf. Quinn and Cameron, 1983). Common structural dimensions are structural form, formalization, centralization and number of organizational levels. Age, size and growth rate are the contextual dimensions most commonly included (Hanks et al., 1993).

The models can be differentiated regarding the assumed drivers for growth and triggers for transition between stages. Some authors see the unfolding of stages as following from the resolution of problematic situations or crises (Hanks et al., 1993). For example, Churchill and Lewis (1983) illustrate the passage from one stage to another in terms of different problems and challenges that need to be addressed, while Greiner (1972) sees the transition between stages as the response to internal crises. Other scholars stress the entrepreneurial nature of organizations and argue that stages are driven by the search for new growth opportunities. Eisenhardt and Bird Schoonhoven (1990), for instance, attribute particular importance to the founding top management team and to their ability to exploit and enhance resources, while McMahon (2001) sees the growth aspiration of

SMEs as a key factor in characterizing their pathway. Smith and Miner (1983) even relate the likelihood of a firm's successfully passing through the initial stages of development to the opportunistic orientation of its founder or entrepreneur.

The concepts can also be differentiated along the assumed development path. Some scholars individuate only a one-way path and suggest that firms progress through certain, specific stages in sequential order (for example Greiner, 1972). Others also consider multiple paths (Adizes, 1988) or contemplate the case in which a firm does not follow the whole development trajectory but halts somewhere in between. Churchill and Lewis (1983), for instance, argue that a firm can remain indefinitely small or medium-sized, given that changes in the environment do not destroy its market niche. McKelvie and Chandler (2002) explain this phenomenon with transaction costs economics.

The shortcomings of models using biological analogies to conceptualize firm growth have been emphasized by many authors. A clear and straightforward critique to these concepts was provided by Edith Penrose in 1952. She states that 'we have no reason what so ever for thinking that the growth pattern of a biological organism is *willed* by the organism itself. On the other hand, we have every reason for thinking that growth of a venture is willed by those who make the decisions' (Penrose, 1952, p. 808). While Penrose's critique refers mainly to the life-cycle concepts, Tornatzky et al. (1983, p. 19) question stage models by arguing that the concept of a stage 'is a distortion of reality'. In the authors' view, the assumption of stages is an intellectual tool which might be useful in simplifying the representation of complex processes, but which says very little about the underlying patterns of decisions and actions. Other critiques relate to the assumption of imminence of growth, which underlies life-cycle and stage models. O'Farrell and Hitchens (1988), for instance, argue that there is no empirical evidence that firms either grow, passing through all the stages, or else fail. In addition, O'Farrell and Hitchens (1988) partly question the unidirectionality of the development process. They wonder whether the sequence of stages is unshirkable or whether, under certain conditions, certain stages could be missed out or their order inverted. Following Stubbart (1992), Melin (1992) points at another problem of stage models: namely their fundamental disregard of individual differences.

Configuration Models of Firm Growth

In an attempt to overcome the shortcomings of assuming a simple linear and sequential logic of firm growth, as inherent in life-cycle and stage models, some scholars have developed complex contingency models, also known as configuration models of firm growth (Kazanjian and Drazin, 1989). Miller and Friesen (1984) can be considered the precursors of this view. After an extensive review of the literature on life-cycle and stage models, these authors identify five common stages (birth, growth, maturity, revival and decline), each of which presents integral complementarities among variables of environment, strategy, structure and decision-making modes. Empirically, Miller and Friesen (1984) find support for the prevalence of certain complementarities between these factors within each stage, but not across stages, in a linear sequence. The authors comment that 'while the stages of the life cycles are internally coherent and very different one another, they are by no means connected to each other in a deterministic way' (Miller and Friesen, 1984, p. 1490). Thus, the passage from one configuration to another would not follow any predetermined path. They even suggest that a maturity phase might be followed by decline and then growth again. However, although Miller and Friesen (1984, p. 1177) attempt to emphasize how 'the latitude for strategic choice may be considerable' and how there would be innumerable developmental paths, this advice has hardly been taken notice of by scholars following the configuration view.

Configuration models have developed in two directions. First, by clustering firms according to demographic characteristics such as their age, size or growth figures, researchers have identified different configurations (or 'gestalts'), each assumed to represent a different stage of the firm's development path (Hanks et al., 1993; McMahon, 2001). Thus, organizations are empirically categorized into a number of configurations. In contradiction to Miller and Friesen's (1984) advice, these configurations are conceptually ranked to at least partly conform to the sequence of stages inherent in life-cycle models (McKelvie and Chandler, 2002). For instance, Hanks et al. (1993) use cluster analysis to derive a taxonomy of growth-stage configurations in a sample of high-technology organizations, and McKelvie and Chandler (2002) provide a similar investigation on a sample of Swedish start-ups. Second, the configuration approach suggested by Miller and Friesen (1984) has also resulted in another type of model, which openly departs from the life-cycle analogy. Wiklund (1998), for instance, acknowledges that life-cycle models could be applicable only to the few firms that display significant growth. Therefore, instead of trying to force firms into one common developmental path, the author focuses on the combination of individual, organizational and environmental characteristics to predict future growth better. Wiklund (1998) provides a complex multilevel model that follows firm development at different points in time.

But even configuration models are not immune to criticism. Taxonomies of configurations, empirically derived and suggestive of life-cycle stages, still share most of the shortcomings inherent in stage models. For example, they display a deterministic view on firm growth and lack attention to the variations in venture development. In addition, most of these studies are cross-sectional and thus only presuppose the temporal link between the different configurations.

THE EMPIRICAL STUDY

Sample

The empirical basis for our study consists of all 30 companies which received the 'Gröna Kvisten' prize (Swedish for 'the green twig') for being successful growth companies. Gröna Kvisten was a prestigious prize handed out during a Swedish TV programme by a qualified jury to profitably growing SMEs in the years 1993 to 1996. Gröna Kvisten was initiated by a well-known Swedish entrepreneur, together with the host of a TV programme called *Stora Pengar* (Swedish for 'Big Money') on channel TV4 in Sweden. Besides TV4, the Gröna Kvisten jury involved *Dagens Industri*, the most important Swedish daily business newspaper, and a board of directors containing people from business, academia and entrepreneurship. The purpose of Gröna Kvisten was to stimulate entrepreneurship in Sweden by enhancing the visibility of successful entrepreneurs and their growth companies in media, thereby creating role models. Growth companies were short-listed for the prize based on the following criteria: (1) the company needed to be a Swedish, entrepreneurially-oriented company; and (2) it needed to have earned a return on capital employed (ROCE) higher than the capital market rate over the previous three years. In a second step, the jury attributed points to the short-listed companies based on more qualitative criteria, such as their environmental profile, market planning, technological development, and management and investment strategies.

As our sample consists of all the 30 companies that have received the Gröna Kvisten prize for their successful growth, all companies in our sample share a number of characteristics: they are all Swedish companies, they have displayed a longer period of high profitability and growth in the early 1990s, and they were (at least then) entrepreneurially oriented. These characteristics make the companies comparable, even though they represent a range of different industries and ownership structures.

As growth is such a societal and political hot topic, many recent empirical studies focus on companies currently displaying (high) growth. In that respect, 'gazelle' companies have received attention in a number of countries. Yet, little is known about their sustainability – high growth is often related to high risk. We follow a different logic: we follow up a group of companies that have received a prize for successful, but often moderate growth, during the decade following their prize-winning. For our research aim, this is more interesting, as groups of companies winning growth prizes nowadays have to display similar patterns during earlier years in order to fulfill selection criteria for such a prize. Thus, our sample gives us the chance to investigate the phenomenon of continuous growth. This in itself can be graded as an important contribution, as many studies on growth are mainly snapshots of young companies or are based on data from a shorter time period. Studies of companies in different maturity phases and over a longer time period have long been requested (for example Miller and Friesen, 1984).

The following data have been collected for this study. We have conducted up to five personal or telephone interviews with each company in the sample, as well as with members of the Gröna Kvisten jury. In addition, we have evaluated the companies' annual reports – as all companies in the sample are incorporated, their annual reports are comparable. Company information such as web pages and publications about the firms has complemented this data. Based on the statistical analyses discussed below, we have grouped the 30 companies into five categories on the basis of the firms' profitability figures between the years 1993 and 2002. Each category displays a different pattern of profitability shared by all companies in that category. It is important to note that this kind of categorization is of course reductionistic, and other measures of growth could lead to different patterns. However, for the purpose of this chapter it seemed important to choose a manner of representing the companies in similar fashion as many contributions on organizational growth have done before (for example McKelvie and Chandler, 2002). The categorization helps us to point out three things. First, given the detailed focus on ten subsequent years, it provides a micro perspective on the firms' profitability development and growth patterns. Life-cycle and stage models present a macro and short-hand illustration of firm development, but say very little about the underlying micro patterns of growth which unfold when looking at more detailed time-spans. As pointed out by Tornatzky et al. (1983, p. 19) such macro representations are 'a distortion of reality'. Second, unlike the suggestion of many stage models, this categorization shows that firms can successfully survive in their businesses even though they are following very different patterns. Third, we illustrate that the interpretation of these patterns without further qualitative information about the company might be misleading. In the following section, we will illustrate the methodology used for deriving categories of similar profitability patterns among the Gröna

Kvisten companies, for the time-span 1993–2002. Thereafter we will present the identified patterns and illustrate them by selected case vignettes of the Gröna Kvisten companies.

Method

We used the inverse or Q-type factor analysis to produce a taxonomy of the Gröna Kvisten companies. Differently from R-factor analysis, Q-factor analysis takes the respondents rather than the variables as a basis, and condenses respondents into distinctly different groups (Ancona and Caldwell, 1992). As pointed out by Miller (1978, p. 525):

> If we view an organization as a point representing its set of scores across all variables in an N-dimensional vector space, then it can be shown that organizations which correlate highly with one another will be clustered together in that space. A factor analysis systematically explores this space, attempting to project factors or 'ideal companies' into areas which are densely occupied by organizations so that as much variance as possible is explained by consecutive factors . . . By definition, any factor . . . will give us groups of ventures which are themselves highly intercorrelated and thus similar in terms of score patterns.

This technique was favoured over the commonly used cluster analysis, because it is more sensitive to patterns among variables (Hair et al., 1995). In other words, it allowed us to identify groups of Gröna Kvisten companies which, over the ten years under study, have demonstrated similar profitability patterns.

Analysis and Results: Identified Patterns of Growth

A Q-factor analysis with a varimax rotation was performed on the 30 Gröna Kvisten companies, using scores on profits from 1993 till 2002. Firms that loaded more than 0.50 on one factor as well as firms whose loadings exhibited the same sign were combined.[1] Three firms were excluded from the analysis as they showed high loadings on more than one factor. Table 1.1 summarizes this analysis and displays the case loadings greater than 0.50.

This analysis identified six distinct groups of companies. Yet, as one group consisted only of two firms, these cases were not considered for the further analysis. For each remaining group, a summated scale of profits was derived by taking the average of the firms' standardized profit scores. The patterns of profits for the five groups of firms are plotted in Figure 1.1.

The pattern of the 'steady growers' depicts companies which have shown a steady increase in profits over the study period. The pattern of the 'steady

Table 1.1 Varimax factor loadings for Gröna Kvisten companies

	Factors			
	1	2	3	4
FIRM 2	0.964			
FIRM 28	0.954			
FIRM 15	0.910			
FIRM 9	0.888			
FIRM 10	−0.837			
FIRM 12	0.797			
FIRM 20	−0.790			
FIRM 6	−0.750			
FIRM 24	0.746			
FIRM 29	−0.703			
FIRM 19	−0.670		0.648	
FIRM 7	0.649			
FIRM 13		0.894		
FIRM 1		0.749		
FIRM 30		−0.718		
FIRM 27		0.692		
FIRM 18		−0.686		
FIRM 23		0.686		
FIRM 8			0.795	
FIRM 26			0.759	
FIRM 3			0.681	
FIRM 21			−0.616	
FIRM 17			0.600	
FIRM 5				0.908
FIRM 25				0.859
FIRM 11				0.607
FIRM 4				0.580

un-growers' is vice versa to that of the steady growers. Since 1993 these companies have mainly experienced a decrease in profits. The pattern of the 'circulators' is more diverse, as these companies display ups and downs in their profit figures. The 'recession blossoms' experienced a period of un-growth until the late 1990s, followed by high growth during a period in which many other companies were hit by recession. This pattern is contrasted by the last group, the 'recessionists', which grew continuously until 2000 or 2001, but have faced a decline in profits since. We will discuss each of these typical patterns. To provide a better understanding of the presented data, we will also present case vignettes of selected companies from the sample.

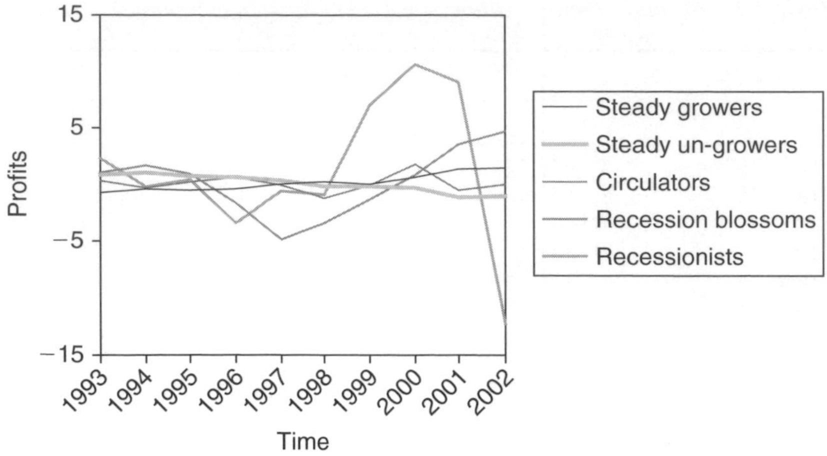

Figure 1.1 Profitability patterns of the Gröna Kvisten companies

The 'steady growers'

These companies (see Table 1.2) display a pattern of continuous growth over the period under investigation, 1993 to 2002. In the year 2000, a severe recession hit Sweden. Nevertheless, these companies continued to grow. Seven out of 30 companies fall into this category. They are from very different industries (groceries, packaging machines, doors, clothing). However, all these companies focus on niches and are rather internationally oriented. In addition, four out of seven are family firms. The companies were founded between 1942 and 1980, and can thus be considered established. These companies follow an explicit growth strategy.

Case vignette: Daloc Daloc, founded in 1942, is the largest company in the Nordic countries to offer doors in wood and steel. The CEO of the company is Inga-Lisa Johansson, who took over the business from her father when she was 25 years old. She and her family are the current owners. When Inga-Lisa took over Daloc in 1970, the company had a 10 per cent market share in Sweden. Some important changes have been introduced since then. Previously, they sold to wholesalers, which led to a lack of communication with customers. Thus, they changed the distribution and selling structure to communicate directly with more than 7000 architects and construction workers.

Inga-Lisa Johansson explains their focus: 'We are satisfying people's needs in terms of protection against fire, war and burglary. This is an increasing need, especially when it comes to burglary' (Söderhjelm and Larsson, 1998, p. 113).

Table 1.2 Steady growers (profits)

Firm	profit 1993	profit 1994	profit 1995	profit 1996	profit 19997	profit 1998	profit 1999	profit 2000	profit 2001	profit 2002
9. Etac AB	11 302	7135	4351	9259	3142	24 042	13 015	32 284	46 674	63 554
28. Trelleborg Rubore AB	12 017	27 223	17 632	19 183	27 337	41 776	39 114	67 418	73 502	66 596
2. Baby Björn AB	1222	1314	1514	4134	6883	19 039	10 478	25 492	43 731	33 290
15. Hörnell	1705	16 187	17 842	12 930	21 832	31 600	46 000	30 692	52 933	71 454
24. Polarrenen AB	41064	40 487	49 901	43 252	71 734	52 104	50 134	67 494	64 881	106 114
7. Daloc Futura AB	17 451	20 592	25 630	20 653	23 172	18 924	19 800	31 821	31 614	26 674
12. HL Display AB	23 122	35 570	19 196	46 166	63 603	70 969	47 125	44 095	81 831	65 353

Daloc focuses on design and security of doors, which apparently is a combination appreciated by the customers. The company was the first in the market to take in designers to develop their doors. Daloc became the market leader during the recession in Sweden in the early 1990s. According to Inga-Lisa Johansson this can be attributed to the continuous focus on sales: 'We had a different strategy than our competitors, and we made sure to take home the orders' (Söderhjelm and Larsson, 1998, p. 114). She views profit maximization as a main goal for the company, as profit is the base for a solid, surviving company that can develop over time. Johansson also finds that profit provides stimulation for work. In 1995, the CEO was not only awarded the Gröna Kvisten prize, but also the Veuve Clicquot award as the female entrepreneur of the year, as well as the gold medal of the Royal Patriotic Society. In 2002, Johansson was selected Swedish entrepreneur of the year.

Case vignette: Polarrenen Polarrenen is a Swedish, family-owned company in the baking industry. The company has roots that go back 100 years. The company started as a producer of traditional northern Swedish bread. This focus has been maintained. Today, Polarrenen is the third-largest producer of bread in Sweden with a 14 per cent market share, baking 29 000 tonnes of bread (as of 2002). In an otherwise shrinking industry, Polarrenen has managed to increase sales and profitability. Much of the growth derives from acquisitions of other companies as well as export. In 1997, it bought Gene, at that time the largest competitor in the field. 'For the Northern baking culture to be able to compete against the big Swedish and international players, coordination is needed', says Kjell Jonsson, CEO of the company (TT Nyhetsbanken, 1997). In 1999, the company made another important acquisition when it bought 51 per cent of Allbröd, which coordinates the bread sales for 21 independent companies. This acquisition secured the company's future distribution coverage of the whole country. The company started to export relatively late. In 2002, exports increased by 60 per cent. Important export markets are Norway, Finland and Spain. The company's head office and production are still located in the depopulated area of northern Sweden. All employees hold a minority of shares in the company, and they can use 300 hours per year for their individual development.

Steady un-growers

The group of the steady un-growers (see Table1.3) has experienced mainly a trend of decreasing profits since 1993. Yet, except for one company, Connecto Electronics, they are still in business. It is this group of companies that according to much of the literature discussed above should no

Table 1.3 Steady un-growers (profits)

Firm	profit 1993	profit 1994	profit 1995	profit 1996	profit 1997	profit 1998	profit 1999	profit 2000	profit 2001	profit 2002
6. Connecto Electronics	9257	13 793	21 206	20 831	19 000	18 000	−4700	−3100	−21 000	N/A
10. Freds La Mote	12 997	20 027	15 582	3111	10 285	13 328	4403	−7491	−12 125	−22 607
29. Unipet	5545	7850	9330	11 346	6567	4084	7533	10 952	−1352	−3204
20. Kriss AB	13 642	10 469	8780	9930	8270	−6409	1210	2896	3163	−3591
19. Kastman & Co AB	2756	3497	549	364	−1402	−1392	−522	−1893	−1497	207

longer exist, as only continued growth is believed to ensure organizational survival. Yet, these companies have successfully survived over the studied period of ten years, they have offered jobs, and contributed to welfare. Thus, steady un-growers play a more important role in the economy than is mostly attributed to them. This group of companies also shows how the evaluation of firm performance on the basis of numbers alone can be misleading. For example, the company Kastman & Co is run by the wife of the former CEO, who has retired. As she is also retiring now, she runs the business of importing clothes on a part-time basis only. Yet, this development is taking place out of choice, rather than due to bad entrepreneurial skills.

Case vignette: Kriss Kriss was founded in 1982 and offers designer clothes for middle-aged women, building on its 'Made in Sweden' image. The profitability figures of Kriss point downward over the past decade, which would make this company look unsuccessful in many purely quantitative studies. However, the company has actually grown from 18 to 80 shops in Sweden and Europe during this period of time – the profitability figures thus mirror the investments made to implement its pronounced strategy of geographic expansion.

Circulators

These companies (see Table 1.4) have displayed more unstable patterns of growth (and ungrowth) over time, and might even have decreased in profits since 1993. However, just like most steady un-growers they are still alive and kicking, even though a number of authors have claimed that firms which do not grow are doomed to fail. Those firms that achieve an acceptable return and avoid further growth to remain in a relative 'comfort zone' have been called 'lifestyle' companies – companies that afford their founders enough revenues without the hazard of further growth. These lifestyle companies have been argued to put their existence in jeopardy, as the level of resources to buffer instability in supplies or demand could quickly exhaust the company's resources (for example Garnsey, 1998, p. 538). In our sample, four companies belong to this category of circulators.

Case vignette: Peak Performance In 1986, Peak Performance was founded as a company based on the core values 'love of sports and love of nature'. Initially the company sold mostly skiwear. In 1989, it broadened the collection to include sports clothes for the summer season as well as a collection of jeans, to avoid becoming a brand of only sports clothes. The company regards the year 1991 as its breakthrough year. In that year, it began to export to Finland, Denmark and Switzerland. Between 1991 and 1995 the company became one of the largest Scandinavian companies

Table 1.4 Circulators (profits)

Firm	profit 1993	profit 1994	profit 1995	profit 1996	profit 1997	profit 1998	profit 1999	profit 2000	profit 2001	profit 2002
1. Albihns AB	15 622	9120	11 551	25 962	8820	5309	8494	24 605	6416	1626
13. Hudson RCI AB	701	1512	17 557	16 850	10 029	−4315	12 280	40 797	6220	17 847
23. Peak Performance	3758	10 027	23 050	25 794	10 980	−74 825	−4088	23 559	2996	8203
27. Team Tejbrant AB	13 622	685	−1653	−497	−442	1983	3113	20 047	−3944	7273

within the field of fashion and sports clothes. In 1996, Peak Performance was ranked as one of the fastest-growing Swedish companies and was listed on the stock exchange. Peak Performance was acquired by the Danish company IC Companys (then Carli Gry) in 1998.

According to financial analysts, the brand image of Peak Performance has always been one of its biggest assets. This consumer-product company has focused on marketing since the company was founded. Its members consider brand building as important in every process. This focus led to the decision to quit working with importers and instead to launch the company themselves in different countries: 'As we are not just selling a sweater, but an image and lifestyle, it is important for us to have control over the total value chain' (then CEO Peter Blorn in Hallerby, 1994). Peak Performance has a reputation for never doing market research even though it is operating in consumer markets with a high level of competition. Its members argue that this is not needed as they are living the propagated lifestyle themselves, and as they produce the products they want to wear themselves. Their marketing activities focus on events and sponsoring of sport events attended by the key target groups. Much of the changes in profitability that make Peak Performance a circulator are due to the changes in accounting practices as a result of the acquisition by the Danish company. Thus, again, the company's numbers alone do not convey the entire picture of its performance.

Recession blossoms

This group of companies (see Table 1.5) displays an interesting pattern. They experienced a period of un-growth until the late 1990s, followed by high growth during a period in which many other companies were hit by recession. Typical for this group of companies is that they are all run by their owners, and they are mainly family-owned.

Case vignette: Berte Qvarn Berte Qvarn is the oldest Swedish company still operating, with its roots going back to 1569. Today, it is a family-owned business, and the current management is in the thirteenth generation. The family owns Berte Qvarn through their holding company Bertegruppen. Bertegruppen also includes a farming business, a seed company and Sia Glass. Sia Glass is the only larger Swedish ice-cream producer, which is competing against companies such as Unilever. Berte Qvarn is a mill, and the company sells flour to grocery shops all over Sweden. The company has managed to remain an independent mill and to grow during a time when the stagnating agriculture industry is focusing on rationalization and large-scale production. The company builds on a strong environmentally-friendly orientation and image, and has been a major driving force in the establishment

Table 1.5 Recession blossoms

Firm	profit 1993	profit 1994	profit 1995	profit 1996	profit 1997	profit 1998	profit 1999	profit 2000	profit 2001	profit 2002
26. Ryftes Grönsaker AB	6533	7764	7478	5324	4731	3118	4068	2745	6794	6114
17. Innovativ Vision AB	4347	3121	1506	−21 798	−6025	−6253	924	2266	1764	−2027
3. Berte Qvarn AB	4864	5822	4100	3710	753	4170	4871	5710	5693	4828
8. Elekta AB	64 084	86 000	61 000	−38 000	−252 000	−179 000	−69 000	69 000	221 000	317 000

of the Swedish eco-label KRAV. They have developed their niche as one of the largest producers of ecological flour, which enables them to be one of only eight remaining mills in Sweden. Since the 1950s, 2400 mills have been closed or acquired in Sweden. Even though the company Berte Qvarn alone might not look very impressive, the family members managing the company have created a number of other companies, which now form Bertegruppen. Thus, just regarding this one company might distort the evaluation of a successful family business holding.

Recessionists

Another pattern identified in our sample is that of companies that displayed a trend of growth over several years until recently. While the profits of these companies might have gone down considerably over recent years, their sales levels mostly are still much higher than in 1993. Four companies in our sample (see Table 1.6 belong to this category. Many quantitative studies on organizational growth would exclude these companies due to their lack of a unidirectional growth process. However, it would do these companies injustice not to consider them as growth companies, as, among other things, they offer more jobs than in 1993.

Case vignette: Besam A typical example of the group of recessionists is Besam, founded in 1962. Its founder developed automatic sliding doors to enhance convenience especially in healthcare (to make it easier to move hospital beds through doors). In this case, the sales figures would tell a different story than the profitability figures, as sales have continuously increased over all years except one. The profitability of Besam has declined in recent years due to heavy investments into new technologies as well as to its takeover by Assa Abbloy.

A number of further issues are striking when analysing our sample. First, hardly any service firms are represented. Only one firm (namely the consulting firm Ahlbihns) is a pure service firm; one other company develops software. Most of the other companies are from very traditional industries, in which they successfully occupy niche markets. This also means that few of the companies are based on high technology. The overall degree of internationalization has clearly increased between 1993 and 2002. In 1993, only five companies sold globally; in 2002, this number had increased to 12.

DISCUSSION

Above, we have presented the different typical patterns of profit growth found in our sample by statistical analysis. This representation is admittedly

Table 1.6 Recessionists

Firm	profit 1993	profit 1994	profit 1995	profit 1996	profit 1997	profit 1998	profit 1999	profit 2000	profit 2001	profit 2002
25. Programma Electronic AB	9199	9202	7058	5102	2513	4786	3250	7990	30 710	−19 822
5. Besam AB	135 380	104 800	112 100	81 500	102 900	100 931	182 939	216 683	200 669	N/A
4. Bertil Bergbom	2924	7152	6124	1265	4970	5222	6953	4476	2875	233
11. Hedmans Invest AB	7544	7203	7762	5710	9413	6907	2287	10 711	7039	2200

reductionistic, and different measures of growth typically employed in growth studies (such as numbers of employees or sales) would lead to different patterns of the same sample. Yet, this problem is inherent by nature in quantitative studies. In this respect, our study demonstrates the limits of quantitative studies of firm growth. Our study also illustrates the limitations of current life-cycle and stage models and the need for more detailed studies of organizational growth processes. The different patterns of growth shown by the Gröna Kvisten firms provide the basis for questioning the usefulness of life-cycle and stage models for understanding firm development. When awarded the prize as successful growth firms (between the years 1993 and 1996), all the companies in the study had successfully passed what in the language of life-cycle or stage models would be regarded as the initial stage, and entered or experienced the period of growth. Thus, they would be supposed to present certain similar structural and contextual features (Quinn and Cameron, 1983). However, the variations in age and ownership structures, as well as in background and previous development, of the Gröna Kvisten firms do not support these assumptions and call for a more micro and process perspective on the actual growth patterns unfolding in those companies.

The patterns identified are not consistent with the single developmental route often considered in the literature. Many of the stage models, indeed, suggest unidirectionality of growth (cf. Van de Ven and Poole, 1995). We illustrated that companies in two of our categories did not display such unidirectionality and still grew substantially. Ample learning seems to take place during the development (cf. Greiner, 1972). For example, one of the Gröna Kvisten companies, Intentia, left its education and consultancy business aside and become a pure software company after having learned that customers would benefit more from a combination of Intentia's knowledge about business processes and software solutions. This also illustrates that the development of the Gröna Kvisten firms does not provide empirical support for the imminent nature of firm growth, which is often assumed by stage and life-cycle models. On the contrary, the different growth patterns identified provide the basis for illustrating a varying set of logics and forms of development, which evolve in an often unpredictable way – while still displaying distinct typical patterns of growth.

Churchill and Lewis (1983) had proposed that firms could also stay small in size within a certain niche. Interestingly, we found that none of the companies remained at the same size (though a few companies had very low growth rates). And even shrinking firms showed a long period of survival. Kazanjian and Drazin (1990) argue that over the course of their existence all firms would be confronted with similar problems, and that it was possible to relate dominant problems with development phases. Yet, dominant problems in the Gröna Kvisten firms do not seem to be the prevalent indicators of new trends. Entrepreneurially-minded individuals, such as Daloc's CEO Inga-Lisa Johansson, are often the driving forces behind such decisions. We can thus share Penrose's (1952) criticism of the analogy of the organizational life-cycle as being too deterministic.

Many of the stage models, but also other entrepreneurship literature, suggest that different development stages require different management and leadership styles and that therefore the founder would have to be replaced by a different CEO when the firm grew. A number of the companies in our sample illustrate that this does not have to be the case. Rather, many cases display continuous growth over a long period of time, while the founder was still the CEO. Our findings also underline the importance of considering the possibility of stability, temporal decline and slow growth into models of organizational growth. Many growing companies do not display unidirectional patterns of growth, yet it would be incorrect not to call them growth companies. Equally, our case studies have shown that – if we assume a stage-model perspective – the transition between stages is not necessarily triggered by crises or other negative situations, as suggested by a number of the models. Rather, a range of different issues can contribute to such a transition, and these do not have to be negative. One of many issues to study in our further analyses of this database is the role of ownership structures for the growth orientation, where for example many of the companies are family-owned.

IMPLICATIONS

More detailed studies of processes and patterns of organizational growth are clearly needed. Unlike the suggestion of many models of organizational growth, even continuously growing firms often do not display unidirectional development paths. In our empirical study of 30 growth firms we could demonstrate how more detailed knowledge about the companies can change the evaluation of their growth paths. We also showed that the discussion of organizational growth should be more differentiated. Even if companies are not growing from year to year; they might be very stable over a long period over time, thus contributing to economic welfare and providing job positions. An important implication of this finding is to rethink the focus on growth as the best option – and especially rapid growth. In total, the companies in this study offered 5648 more jobs in 2002 than in 1993.

By analysing the composition of our categories, interesting implications for policy-makers can be drawn. First, the companies that showed higher and stable growth are mainly manufacturing firms. This evidence is in sharp contrast with the common assumption that firms with higher growth potentials would be technology-based ventures (for example Keeble and Wilkinson, 2000). Second, the companies that were growing steadily were founded between 1942 and 1980. This finding suggests that the political focus on young firms as major engines of job creation and growth might be somewhat simplistic.

NOTE

1. In R-factor analysis, a negative loading indicates a negative relationship between the variables to the factor. One common approach in Q-factor analysis is to consider all cases with negative loading on one factor as being a cluster on their own.

REFERENCES

Adizes, I. (1988). *Corporate Lifecycles: How and Why Corporations Grow and Die and What to Do About It*. Englewood Cliffs, NJ: Prentice-Hall.
Aldrich, H. (1999). *Organizations Evolving*. Sage: London and Thousand Oaks, CA.
Ancona, D.G. and Caldwell, D.F. (1992). Bridging the external activity and performance in organizational teams. *Administrative Science Quarterly*, **37**: 634–65.
Barth, H. (2001). Tillväxthinder i mindre företag. In Davidsson, P. *Tillväxtföretagen i Sverige*. Stockholm: SNS Förlag, pp. 234–49.
Baum, J.R., Locke, E.A. and Smith, K.G. (2001). A multidimensional model of venture growth. *Academy of Management Journal*, **44**(2): 292–303.
Churchill, N.C. and Lewis, V.L. (1983). The five stages of small business growth. *Harvard Business Review*, **61**(3): 30–50.
Eisenhardt, K.M. and Bird Schoonhoven, C. (1990). Organizational growth: Linking founding team, strategy, environment, and growth among US semiconductor ventures, 1978–1988. *Administrative Science Quarterly*, **35**(3): 504–29.
Galbraith, J. (1982). The stages of growth. *Journal of Business Strategy*, **3**(1): 70–79.
Garnsey, E. (1998). A theory of the early growth of the firm. *Industrial and Corporate Change*, **7**(3): 523–56.
Greiner, L.E. (1972). Evolution and revolution as organizations grow. *Harvard Business Review*, **76**(3): 37–46.
Hair, J.F., Anderson, R.E., Tatham, R.L. and Black, W.C. (1995). *Multivariate Data Analysis*. Englewood Cliffs, NJ: Prentice Hall.
Hallerby, L. (1994). Peak på modet hos ungdomar. *Svenska Dagbladet*, 16 August.
Hanks, S.H., Watson, C.J., Jansen, E. and Chandler, G.N. (1993). Tightening the life-cycle construct: A taxonomic study of growth stage configurations in high-technology organizations. *Entrepreneurship Theory and Practice*, **18**(2): 5–29.
Kazanjian, R.K. (1988). Relation of dominant problems to stages of growth in technology-based new ventures. *Academy of Management Journal*, **31**(2): 257–79.
Kazanjian, R.K. and Drazin, R. (1989). An empirical test of stage of growth progression model, *Management Science*, **35**(12): 1489–503.

Kazanjian, R.K. and Drazin, R. (1990). A stage-contingent model of design and growth for technology based ventures. *Journal of Business Venturing*, **5**(3): 137–50.
Keeble, D. and Wilkinson, F. (2000). High-technology SMEs, regional clustering and collective learning: An overview. In Keeble, D. and Wilkinson, F. (eds). *High-Technology Clusters, Networking and Collective Learning in Europe*. Aldershot, UK: Ashgate Publishing, pp. 1–20.
Levinson, D. (1978). *Seasons of a Man's Life*. New York: Knopf.
McKelvie, A. and Chandler, G.N. (2002). Patterns of new venture development. In Bygrave, W.D., Brush, C.G., Davidson, P., Fiet, J., Greene, P.G., Harrison, R.T., Lerner, M., Meyer, G.D., Sohl, J. and Zacharakis, A. (eds). *Frontiers of Entrepreneurship Research*. Wellesley, MA: Babson College, pp. 309–20.
McMahon, R.G.P. (2001). Business growth and performance and the financial reporting practices of Australian manufacturing SMEs. *Journal of Small Business Management*, **39**(2): 152–64.
Melin, L. (1992). Internationalization as a strategy process. *Strategic Management Journal*, **13**: 99–118.
Miller, D. (1978). The role of multivariate 'Q-Techniques' in the study of organization. *Academy of Management Review*, **3**(3): 515–31.
Miller, D. (1986). Configurations of strategy and structures: Towards a synthesis. *Strategic Management Journal*, **7**: 233–49.
Miller, D. and Friesen, P.H. (1984). A longitudinal study of the corporate life-cycle. *Management Science*, **30**(10): 1161–83.
Neumair, U. (1998). A general model of corporate failure and survival: A complexity theory approach. Unpublished doctoral dissertation, University of St Gallen.
O'Farrell, P.N. and Hitchens, D.M.W.N. (1988). Alternative theories of small-firm growth: A critical review. *Environment and Planning A*, **20**(2): 1365–83.
O'Rand, A.M. and Krecker, M.L. (1990). Concepts of the life-cycle: Their history, meanings, and uses in the social sciences. *Annual Review of Sociology*, **16**(1): 241–62.
Penrose, E.T. (1952). Biological analogies in the theory of the firm. *American Economic Review*, **42**(5): 804–19.
Penrose, E.T. (1995/1959). *The Theory of the Growth of the Firm*, 3rd edn, Oxford: Oxford University Press.
Quinn, R.E. and Cameron, K.S. (1983). Organizational life cycles and shifting criteria of effectiveness: Some preliminary evidence. *Management Science*, **29**(1): 33–51.
Scott, M. and Bruce, R. (1987). Five stages of growth in small business. *Long Range Planning*, **20**(3): 45–52.
Smith, K.G., Mitchell, T.R. and Summer, C.E. (1985). Top level management priorities in different stages of the organizational life cycle. *Academy of Management Journal*, **28**(4): 799–820.
Smith, N.R. and Miner, J.B. (1983). Type of entrepreneur, type of firm, and managerial motivation: Implications for organizational life cycle theory. *Strategic Management Journal*, **4**: 325–40.
Söderhjelm, T. and Larsson, Å. (1998). *Att våga: 23 berättelser om svenska framgångsrika entreprenörer*. (To dare: 23 stories about Swedish successful entrepreneurs) Stockholm: IVA.
Stubbart, C. (1992). The deceptive allure of developmental models of strategic

process. Paper presented at the annual Strategic Management Society Conference, London.

Tornatzky, L.G., Eveland, J.D., Boyland, M.G., Hetzner, W.A., Johnson, E.C., Roitman, D. and Schneider, J. (1983). *The Process of Technological Innovation; Reviewing the Literature*. Washington, DC: National Science Foundation, TT Nyhetsbanken (1997). Polarbröd köper Gene 8 August.

Van de Ven, A.H. and Poole, M.S. (1995). Explaining development and change in organizations. *Academy of Management Review*, **20**(3): 510–40.

Whetten, D.A. (1987). Organizational growth and decline processes. *Annual Review of Sociology*, **13**: 335–58.

Wiklund, J. (1998). *Small Firm Growth and Performance: Entrepreneurship and Beyond*. JIBS Dissertation Series No. 003: Jönköping: Jönköping International Business School.

Wiklund, J., Davidsson, P. and Delmar, F. (2001). Hur förväntningar påverkar småföretagares tillväxtvilja. In Davidsson, P., Delmar, F. and Wiklund, J. (eds). *Tillväxtföretagen i Sverige*. Stockholm: SNS Förlag.

2. New business early performance: differences between firms started by novice, serial and portfolio entrepreneurs

Gry Agnete Alsos, Lars Kolvereid and Espen John Isaksen

INTRODUCTION

There has been a growing research interest in the field of habitual entrepreneurs, that is, entrepreneurs that start more than one business during their career. Multiple business founders are interesting since they are often expected to be competent entrepreneurs. MacMillan (1986) argued that habitual entrepreneurs develop an experience curve of entrepreneurship. They learn from their former experiences, have the opportunity to analyse what went wrong and what went right, and to develop a 'methodology' for entrepreneurship. If such an experience curve exists, the experiences from former businesses give habitual entrepreneurs advantages over inexperienced novice entrepreneurs when it comes to new business start-ups. Research interest has been fuelled by the expectation that firms started by experienced entrepreneurs will have superior or enhanced performance. While this suggestion is intuitively appealing, to date there is little empirical support for such a relationship. One explanation may be that previous studies have not controlled for potential differences in business ideas. Ucbasaran et al. (2003) found that habitual entrepreneurs identified opportunities with higher levels of innovativeness than novices. Experienced entrepreneurs may have more complex business ideas which require a longer introduction period with low returns. Another reason may be that many previous studies have failed to acknowledge the heterogeneity among habitual entrepreneurs. The important difference between serial and portfolio founders is that the latter group still own and manage their original business and are able to draw upon resources in the existing firm when starting a new business. Portfolio entrepreneurs may use their original firm as a seedbed for subsequent new ventures (Carter, 1998). In a previous study, Alsos and Kolvereid (1998) found that portfolio nascent entrepreneurs were more often successful in founding a new business than both novice and serial nascent entrepreneurs, indicating that the value of still owning and running an existing business is larger than past experience from prior ventures. An existing business may be a better source of fresh experience and relevant know-how than earlier businesses.

The literature on habitual entrepreneurship has speculated about, but has hitherto found little empirical evidence of, experienced business founders performing better than their inexperienced counterparts. There is a need to investigate what constitutes the potential advantages of experienced entrepreneurs. If there is 'an experience curve of entrepreneurship', what do habitual entrepreneurs learn from their experience that give them advantages when starting the entrepreneurial process over again? To be a novice is a temporary condition, as novice entrepreneurs will become experienced after learning from their first start-up. Performance differences between novice and habitual entrepreneurs are, however, likely to be found in the early stages of business development.

Entrepreneurship is about identifying and exploiting opportunities and organizing resources (Landström and Johannisson, 2001; Stevenson and Jarillo, 1990). We suggest that experienced entrepreneurs may have acquired knowledge and resources from their former business, and that this gives them better access to both new opportunities and resources. Since access to opportunities and resources is central to the possibility of success of a new business, this is expected to lead to higher performance of new businesses started by experienced entrepreneurs. Particularly, serial and portfolio entrepreneurs may be able to 'grow' their new businesses more rapidly from the start because of their presumed better access to resources. The following research questions are explored:

1. Do novice, serial and portfolio entrepreneurs differ when it comes to their ability to identify opportunities and acquire resources when starting a new business?
2. Do such differences lead to different performance in new businesses started by novice, serial and portfolio entrepreneurs?

Based on longitudinal data of a representative sample of new business formations, the present research will explore the differences between novice, serial and portfolio entrepreneurs in the process of starting a new business. Portfolio entrepreneurs are defined using multiple ownership and management as criteria: these are persons who own and manage more than one business. Serial entrepreneurs are entrepreneurs who have owner-management experience from more than one business, but only one at a time, and novice entrepreneurs are entrepreneurs with no prior owner-management experience (Rosa and Scott, 1999; Westhead and Wright, 1998b).

LITERATURE REVIEW

It can be argued that resources are especially critical for new and small businesses due to the shortage of these and the difficulties connected to raising financial capital and sourcing skilled employees as well as other assets (Brush and Chaganti, 1997; Cooper and Dunkleberg, 1986). Aldrich and Fiol (1994) pointed at the 'liabilities of newness and smallness' when it comes to the acquisition of resources. The acquisition of resources is a central element in starting a new business; some even claim it is the most central one (Aldrich, 1999; Landström and Johannisson, 2001). The entrepreneur's ability to collect the necessary resources and combine these into a new business may be vital for whether the new firm will come into existence, and what degree of success it will subsequently attain.

Serial and portfolio entrepreneurs may have accumulated resources through their former businesses that might be drawn upon in the process of starting a new business (Scott and Rosa, 1996). These resources may include knowledge resources that accrue from experiential learning, networks and contacts, and financial capital. In addition, portfolio entrepreneurs possess resources through their existing business that might be used in the start-up of the new business, such as organizational routines, employees, suppliers and customers, as well as physical resources such as buildings and equipment. In these cases the existing business can work as a 'seed-bed' for the new business in its infancy (Carter, 1998). In their study of portfolio entrepreneurs in the farm sector, Alsos and Carter (2003) found an extensive transfer of resources from the existing to the new business. Further, the extent of such resource transfer was associated with the performance of the new business. Moreover, Westhead et al. (2003) found that portfolio entrepreneurs have more diverse experiences and more resources than both serial and novice entrepreneurs, and argue that portfolio entrepreneurs constitute a particularly interesting type of entrepreneurs.

Experience may bring a wide range of contacts, which might be useful in new business start-ups. Through a well-developed network, entrepreneurs may gain access to resources they would otherwise have difficulties obtaining. Such resources may include financial capital or physical resources, or information and knowledge valuable both for identification of opportunities and for founding and developing a new business. Experienced entrepreneurs with a well-developed social network may be better able to establish good start-up teams for developing new business opportunities. Previous studies have found that experienced entrepreneurs, and in particular portfolio entrepreneurs, are more likely to start a new business with partners (Birley and Westhead, 1993; Westhead and Wright, 1998b). As a lead entrepreneur, the experienced entrepreneur may bring together a group of entrepreneurs for opportunity exploitation, relying on the track record of the lead entrepreneur. Further, experienced entrepreneurs may also be invited to be part of start-up teams of other lead entrepreneurs.

Westhead and Wright (1998a) argue that the experience of the entrepreneur can have a considerable influence on the ways the new business is financed, and that successful habitual entrepreneurs can have a greater access to funds than novice entrepreneurs. For instance, successful habitual entrepreneurs may have more financial resources available to invest in equity capital than novices do. In their study of independent business owners in Great Britain, Westhead and Wright (1998b) found that serial entrepreneurs were more likely to use finance from personal sources (perhaps because they have large financial assets after the sale of the previous business), and that portfolio founders were more likely to obtain finance from customers and suppliers (perhaps because they have ties to them through their existing business). Moreover, experience from previous or current business ownership may have developed their network when it comes to investors, banks and other sources of finance. Finally, a track record as a successful entrepreneur may attract more investors to new business projects.

Several authors have argued that habitual entrepreneurs are particularly good at recognizing and developing opportunities (MacMillan, 1986; McGrath, 1996; McGrath and MacMillan, 2000). Founding and running a business may give access to information and knowledge which becomes the basis of new business ideas. Ronstadt (1988, p. 31) introduced 'the corridor principle' and suggested that 'the mere act of starting a venture enables entrepreneurs to see other venture opportunities they could neither see nor take advantage of until they had started their initial venture'. McGrath (1996) argued that entrepreneurs with access to a large and well-functioning network, for instance through an existing business, will probably have access to a large number of good 'shadow options', that is, latent business ideas. Also Singh et al. (1999) stated that a large social network, with many weak ties going beyond close friends and family, relates positively to idea identification and opportunity recognition. Further, McGrath (1996) advocated that experienced entrepreneurs often have a larger ability to recognize and take advantage of latent business ideas, since experience increases their sense-making ability.

Ucbasaran et al. (2003) investigated information search and opportunity identification among novice and habitual entrepreneurs. They found that while there were no differences in the intensity of information search and number of sources used, habitual entrepreneurs identified more opportunities given a certain amount of information. They also found that habitual entrepreneurs had different attitudes to opportunity identification than their less experienced counterparts. Habitual entrepreneurs put more focus on problem-solving activities as a source of opportunities, they enjoyed opportunity identification more and they assessed that one opportunity often led to another. The latter is in congruence with Ronstadt's (1988) concept of 'the corridor principle'.

Based on this review of the literature the following hypotheses were developed:

Hypothesis 1: Serial and portfolio entrepreneurs are better than novices in acquiring resources to the new business.

Hypothesis 2: The resources acquired are significantly related to subsequent early business performance.

METHOD

Data for this study was gathered from new business founders drawn from the Norwegian central coordinating register for legal entities. This register coordinates information that exists in other government registers, including: (1) the register of employers; (2) the register of business enterprises; and (3) the Value Added Tax register. Hence, the central coordinating register contains all businesses that have employees, all limited liability companies and partnerships, and all sole proprietorships obliged to pay VAT.[1] Businesses that register are assigned a unique organization number that identifies the business. The four most common legal forms of new businesses in the register are sole proprietorships, partnerships with mutual responsibility, partnerships with shared responsibility and unlisted limited liability companies. Since a total of 98.6 per cent of Norwegian new registrations in 2002 chose one of these four legal forms (Statistics Norway, 2004), other less common legal forms were disregarded. All new businesses that registered with the central coordinating register during weeks 21–24 2002 were approached. In other words, the whole population of new business registrations during these four weeks constituted the sampling frame. With only one week's delay, the register delivered lists of new businesses that were registered each of these weeks. Within a week after the register supplied these lists, a questionnaire was mailed out in four rounds to 603 businesses registered in week 21, 866 businesses registered in week 22, 747 businesses registered in week 23, and 905 businesses registered in week 24. A reminder with a new copy of the questionnaire was sent out in four rounds three weeks after the initial mailings. A total of 3121 businesses were approached. Of the questionnaires posted, 126 were returned unreachable, while we received 1048 competed questionnaires – a response rate of 35 per cent.

The second round of data collection took place during weeks 5–8 in 2004 (that is, about 19 months after the initial mailing). A professional survey agency was engaged to telephone the respondents to the mail survey in order to find out what had happened to the businesses since the first round of data collection. Among the 1048 businesses that responded to the mail survey, 29 businesses were excluded since they had been deregistered from the central coordination register. Another six businesses were excluded because they had more than 50 per cent missing data on the first round of data collection. Finally, 33 respondents were excluded since the business or the contact person was not listed in any of the available telephone directories. The survey agency attempted to reach all the remaining 980 respondents. Among these, 275 persons were inaccessible and 54 others refused to participate. A total of 3924 telephone calls were made in order to collect follow-up data from a total of 651 of the business founders, 66 per cent of the 980 founders on the list. A total of 104 questionnaires not completed by the founder and owner-manager were removed. Only respondents who submitted complete data sets are included in the present analysis, leaving 410 cases for the analysis of total employment and 354 cases for the analysis of sales turnover in the business. Thorough response bias tests did not reveal any significant differences between respondents and non-respondents. Moreover, the final sample did not differ significantly from the entire cohort of businesses started in Norway in 2002 with regard to legal status or localization. Hence, there is good reason to believe that the sample is representative for the population of new business start-ups in Norway.

Measures

Dependent variables: new business performance

Turnover in 2003 (the first full year in business) and hired employment (other than the respondent) at period two (19 months after registration) were selected to measure of performance. Both variables were highly skewed. Therefore, they were both transformed by taking the logarithm of the responses after adding a constant of 10 000 for turnover and 0.1 for employment.

Types of entrepreneurs

Novice, serial and portfolio entrepreneurs were defined using two questions: whether the respondent at present owned and managed another business in addition to the newly registered business, and whether the respondent had previously owned and managed another business. Respondents who answered 'no' to both these questions were categorized as novice entrepreneurs. Respondents who answered 'no' to the first question and 'yes' to the second one were categorized as serial entrepreneurs, while respondents who answered 'yes' to the first question were categorized as portfolio entrepreneurs. In the final sample of 410 respondents, 68.5 per cent were novices, 13.7 per cent were serial and 17.8 per cent were portfolio entrepreneurs.

Control variables: new business characteristics

Novelty was included as a control variable since Ucbasaran et al. (2003) found experienced entrepreneurs to have more innovative business ideas. Novelty was measured by an additive scale including three items. Respondents were asked to indicate on a seven-point scale whether they agreed or disagreed with the following statements: 'Customers will experience our product or service as new and unknown', 'Few or no competing businesses offers a similar product or service', and 'The technology or production of our product/service is not easily accessible'. The three items load on the same factor in a principal component analysis representing a cumulative variance of 62 per cent and a Cronbach's alpha of 0.70. This measure is adopted from the one used by the *Global Entrepreneurship Monitor* (Reynolds et al., 2002).

Entry mode was also included as a control variable since experienced entrepreneurs may be more involved in acquisitions than novices. The variable '*de novo*' was included, giving the value 1 to the *de novo* entries (businesses started from scratch) and 0 to acquisitive entries (businesses acquired or inherited).

Resources

Start-up team, opportunities, and amount of financial capital raised were used to measure acquired resources. Respondents were asked to state whether they alone were responsible for the founding of the business (value 0), or whether they started it with other partners (value 1), to measure the existence of a start-up team. The access to opportunities was measured by the number of opportunities the respondent had identified in the last five years (not including the new business). The measure of financial capital was calculated by adding the total debt and deposited equity of the newly registered business. The variable was grouped in seven categories as follows: no financial capital (1), 1 to 10 000 NOK (2), 10 001 to 50 000 (3), 50 001 to 100 000 NOK (4), 100 001 to 200 000 NOK (5), 200 001 to 1 000 000 NOK (6), and more than 1 000 000 NOK (7).

RESULTS

Prior to the formal testing of the hypotheses, descriptive statistics and correlations were run. The results are shown in Table 2.1. Table 2.1 gives preliminary support to both hypotheses, and shows that multicollinearity is not a problem. Hypothesis 1 was tested using ANOVA. The results are presented in Table 2.2.

Novice entrepreneurs are found to be significantly less likely to have organized a team of entrepreneurs to start the business, than are serial and portfolio entrepreneurs. Only 19 per cent of the businesses started by novice entrepreneurs are team start-ups, compared to 34 per cent and 41per cent of the businesses started by serial and portfolio entrepreneurs respectively. Further, novices are found to identify significantly less opportunities than serial and portfolio entrepreneurs. Portfolio entrepreneurs are also found to identify significantly more business opportunities than serial entrepreneurs. The mean number of business opportunities identified is 0.88 for novice entrepreneurs, 1.5 for serial entrepreneurs and 2 for portfolio entrepreneurs. Serial and portfolio entrepreneurs were also able to raise significantly more capital for investment in the new business than novice entrepreneurs. Further, independent sample t-tests were conducted to explore differences in means between novices and habitual entrepreneurs. The results show significant differences between the types of entrepreneurs ($p < 0.01$) for all three resource types, and thus support the results from the ANOVA analysis. In total, these results indicate that serial and portfolio entrepreneurs are able to get access to more resources and opportunities than novice entrepreneurs. These findings support hypothesis 1.

The next question is whether these opportunities and resources lead to better performance of the new businesses. Performance is measured by the achieved sales turnover of the new business as well as employment of others. To test whether the different types of founders were associated with different levels of performance, multivariate regression analysis was used.

Table 2.3 shows results from a hierarchical linear regression analysis with sales turnover as the dependent variable. Model 1 shows the effect of the control variables. The model is highly significant giving an adjusted R square of 0.13. As expected both control variables are significant with a negative beta-value in the model, indicating that more novel business ideas and *de novo* entries have reached significantly less sales in the first whole year in business than less novel and acquisitive entries. In model 2, serial and portfolio entrepreneurship are included. Both variables have significant and positive impact in the model, indicating that both serial and portfolio

Table 2.1 Descriptive statistics: mean, standard deviation, correlations and VIF-values

	Mean	Standard deviation	1	2	3	4	5	6	7	8	9	10	VIF values
1 Novice entrepreneur	0.69	0.46	1.00										
2 Serial entrepreneur	0.14	0.35	−0.587**	1.00									1.086
3 Portfolio entrepreneur	0.18	0.38	−0.687**	−0.185**	1.00								1.153
4 Novelty	2.91	1.63	−0.053	−0.014	0.078	1.00							1.043
5 *De novo*	0.88	0.33	0.036	−0.069	0.018	0.161**	1.00						1.138
6 Start-up team	0.25	0.44	−0.201**	0.081	0.171**	0.012	−0.145**	1.00					1.141
7 Opportunities	1.17	1.70	−0.248**	0.079	0.230**	0.044	−0.017	0.140**	1.00				1.100
8 Financial capital	3.67	1.99	−0.219**	0.152**	0.129**	−0.112*	−0.313**	0.306**	0.179**	1.00			1.268
9 Turnover (log)	12.38	1.91	−0.166**	0.138**	0.078	−0.283**	−0.277**	0.237**	0.116*	0.469**	1.00		
10 Employees (log)	−1.59	1.30	−0.126*	0.096†	0.067	−0.148**	−0.187**	0.256**	0.171**	0.390**	0.575**	1.00	

Notes:
n = 410 (except for turnover, where n = 354).
Statistic significance: † indicates $p < 0.10$, * indicates $p < 0.05$ and ** indicates $p < 0.01$.

Table 2.2 Differences between novice, serial and portfolio entrepreneurs in access to resources (means and F-value)

	Novice entrepreneurs	Serial entrepreneurs	Portfolio entrepreneurs	F-value
Start-up team	0.19	0.34	0.41	9.030**[ab]
Opportunities	0.88	1.50	2.00	14.968**[abc]
Financial capital	3.37	4.43	4.22	10.427**[ab]
N	281	56	73	

Notes:
n = 410.
Statistic significance: † indicates $p < 0.10$, * indicates $p < 0.05$ and ** indicates $p < 0.01$.
[a] indicates significant difference between novice and serial entrepreneurs, [b] indicate significant difference between novice and portfolio entrepreneurs, and [c] indicate statistical difference between serial and portfolio entrepreneurs.

Table 2.3 Hierarchical linear regression: turnover (log) as dependent variable

	Model 1	Model 2	Model 3
Control variables			
Novelty	−0.244**	−0.256**	−0.234**
De novo	−0.237**	−0.225**	−0.094†
Experience			
Serial entrepreneur		0.143**	0.081†
Portfolio entrepreneur		0.129**	0.051
Resources			
Start-up team			0.092†
Opportunities			0.018
Financial capital			0.361**
Model characteristics			
F-value	27.260**	17.169**	21.194**
R^2	0.134	0.164	0.300
Adjusted R^2	0.130	0.155	0.286
ΔR^2		0.030	0.136
Δ F-value		6.261**	22.357**

Notes:
n = 351.
Statistic significance: † indicates $p < 0.10$, * indicates $p < 0.05$ and ** indicates $p < 0.01$.

entrepreneurs reach significantly higher sales turnover than novice entrepreneurs. The change in R square is 0.030 and is significant. In model 3 the variables measuring resources are included. The resulting increase in R square is 0.136 up to a total adjusted R square of 0.286. The change is highly significant. Financial capital is highly significant in the model, indicating an association between the amount of capital invested in the business and the achieved short-time turnover. Further, the presence of a start-up team is positive and significant at the 10 per cent level. The effect of serial and portfolio entrepreneurs is considerably reduced when resources are included. Portfolio entrepreneurship is not longer significant, while serial entrepreneurship is significant now only on the 10 per cent level. This indicates that access to resources is mediating the relationship between experience and performance. More specifically, serial and portfolio entrepreneurs reach higher turnover in their new businesses mainly because they are better able to get access to valuable resources.

Table 2.4 shows the results from a hierarchical linear regression analysis with employment as the dependent variable, following the same steps as the model above. Here also, the first model shows a negative association

Table 2.4 Hierarchical linear regression: employees (log) as dependent variable

	Model 1	Model 2	Model 3
Control variables			
Novelty	−0.121**	−0.129**	−0.112**
De novo	−0.168**	−0.161**	−0.052
Experience			
Serial entrepreneur		0.101*	0.025
Portfolio entrepreneur		0.098*	−0.005
Resources			
Start-up team			0.144**
Opportunities			0.102*
Financial capital			0.295**
Model characteristics			
F-value	10.584**	7.104**	14.174**
R^2	0.049	0.066	0.198
Adjusted R^2	0.045	0.056	0.184
ΔR^2		0.016	0.132
Δ F-value		3.495*	22.117**

Notes:
n = 407.
Statistic significance: † indicates $p < 0.10$, * indicates $p < 0.05$ and ** indicates $p < 0.01$.

between novelty and *de novo* entry and performance, but this model is somewhat weaker than the turnover model with an adjusted R square of 0.045. Including serial and portfolio entrepreneurship in model 2 leads to an increase in R square of 0.016, which is a statistically significant change. Both types of experience are significant and positive in the model. Including the resource variables in model 3 removes the effect of entrepreneurial experience. The presence of a start-up team, the identification of more opportunities and access to financial capital are positively and significantly associated with the level of employment in the new businesses. Thus, the resources are here too mediators in the relationship between entrepreneurial experience and performance. The final model has an adjusted R square of 0.184 and is highly significant.

DISCUSSION

The present study found that experienced business founders are better than novices at obtaining resources during new business start-ups. Hence, the first hypothesis is supported. Further, supporting the second hypothesis, the more resources entrepreneurs acquire, the higher the subsequent performance of the business. The hierarchical regression analysis also showed that the dummy variables for serial and portfolio entrepreneurs failed to have any significant effect on performance when resource access was included in the model. These results indicate that serial and portfolio entrepreneurs have higher performance than novices because they are better at obtaining resources for the new venture. However, experienced entrepreneurs are not found to be able to utilize the resources they acquire any better than their novice counterparts.

The results of this study give interesting contributions to the literature on entrepreneurial experience and habitual entrepreneurship. First, this is one of very few studies that are actually able to show performance differences between experienced and inexperienced entrepreneurs. Acknowledging the need to control for the nature of the business idea, the results show that the new businesses of serial and portfolio entrepreneurs actually perform better. Second, the study begins to reveal what constitute the advantages of experienced entrepreneurs. Basically, these entrepreneurs seem to be better at getting access to resources which again help them build businesses with higher performance.

One important limitation of the present research is that we have only looked at one business and not the entire portfolio of businesses controlled by portfolio entrepreneurs. As Scott and Rosa (1996) argued, the performance of the latest venture of portfolio entrepreneurs may not give the true picture of their contribution to value creation, as they still create value through their previous businesses. However, to explore the potential experience curve of entrepreneurship, to look at the performance of their latest business is appropriate to reveal how they perform after they have learnt. Another potential limitation is the relativly short time-span between the initial data collection and the follow-up survey. Novel business ideas may require a longer period of time before the start to flourish. Further, an interesting question is how long the resource advantage of experienced entrepreneurs will give advantages. Are novice entrepreneurs eventually able to 'fill the gap'? After all, they too become experienced as time goes by. Future studies should also look at performance differences at later stages of the businesses' development.

Policy-makers should acknowledge the fact that a substantial proportion of new business formations are made by experienced serial and portfolio entrepreneurs, using their experience in the process of exploiting new business opportunities and setting up new businesses. They should also take into account that experienced entrepreneurs generally achieve higher performance in their new firms, at least on a short-term basis, because they are better at obtaining the resources needed. When supporting novice business owners, their disadvantage when it comes to resource acquisition should be recognised. Support directed towards giving these entrepreneurs access to the necessary resources, particularly financial resources, may help novice entrepreneurs to increase the performance of their firms to the level of their experienced colleagues, as there is no evidence that novice entrepreneurs utilize the accumulated resources in an inferior way. New entrepreneurs should look at the way in which serial and portfolio entrepreneurs gather resources and try to learn from this.

The findings of the present study also raise new questions that should be dealt with in future research in this area. For instance, one should look into the process of resource acquisition and explore how experienced entrepreneurs are able to get access to a larger amount of resources. It is reasonable to assume that some of these resources are obtained from their previous or existing ventures. This raises a question about the nature and effects of resource transfer between the ventures of experienced entrepreneurs. As Iacobucci and Rosa (2004) suggested, the creation of new businesses on the basis of previous or existing businesses of experienced entrepreneurs can be regarded as evolutionary entrepreneurial systems where the relationship between the different business opportunity exploited by the entrepreneur and the dynamics of the entrepreneurial team(s) involved may be important antecedents of new business performance. Further studies into the motivational and processual aspects of serial and portfolio entrepreneurship are needed (Carter and Ram, 2003; Westhead et al., 2003). Moreover, there is a need to look into the influence of the performance of previous and existing businesses of experienced entrepreneurs, as one can assume it is easier to obtain resources from previous successful businesses than from failing businesses.

NOTE

1. At the time of the initial data collection in 2002, this included, with few exceptions, all sole proprietorships (as well as other businesses) with an annual turnover of NOK 30 000 or more. (1 NOK = approx. US$0.14 or 0.12 euros.)

REFERENCES

Aldrich, H. (1999). *Organizations Evolving*. London: SAGE Publications.

Aldrich, H.E. and Fiol, M. (1994). Fools rush in? The institutional context of industry creation. *Academy of Management Review*, **94**(4): 645–70.

Alsos, G.A. and Kolvereid, L. (1998). The business gestation process of novice, serial and parallel business founders. *Entrepreneurship Theory and Practice*, **22**(4): 101–14.

Birley, S. and Westhead, P. (1993). A comparison of new businesses established by 'novice' and 'habitual' founders in Great Britain. *International Small Business Journal*, **12**(1): 38–60.

Brush, C.G. and Chaganti, R. (1997). Resources in new and small ventures: Influences on performance outcomes. Paper presented at Babson-Kauffman Entrepreneurhip Research Conference, Wellesley, MA.

Carter, S. (1998). Portfolio entrepreneurship in the farm sector: Indigenous growth in rural areas? *Entrepreneurship and Regional Development*, **10**: 17–32.

Cooper, A.C. and Dunkleberg, W.C. (1986). Entrepreneurship and paths to business ownership. *Strategic Management Journal*, **7**: 53–68.

Iacobucci, D. and Rosa, P. (2004). Business groups as evolutionary entrepreneurial systems. Paper presented at Babson–Kauffman Entrepreneurship Research Conference, 3–5 June, Glasgow, Scotland.

Landström, H. and Johannisson, B. (2001). Theoretical foundations of Swedish entrepreneurship and small-business research. *Scandinavian Journal of Management*, **17**: 225–48.

MacMillan, I.C. (1986). To really learn about entrepreneurship, let's study habitual entrepreneurs. *Journal of Business Venturing*, **1**: 241–3.

McGrath, R.G. (1996). Options and the entrepreneur: Toward a strategic theory of entrepreneurial wealth creation. *Academy of Management Proceedings* '96: 101–5.

McGrath, R.G. and MacMillan, I.C. (2000). *The Entrepreneurial Mindset: Strategies for Continuously Creating Opportunity in an Age of Uncertainty*. Boston, MA: Harvard Business School Press.

Reynolds, P.D., Bygrave, W.D., Autio, E., Cox, L.W. and Hay, M. (2002). *Global Entrepreneurship Monitor 2002 Executive Report*. Wellesley, MA: Babson College, Kauffman Foundation and London Business School.

Ronstadt, R. (1988). The corridor principle. *Journal of Business Venturing*, **3**(1): 31–40.

Rosa, P. and Scott, M. (1999). The prevalence of multiple owners and directors in the SME sector: Implications for our understanding of start-up and growth. *Entrepreneurship and Regional Development*, **11**: 21–37.

Scott, M. and Rosa, P. (1996). Opinion: Has firm level analysis reached its limits? Time for rethink. *International Small Business Journal*, **14**(4): 81–9.

Singh, R.P., Hills, G.E., Hybels, R.C., and Lumpkin, G.T. (1999). Opportunity recognition through social network characteristics of entrepreneurs. *Frontiers of Entrepreneurship Research*. Wellesley, MA: Babson College.

Statistics Norway (2004). 1 July, available at http://www.ssb.no.

Stevenson, H.H. and Jarillo, J.C. (1990). A paradigm of entrepreneurship: Entrepreneurial management. *Strategic Management Journal*, **11**: 17–27.

Ucbasaran, D., Westhead, P., Wright, M. and Binks, M. (2003). Does entrepreneurial experience influence opportunity identification? *Journal of Private Equity*, **7**(Winter): 7–14.

Westhead, P., Ucbasaran, D. and Wright, M. (2003). Differences between private firms owned by novice, serial and portfolio entrepreneurs: Implications for policy makers and practitioners. *Regional Studies*, **37**(2): 187–200.

Westhead, P. and Wright, M. (1998a). Novice, portfolio, and serial founders in rural and urban areas. *Entrepreneurship Theory and Practice*, **22**(4): 63–100.

Westhead, P. and Wright, M. (1998b). Novice, portfolio, and serial founders: Are they different? *Journal of Business Venturing*, **13**(3): 173–204.

3. Small firms' relationships and knowledge acquisition: an empirical investigation

Mariachiara Colucci and Manuela Presutti

INTRODUCTION

The rapid changing of competitive environments is forcing firms to seek more creative and flexible means to manage the competition. Many firms have responded to these challenges by building collaborative relationships with external partners, such as customers and suppliers, to share development costs and to reduce the time to market (Larson, 1992; Gulati, 1999). In fact firms, rather than considering antagonism with other actors in the industry, have begun to build cooperative relationships with a multiplicity of external partners, encompassing customers, suppliers, investors and other organizations (Birley, 1985; Dyer and Singh, 1998). The ability to build and maintain inter-network relationships is increasingly viewed as the key factor to obtain competitive advantage, especially for small firms (Covin and Slevin, 1990; McDougall et al., 1994). Small firms consider their partners as a resource to get access to external resources and knowledge in order to compensate for their restricted internal portfolio of tangible and intangible resources (Yli-Renko et al., 2001).

In business-to-business settings, in particular, vertical dyadic relationships between suppliers and their customers have been attracting rising interest from researchers (Anderson et al., 1994; Ford, 2002). The basic assumption of the literature on this topic is that buyers and sellers play important roles for the performance of each other; therefore, it seems necessary for these players to make mutual adaptations to facilitate the ongoing business relationships (Hakansson, 1982). In this perspective, some authors have expressed the motivation to collaborate between supplier and customer as a strategic instrument that is useful to create opportunities for the acquisition and exploitation of knowledge (Hakansson, 1982; Larson, 1992). Yet, not many studies have examined the role of social capital in improving the management of these business relationships between small firms (Yli-Renko et al., 2001). Relatedly, apart from studies focused on trust, little attention has been turned to the direct influence of social capital on business relationships between suppliers and customers.

In this chapter we consider social capital as a resource which improves the value of business relationships implemented by a start-up (Lin, 2001; Burt, 1997). Therefore, we suppose that the advantages of a small firm are often related not only to the value of its network of relationships, but above all to its capability to develop some valuable social networks with customers. In order to illustrate the potential influence of social capital on the management of small firm vertical dyadic relationships, we consider a strategic dimension of the business network, characterized by a greater knowledge transfer that arises among business partners. In other words, we suggest that social capital facilitates external knowledge acquisition in customer relationships of small firms.

Our chapter is structured in six sections, as follows. As a first step, we offer a theoretical background on both vertical dyadic relationships and social capital, presenting relevant theoretical contributions concerning these topics with a particular focus on small firms. Based on a literature review, we develop a conceptual framework and the hypotheses that led our research. Consistently, in the third section we explain the research methodology and the main characteristics of the selected empirical sample. Then the proceedings of the statistical analysis are drawn, and the results on the validation of our hypotheses are provided. Finally, the last two sections allow us to propose some concluding remarks, as well as to propose some suggestions for further research.

THEORETICAL BACKGROUND: SMALL FIRMS, VERTICAL DYADIC RELATIONSHIPS AND SOCIAL CAPITAL

In recent years increasing attention has been given to the social and economic external context in which business partners operate (Granovetter, 1985; Aldrich and Zimmer, 1986; Birley et al., 1990; Jarillo, 1989). As a consequence, the concept of the network has gained momentum as one of the most powerful means of analysis within the management research field. In fact, a network approach builds on the general notion that economic action does not take place in a barren social context but is instead embedded in a social network of relationships (Gulati, 1999). Along this perspective, organizations are considered to be interconnected with other actors, through a wide array of social and business relationships (Burt, 1992; Gulati, 1999).

Particularly, entrepreneurship scholars have recognized the importance of networks for the growth of small and new firms (Birley, 1985; Dollinger, 1984), especially in amassing the resources needed for a business (Starr and MacMillan, 1990). Networking is increasingly seen as 'primarily a means of raising required resources' (Ramachandran and Ramnarayan, 1993, p. 515). Since new firms usually have few employees and possess only limited resources, intensive networking improves their access to information, capital, personnel, customers, and so on (Starr and MacMillan, 1990; Van de Ven, 1993, p. 226). The resources of critical importance to new and small businesses include entrepreneurial capability, relevant knowledge bases and expertise, and financial capital (Cooper et al., 1991). Most measurements of available resources consider only those contained within the organization. We believe that social resources, 'embedded in one's social network . . . not possessed goods of the individual [but] accessible through one's direct and indirect ties' (Lin et al., 2001), are also critical to success because they afford access to other types of resources.

Along these lines, interfirm network relationships are increasing in importance among suppliers and their customers and have become an integral part of business-to-business operating strategies (Borgatti et al., 1998; Granovetter, 1985; Hakansson, 1982). Traditionally, in the literature, the business inter-organizational networks are widely accepted as an organizational arrangement that represents an intermediate alternative to hierarchically organized firms and market mechanisms, which have been proposed as the two principal tools to obtain resources (Coase, 1937; Williamson, 1975). Within the network theoretical framework, vertical networks are seen as those members of the value-adding system involving suppliers down to final users.

Recently these collaborative relationships of small firms with suppliers have been termed 'partnerships', underlining that partnership sourcing works because both parties have an interest in each other's success. The dyadic buyer–seller relationship is taken as the unit of analysis and it is on the base of the famous framework developed by the IMP Group (Industrial Marketing and Purchasing) in the 1980s and 1990s (Ford, 2002; Anderson et al., 1994). Within this framework, the actors are seen as embedded in contexts where they rely on the controlled resources and activities carried out by other actors, while the networks are seen as organically evolving. Relatedly, the network itself consists of the collaborative and competitive patterns that emerge as a result of conducted business activities. This idea rests on the hypothesis that boundaries among firms and environment are vanishing more and more, and that the implementation of strong relationships with business partners allows the reduction of uncertainty within the environment itself (Gulati, 1999). Thus, the nature of business relationships is more than just teamwork.

This interactive approach to the analysis of vertical partnerships is based on the idea that, differently from the markets of goods consumption, industrial relationships are deeply characterized by trust and loyalty, which breed a formalization of strong and long-term relationships between suppliers and customers. According to the embeddedness perspective (Granovetter, 1985), the vertical dyadic relationship between a firm and its main customers may represent the relevant level of analysis. Firms and customers are not atomistic entities free to undertake any competitive action within their own resource constraints; rather, they are embedded in a network of relationships that may influence their competitive behaviour (Uzzi, 1997).

The embeddedness of interpersonal ties may be viewed as a continuum ranging from one extreme of high social embeddedness to the other extreme of low embeddedness, or arm's-length in nature. According to Granovetter (1985), embeddedness refers to the notion that behaviours and institutions are constrained by ongoing social relations. Embedded relationships involve repeated interactions over long-term horizons and are characterized by mutual cooperation and high levels of trust. These relationships are therefore 'value-laden', within which members develop shared languages and interpretive schemas that become linked to a sense of identity. Such relationships and linkages between actors may augment the transfer of fine-grain knowledge and joint problem-solving arrangements between firms (Uzzi, 1997).

According to previous studies, the development of business networks can be improved by the presence of an important relational asset, that is, social capital (Bourdieu, 1983; Coleman, 1990). The term 'social capital' was originally used to describe the relational resources, embedded in cross-cutting personal ties, that are useful for the development of individuals in the social organization community (Jacobs, 1965). James Coleman was the first to develop a comprehensive theory of social capital (1990) and his work then inspired the diffusion of the use of the theory in relation to the study of actors who are pursuing interest-driven goals. Recent research has applied social capital theory to analyse the set of relationships that a single actor (individual or firm) has instituted with other people, and to identify the ways with which these relationships are exploited to reach personal goals. The common idea of these studies is to consider the social capital as a factor influencing, in a positive way, the action of actors, simplifying the process of tacit knowledge creation (Nonaka, 1991), the spread of relevant information, and the creation of trust relationships. However, although a large body of research has emerged on social capital, and a growing group of researchers are now using social capital in their specific field of research, consensus on the definition of this concept has yet to be established.

In our studies, the social capital concept, according to a wide definition of 'social structural arrangements which facilitate the attainment of goals' (Lin, 2001), includes positional advantages achieved in business networks, such as knowledge acquisition, useful to improve the management of relationships. Among the various resources available to the firm, in fact, knowledge is arguably the most important one (Spender, 1996), and the accumulation of knowledge through inter-organizational networks constitutes a driving force in the development and growth of small firms (Penrose, 1959; Spender, 1996). In fact, knowledge acquisition opens new strategic and productive opportunities and it enhances the firm's ability to exploit these opportunities. Moreover, the acquisition of knowledge is predominantly seen as a social process (Kogut and Zander, 1992) so that social capital may be critical for the profitable management of business networks (Deeds et al., 1999).

CONCEPTUAL FRAMEWORK: HYPOTHESES

Our conceptual framework moves from the idea that the aspects of social capital embedded in business relationships among small firms and their customers positively influence these vertical relationships, enhancing knowledge acquisition (Lane and Lubatkin, 1998). In particular, we follow Nahapiet and Ghoshal (1998) in arguing that social capital facilitates knowledge acquisition by affecting conditions necessary for the value improvement of vertical business networks between firms and customers. We consider the strategic and innovative dimension of business relationships, characterized by the greater knowledge that transfer gives rise to between business partners. Central to this argument is that social capital improves the management of relationships, influencing the knowledge available for the small firm through its network of relationships (a 'structural' dimension), the knowledge actually disclosed to the small firm (a 'relational' dimension), and the efficiency of the resulting knowledge transfer and exchanges (a 'cognitive' dimension).

Based on these argumentations, we can formulate a first generic proposition:

Proposition: The greater the social capital between a small firm and a customer, the greater will be the value of correlated business networks, measured by the small firm's knowledge acquisition from the relationship.

According to Nahapiet and Ghoshal (1998) and Yli-Renko et al. (2001), we distinguish three different dimensions of social capital: the level of social interaction between the actors (Larson, 1992; Ring and Van de Ven, 1994) – cognitive dimension; the quality of the relationship in terms of goodwill, trust and reciprocity (Dyer and Singh, 1998; Larson, 1992) – relational dimension; the level of network ties created through the relationship (Uzzi, 1997; McEvily and Zaheer, 1999) – structural dimension. Concerning the cognitive dimension, we suppose that greater levels of social interaction between a small firm and its customers may increase the knowledge acquired through the relationship reinforcing role interactions (Ring and Van de Ven, 1994), or by intensifying the firm's ability to recognize and evaluate pertinent knowledge (Cohen and Levinthal, 1990; Lane and Lubatkin, 1998). In fact, this dimension provides better access to understanding of the customer operations and more effective communicative means with the customer (Yli-Renko et al., 2001). In this sense, social interaction permits the increase of the relative capacity and effectiveness of a small firm in both recognizing and absorbing external knowledge from customers. Thus, we propose:

Hypothesis 1: The greater the social interaction between a customer and a small firm, the greater will be the value of correlated business networks, measured by the small firm's knowledge acquisition from the relationship.

Focusing attention on the relational dimension, we suppose that shared expectations, goals and common norms between a small firm and its customers reduce the need for formal monitoring, allowing firms to invest more effort into knowledge acquisition from business relationships (Dyer and Singh, 1998; Larson, 1992; Nahapiet and Ghoshal, 1998). In fact, the quality of a relationship can be seen in the extent to which firms and customers develop common goals, norms and reciprocal expectations regarding the goodwill trustworthiness of the exchange partner (Tsai and Ghosal, 1998). Accordingly, we propose that:

Hypothesis 2: The greater the quality of the relationship with customers, the greater will be the value of correlated business networks, measured by the small firm's knowledge acquisition from that relationship.

Finally, we consider the structural dimension affirming that customers, acting as a link to a broad marketplace, are important for the transmission of novel information since they connect the small firms with other external partners. Therefore, this factor can amplify the possibility of obtaining a greater level of knowledge through these networks. Customer ties enhance knowledge acquisition, broadening knowledge exposure and deepening learning skills, and then providing greater opportunities for knowledge acquisition. Along these lines, we propose:

Hypothesis 3: The greater the level of customer network ties provided by the single customer, the greater will be the value of correlated business networks, measured by the small firm's knowledge acquisition from the relationship.

METHOD

Sample and Data

The principles underpinning the sample identification, coherently with our research hypotheses, are: (1) positive rates of new firms' creation; (2) firms not more than eight years old (start-ups); (3) a business market where the knowledge transfer is considered complex and linked to tacit systematic know-how and therefore hard to transfer. In this situation, firms develop strong and long-lasting business relations characterized by high levels of mutual knowledge.

We decided to apply these three principles in one of the most important areas in the centre of Italy, near Rome, characterized by a high concentration of young firms with significant technological capabilities and a high-performing competitive presence in both national and foreign markets. The high-tech firms located here are of considerable importance in the Italian economy, as is shown by the fact that since the end of the 1980s this area has been recognized as the third most important Italian industrial conglomeration in the field of electronics. About 1200 small and medium-sized firms in the ICT sectors, which employ around 20 000 workers, belong to this area. According to data collected during the year 2000 by the Chamber of Commerce of Rome, the different sectors located in this area, are electronics (397 firms), media (220 firms) and new economy (583 firms). Among these three sectors, we preferred to devote our attention in particular to the electronics one, which, according to the definition by ANIE (National Federation Electronics Firms), is constituted by the computer industry, electronics (in a narrow sense), and telecommunications.

Using the data bank of the Chamber of Commerce of Rome and SITC classification codes, we noticed that, from 1985 to 2000, a total of 120 firms in the high-tech electronics sector started up and only about 60 of them have survived. We focused only on young firms because such firms have been thought to benefit or suffer most from key external relationships (Eisenhardt and Schoonhoven, 1996). So, we excluded firms more than eight years old, according to previous research on entrepreneurial firms

(Covin and Slevin, 1990). In this way, we identified a total of 50 start-ups. Before starting the empirical research, we did a preliminary detailed exploratory study through free interviews with selected actors of the cluster, so that we could reconstruct at least from a qualitative prospective the map of the relationships among the principal actors.

The data to test our hypotheses come from a direct survey. The survey process proceeded in four phases: (1) developing the measurement scales by conducting literature reviews; (2) developing the questionnaire structured in the closed question–answer form; (3) pre-testing randomly the questionnaire on three sample firms; and (4) collecting data. Our key informant was the entrepreneur, who can be considered representative of the whole start-up, according to entrepreneurship literature which conjectures that during the first step in the life-cycle of a firm the personal and social networks of the entrepreneur normally coincide with the total network of the start-up (Birley et al., 1990).

We contacted firms by phone to obtain the names of respondents – the entrepreneurs – and to be sure they agreed to complete the survey. Of 50 firms contacted – including follow-up mailings – 48 responded, yielding a response rate of 96 per cent. A comparison of differences in the mean values of the responding and non-responding companies based on three years' average sales revenues, company age, and number of employees did not reveal any significant non-response bias.

The questionnaire was explicitly focused on the relationship between a firm and its customers, because, as mentioned in the theoretical background, we chose this vertical dyadic relationship as the unit of analysis. Rather than imposing a numerical limit, we preferred to leave the entrepreneurs free to quote their more important customers, imposing only a maximum number of ten. Finally, the data set included 212 observations, that represent the sum of customers spontaneously listed by the 48 entrepreneurs interviewed.

On average, firms in the sample were about five years old, they realized about 230 000 euros in annual revenue, and about 15 per cent of total revenue in foreign markets; firms have six employees and spent about 2 per cent of their revenue on R&D.

Measures

Measures were developed on the basis of previous studies. We used multi-item measures for all the independent variables because their use provides considerable advantages over single-item measures (for example Churchill, 1979). Items on the questionnaire were measured using four-point Likert scales anchored by 'strongly disagree' and 'strongly agree'.

Dependent Variable: Knowledge Acquisition from the Relationship

We measured knowledge acquisition with one statement reflecting the strategic information that the young technology-based firm may acquire from its customers (that is, the firm is able to obtain a great amount of market knowledge from customers), using a four-point Likert scale, anchored by 'strongly disagree' and 'strongly agree'. The item was based on Nooteboom et al. (1997) and Von Hippel (1988).

Independent Variables: The Social Capital Construct

In measuring social capital we based this on a personal elaboration of the framework developed by Nahapiet and Ghoshal (1998), integrated by a recent study of Yli-Renko et al. (2001), in which this concept is analysed according to the three following dimensions: (1) cognitive dimension, which is built on the resources acquired via the sharing of codes, paradigms and languages, that facilitate the understanding of common goals among partners and drive actions in the social system (Brass, 1995); (2) relational dimension, which describes the type of personal relationships that the single actors develop with other external actors through continuous interactions over time, giving particular attention to feelings of respect and trust (Krackhardt, 1996, 2000; Nooteboom et al., 1997); (3) structural dimension, constituted by the social ties between different actors and by the location of a single actor in the complex social structure (Burt, 1992).

In order to make the social capital construct empirically measurable, we proceeded as follows. First of all, we sorted this concept out into different dimensions of analysis, which we analysed through the following three indicators: (1) network ties between start-ups and customers, as far as the structural dimension of social capital is concerned; (2) relationship quality, related to relational dimension; (3) social interaction concerning the cognitive dimension. Actually, according to literature about social capital and trust, which suggests that the sharing of common aims among partners in a relationship can be reinforced by the development of trust, which in turn is simplified by frequent social interactions (Uzzi, 1997; Tsai and Ghoshal, 1998), we expect a strong correlation between cognitive and relational dimensions of social capital. However, we prefer to analyse these dimensions separately at the empirical level (Nahapiet and Ghoshal, 1998).

In the second place, we articulated the three indicators described above through a series of explanatory dimensions. For network ties to be measured, we used the two following dimensions: (1) number of new economic ties, to develop the start-ups; (2) level of relevant information embedded in every relationships. From this perspective, we consider networks with customers to be a possible source of social capital as long as they can create meaningful links between the firm and the broad market (Lane and Lubatkin, 1998), but also as they reinforce the image and reputation of young enterprises (Eisenhardt and Schoonhoven, 1996).

We analysed the relationship quality through the dimension: level of trust within a network – which is measured in the following four ways – (1) sharing of common expectations and aims; (2) lack of opportunistic behaviour; (3) creation of common investments (commitment); (4) development of informal relationships. According to this perspective, the relationship quality between firms and customers seems to depend on participants developing common aims or creating mutual expectations. The social capital, as a resource, makes the different actors of an economic relationship expect some positive results from these transactions. By minimizing opportunistic behaviour, the social capital reduces the costs caused by the activities of control and monitoring. In fact, according to Larson (1992), it is possible to remark that relationships based on trust permit time savings by removing the need for monitoring and bargaining over agreements, so as to encourage strong investments in the absorption and use of knowledge (Barney and Hansen, 1994; Lane and Lubatkin, 1998). Other studies have found that relationship quality allows the actors involved in an economic transaction to act in an informal way, without explicit and detailed contracts but through social norms based upon mutual expectations (Nooteboom et al., 1997). Finally, we analysed the social interaction through the dimension: the level of personal knowledge between firms and customers (Tsai and Ghoshal, 1998; Yli-Renko et al., 2001). This dimension reflects the extent to which the tie is characterized by personal and social ties inside industrial markets, showing a reciprocal influence between an economic and a social dimension of actors. Figure 3.1 shows the operationalization of the social capital construct.

Control Variable

Research on social capital has shown that the development of profitable social ties of a small firm, such as a start-up, can be strongly influenced by the length of the relationship (Burt, 1992; Coleman, 1990). In fact, in the literature there is consensus on the impact of the relationship durability on the strength of business tie, generating profitable levels of social capital embedded in this tie.

Analysis

As a first step of measure validation, the responses to the 14 Likert-type items (see Table 3.1) were factor-analysed by the principal axis method. Only

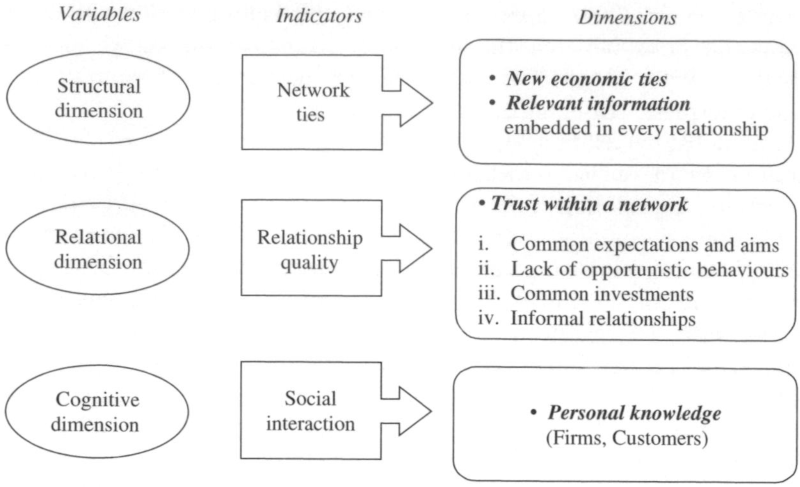

Figure 3.1 Independent variables used in the empirical analysis

two factors, of the three hypothesized, reached the eigenvalue criterion of 1 or higher. This factor structure was then rotated via the varimax procedure with Kaiser normalization, showing that each item's factor loading exceeded the cut-off point of 0.500. As can be seen in Table 3.1 the first factor includes 11 items that globally measure both the level of trust and the cognitive identification among partners, thus labelled as 'relational-cognitive dimension'. The second factor, which includes three items that measure the extent to which the client becomes a link to new business ties, was classified as 'structural dimension'. Finally, scale reliabilities for the two composites were calculated. The coefficient alphas for the item sets were all greater than 0.8, showing a high degree of internal reliability (Nunnally, 1978).

After exploring the factor structure of the data, we then submitted measures to confirmatory factor analysis (CFA), that was accomplished with the SAS system (PROC CALIS). The CFA showed that the two measurement models fit the data reasonably well, with the Bentler-Bonett Fit Index (NFI). In both models, the indicators loaded upon the appropriate factor, with t-values that overall ranged between 11.093 and 20.530. Finally the factor loadings were well above the cut-off value of 0.300 (see Table 3.1).

HYPOTHESES TEST AND RESULTS

The correlation matrix displayed reveals the potential for multicollinearity among predictor variables (Table 3.2). However, the variance inflation

Table 3.1 Description of measures, measure validation and coefficient alphas

	Description of measures/(Coefficient alpha)	Loadings[1]	Factor loadings[2]
	Hp 1/2: Relational/cognitive Dimension ($\alpha = 0.98$)		NFI = 0.870
Relational dimension	• The customer is a relative of the entrepreneur/ someone who works in the firm	0.840	0.978
	• The customer often comes in the head office without working reasons	0.861	0.976
	• The firm has frequent relationships with the customer	0.825	0.999
	• The purchase order relates to a non-working environment	0.648	0.983
	• The entrepreneur met the customer before starting the business	0.811	0.943
Cognitive dimension	• The entrepreneur has an informal relationship with the customer	0.848	0.884
	• The firm grants an extension of the payment to its customer	0.882	0.999
	• The firm takes into consideration the order of the customer without receiving his formal request	0.838	0.979
	• The transaction with the customer is based on informal procedures	0.872	0.876
	• The firm sends the products to the customer before receiving the entire payment	0.828	0.672
	• The transaction with the customer is based on usual procedures without formal agreements	0.850	0.760
	Hp 3: Structural Dimension ($\alpha = 0.89$)		NFI = 1.000*
	• The customer has given other people an opening (new contacts)	0.704	0.819
	• The firm has got new customers thanks to its customer	0.897	0.979
	• The firm has got new suppliers thanks to its customer	0.751	0.812
	Control variable		
	• Relationship length		
	Dependent variable: knowledge acquisition		
	• The firm gets most of its valuable information on customers needs and trends from the customer		

Notes:
[1] Extraction method: principal axis factoring. Rotation method: varimax with Kaiser normalization.
[2] Estimation method: maximum likelihood.
* The model is just-identified.

Table 3.2 Correlation matrix[a]

Variables	1	2	3	VIF values
1. Knowledge acquisition	1.00			
2. Relational/cognitive	−0.672	1.00		2.44
3. Structural	0.639	−0.760	1.00	2.40
N = 212				

Note: [a]All correlations are significant at $p < 0.0001$.

Table 3.3 Results of regression analysis

Variables	Coefficient	t-Value
Intercept	3.170***	26.82
Relational/Cognitive	−0.407***	−4.02
Structural	0.204**	3.60
Relationship length (level 1)	−0.323	−1.46
Relationship length (level 2)	0.170	−1.52
Relationship length (level 3_reference variable)	0.000	–

Note: $**p < 0.001$; $***p < 0.0001$.

factor (VIF) analysis indicated no significant parameter distortion due to multicollinearity, showing VIF values under the recommended cut-off point of 2.5 (Allison, 1999).

A multiple regression analysis was used to test the hypotheses. In order to determine the most appropriate model-to-data agreement, in a preliminary analysis we investigated the interclass correlation coefficient (ICC). To account for the clustering of the data we estimated a random coefficient regression model, using the PROC MIXED procedure implemented in the SAS system. This procedure is based on the restricted maximum likelihood (REML) estimation method, also known as the residual maximum likelihood (Byrk and Raudenbush, 1992). The results of the regression analysis are summarized in Table 3.3.

As it appears in the table, both predictor variables are statistically significant at, respectively, $p < 0.0001$ and $p < 0.0004$. These results are consistent with the central proposition of the study that the relational/cognitive dimension and the structural one may affect knowledge acquisition in the dyadic vertical relationships, thus indicating that they are meaningful dimensions of the social capital construct. However, while the structural dimension seems to enhance the acquisition of knowledge as hypothesized, the relational/cognitive dimension shows a negative relation with the acquisition of knowledge, contrary to our expectations. Finally, the relationship length, the control variable, does not have a statistically significant effect on the knowledge acquisition.

DISCUSSION AND CONCLUSIONS

The starting point for this study was to explore the link between social capital, conceptually articulated in distinct dimensions, and the acquisition of knowledge in vertical dyadic relationships between a small firm (start-up) and its customers. Our empirical results show how the value of business relationships, in terms of knowledge acquisition, seems to be reinforced by high levels of structural dimensions of social capital, while it is negatively influenced by high levels of relational and cognitive dimensions. Actually, the process of diffusion and circulation of strategic information between business partners, that improves knowledge acquisition, seems hindered by strong levels of trust. Vice versa, the acquisition of knowledge benefits from the capability of customers to open the firm towards other significant partners who are able to reinforce the knowledge acquisition processes.

In particular, considering jointly hypotheses 1 and 2 (relational and cognitive dimension, and knowledge acquisition) the data show that high levels of relational and cognitive dimensions of social capital limit the process of diffusion both of knowledge and of other profitable information among partners, reducing the possibility for a firm of growing through the business relationships. Our results confirm what is upheld in most recent studies on social capital and innovation (for example Malmberg and Maskell, 2002; Audretsch and Feldman, 1996), which underline the existence of information redundancy inside such closed economic ties, and consequently of inertia mechanisms in processes aimed to improve the knowledge acquisition from a business tie. According to this perspective, we can explain the negative impact of the relational/cognitive dimension on knowledge acquisition, in the view of Uzzi (1997) who has pointed out the possible existence of 'overembeddedness' within strong and closed networks with high levels of trust. Further empirical studies have shown that excessively closed relationships can isolate small firms from external sources of knowledge and information, suggesting that high levels of social capital are not always able to foster knowledge exchange (Dyer and Singh, 1998; Nahapiet and Ghoshal, 1998).

Redundancy of information is the direct consequence of the creation of coexistent and structurally equivalent connections; indeed, people linked by strong networks have the same sources of information. Nevertheless, such relationships bring the immediate advantage of trust development and decrease of transaction costs related to the management of business relations. Our results are in line with empirical work which shows that highly embedded business networks exclude collaborative opportunities with potential external partners. In order to realize radical innovation, business networks need to regroup their members to access new knowledge. In this sense, it seems that a high degree of embeddedness of business networks is related to the capacity for incremental innovation, whereas a low degree of embeddedness is tied to the capacity for radical innovation and for new sources of knowledge. In fact, a lower embeddedness of business networks corresponds to fewer transaction-related saving costs. The extent of dependence on information provided by business networks is not so significant. Given low embeddedness, start-ups may easily and objectively estimate the value of members of the business networks. On the contrary, with strong relationships, when facing new opportunities, there is the tendency to repeat collaborative and well-known relationships with old partners, being reluctant to reconstruct new business networks.

The analysis confirms the positive relationship between the structural dimension of social capital, and knowledge acquisition (hypothesis 3), reinforcing the idea that this factor is very important to improve the value of vertical networks among business actors. In other words, customers that are able both to act as a link to a broad marketplace and to promote the transmission of novel valuable information, become important sources of opportunities for firms' knowledge acquisition. Relatedly, our result is line in with recent empirical studies which have emphasized that exposure to many different external contacts is essential to learning in new competitive environments (McEvily and Zaheer, 1999). In fact, as some authors have pointed out, the exposure to a variety of customers, within industrial markets, enhances the ability of firms to assess and to evaluate the knowledge available from business partners like customers (Zahra et al., 2000).

IMPLICATIONS, LIMITATIONS AND FUTURE DIRECTIONS

In conclusion, our findings can offer some interesting reflections in the research field concerning small firms, social capital and networks. Firstly, whereas past research has focused on social capital as a macro-level concept in industrial networks (Burt, 1992) or as a micro-level concept within organizations (Moran and Ghoshal, 1996; Tsai and Ghoshal, 1998), we have demonstrated at an empirical level that the concept of social capital is also applicable to the inter-organizational strategy of small firms, according to a recent study (Yli-Renko et al., 2001). Secondly, as pointed out above, while previous research has often analysed only a single dimension of social capital, our results indicate that it is better to divide this concept into two different dimensions, since we have reached opposite conclusions according to structural and relational dimensions.

Our empirical findings indicate that different social assets may have different effects on relationship outcomes, such as knowledge acquisition (Uzzi, 1997). Moreover, this study indicates that a profitable management of business relationships may offer significant learning opportunities for a start-up. Since start-ups generally lack resources to aid their growth, social relationships can be useful in getting access to several forms of significant knowledge which are critical to promote a rapid learning process. At the same time, since our results indicate that distinct dimensions of social capital have differential effects on knowledge acquisition, we argue that finding the optimal level of social capital is a challenge for young firms. In particular, we refer to the possibility that, in order to exploit the benefits of social capital widely, some corrective mechanisms should be introduced, which could avoid overembeddedness negative effects (Dyer and Nobeoka, 2000).

Various limitations characterize our research. First of all, we collected data from inside a high-tech cluster located in central Italy, hence the choice of this sector and of this specific geographic location may limit the applicability and the generalization of our results in other contexts. We also remark that relatively young age of these firms and the lack of suitable resources are probably two factors which foster the creation of external relations and the possible influence on knowledge acquisition and on innovation performance. Moreover, our sample is particularly technology-intensive and therefore it is difficult to discern how well our results would generalize to a broader sample. Probably, future studies focused in other industries and country settings may shed light on the possibility to generalize the theoretical implications discussed above.

Finally, we are sure that a better conceptualization of the link between social capital and knowledge acquisition may be more rigorously achieved by introducing other control variables.

ACKNOWLEDGEMENTS

The authors thank the anonymous reviewers and the participants at the RENT Conference 2004 for their comments and suggestions on a previous draft of the chapter. The authors are solely responsible for any errors and omissions.

REFERENCES

Aldrich, H. and Zimmer, C. (1986). Entrepreneurship through social networks. In Sexton, D.L. and Smilor, R.W. (eds). *The Art and Science of Entrepreneurship*. Cambridge, MA: Ballinger, pp. 3–23.

Allison, P.D. (1999). *Logistic Regression Using the SAS System. Theory and Application*. Cary, NC: SAS Institute.

Anderson, J.C., Hakansson, H. and Johanson, J. (1994). Dyadic business relationships within a business network context. *Journal of Marketing*, **58**: 1–15.

Audretsch, D. and Feldman, M. (1996). R&D spillovers and the geography of innovation and production. *American Economic Review*, **86**: 641–51.

Barney, J.B. and Hansen, M.H. (1994). Trustworthiness as a source of competitive advantage. *Strategic Management Journal*, **15**(2): 175–90.

Birley, S. (1985). The role of networks in the entrepreneurial process. *Journal of Business Venturing*, **1**: 107–17.

Birley, S., Cromie, S. and Myers, A. (1990). *Entrepreneurial networks in Northern Ireland*. Belfast: Ulster Business School.

Borgatti, S.P., Candance, J. and Everett, M.G. (1998). Network measures of social capital. *Connections*, **21**(2): 27–36.

Bourdieu, P. (1983). The form of capital. In Richardson, J.G. (ed.). *Handbook of Theory and Research for the Sociology of Education*. New York: Greenwood, pp. 241–58.

Brass, D. (1995). A social network perspective on human resources management. In Ferris, G.R. (ed.). *Research in Personnel and Human Resources Management*, vol. 13. Greenwich, CT: JAI Press, pp. 39–79.

Burt, R.S. (1992). *Structural Holes: The Social Structure of Competition*. Cambridge, MA: Harvard University Press.

Burt, R.S. (1997). A note on social capital and network content. *Social Networks*, **19**: 355–73.

Byrk, A.S. and Raudenbush, S.W. (1992). *Hierarchical Linear Models: Applications and Data Analysis Methods*. Newbuy Park, CA: Sage Publications.

Churchill, G.A. Jr (1979). A paradigm for developing better measures of marketing constructs. *Journal of Marketing Research*, **16**(February): 64–73.

Coase, R.H. (1937). The Nature of the Firm. *Economica*, **4**(16), November: 386–405.

Cohen, W.M, Levinthal, D.A. (1990). Absorptive capacity: A new perspective on learning and innovation. *Administrative Science Quarterly*, **35**: 128–52.

Coleman, J.S. (1990). *Foundations of Social Theory*. New York: Harvard University Press.

Cooper, A.C., Gimeno-Gascon, F.J. and Woo, C.Y. (1991). A resource-based prediction of new venture survival and growth. In Wall, J.L. and Jauch, L.R. (eds). *Best Paper Proceedings*. Miami Beach, FL: Academy of Management.

Covin, J.G. and Slevin, D.P. (1990). New venture strategic posture, structure, and performance: An industry life cycle analysis. *Journal of Business Venturing*, **5**: 123–35.

Deeds, D.L., De Carolis, D. and Coombs, J. (1999). Dynamic capabilities and new product development in high technology ventures: An empirical analysis of new biotechnology firms. *Journal of Business Venturing*, **15**: 211–19.

Dollinger, M.J. (1984). Environmental boundary spanning and information processing effects on organizational performance. *Academy of Management Journal*, **27**(2): 351–68.

Dyer, J.H. and Nobeoka, K. (2000). Creating and managing a high performance knowledge-sharing network: The Toyota Case. *Strategic Management Journal*, **21**: 345–67.

Dyer, J.H. and Singh, H. (1998). The relational view: Cooperative strategy and sources of interorganizational competitive advantage. *Academy of Management Review*, **23**: 660–79.

Eisenhardt, K.M. and Schoohoven, C. (1996). Resource-based view of strategic alliance formation: Strategic and social effects in entrepreneurial firms. *Organization Science*, **7**: 136–50.

Ford, D. (2002). *Understanding Business Marketing and Purchasing*. London: Thomson Learning.

Granovetter, M.S. (1985). Economic action and social structure: The problem of embeddedness. *American Journal of Sociology*, **91**: 81–150.

Gulati, R. (1999). Network location and learning: The influence of network resources and firm capabilities on alliance formation. *Strategic Management Journal*, **20**: 397–420.

Hakansson, H. (1982). *International Marketing and Purchasing of Industrial Goods: An Interaction Approach*. IMP Project Group. London: John Wiley & Sons.

Jacobs, J. (1965). *The Death and Life of Great American Cities*. New York: Penguin Books.

Jarillo, J.C. (1989). On strategic networks. *Strategic Management Journal*, **9**: 31–41.

Kogut, B. and Zander, U. (1992). Knowledge of the firm. Combinative capabilities and the replication of technology. Special Issues: Management of technology. *Organization Science*, **3**: 383–97.

Krackhardt, D. (1996). The strength of strong ties: The importance of philos in organizations. In Nohria, N. and Eccles, R.G. (eds), *Networks and Organizations: Structure, Form, and Action*, Boston, MA: Harvard Business School Press, pp. 261–89.

Krackhardt, D. (2000). The network as a knowledge: Generative rules and the emergence of structure. *Strategic Management Journal*, **21**: 405–25.

Lane, P.J. and Lubatkin, M. (1998). Relative absorptive capacity and interorganizational learning. *Strategic Management Journal*, **19**: 461–77.

Larson, A. (1992). Network dyads in entrepreneurial settings: A study of the governance of exchange relationships. *Administrative Science Quarterly*, **37**: 76–104.

Lin, N. (2001). Building a network theory of social capital. In Lin, N., Cook, K. and Burt, R.S. (eds). *Social Capital. Theory and Research*. New York: Aldine De Gruyter.

Lin, N., Cook, K. and Burt, R. (2001). *Social Capital*. New York: Walter de Gruyter.

Malmberg, A. and Maskell, P. (2002). The elusive concept of localization economies: Towards knowledge based theory of spatial clustering. *Environment and Planning*, **34**: 429–49.

McDougall, P., Shane, S. and Oviatt, B. (1994). Explaining the formation of international new ventures: The limits of international business research. *Journal of Business Venturing*, **9**: 469–87.

McEvily, B. and Zaheer, A. (1999). Bridging ties: A source of rim heterogeneity in competitive capabilities. *Strategic Management Journal*, **20**(12): 1133–56.

Moran, P. and Ghoshal, S. (1996). Value creation by firms. In Keys, J.B. and Dosier, L.N. (eds). *Best Paper Proceedings*. Cincinnati, OH: Academy of Management, pp. 41–5.

Nahapiet, J. and Ghoshal, S. (1998). Social capital, intellectual capital and the organizational advantage. *Academy of Management Review*, **23**: 242–66.
Nonaka, I. (1991). The knowledge creating company. *Harvard Business Review*, **69**(6): 96–104.
Nooteboom, B., Berger, H. and Noorderhaven, N. (1997). Effects of trust and governance on relational risk. *Academy of Management Journal*, **40**: 308–38.
Nunnally, J.C. (1978). *Psychometric Theory*, 2nd edn. New York: McGraw Hill.
Penrose, E. (1959). *The Theory of the Growth of the Firm*. Oxford: Blackwell.
Ramachandran, K. and Ramnarayan, S. (1993). Entrepreneurial orientation and networking: Some Indian evidence. *Journal of Business Venturing*, **8**(6): 513–24.
Ring, P.S. and Van de Ven, A.H. (1994). Development processes of cooperative inter-organizational relationships. *Academy of Management Review*, **19**: 90–118.
Spender, J.C. (1996). Making knowledge the basis of a dynamic theory of the firm. *Strategic Management Journal*, **17**: 45–62.
Starr, J.E. and MacMillan, I.C. (1990). Resource cooptation via social contracting: Resource acquisition strategies for new ventures. *Strategic Management Journal*, **11**(1): 79–92.
Tsai, W. and Ghoshal, S. (1998). Social capital and value creation: The role of intrafirm networks. *Academy of Management Journal*, **41**: 464–76.
Uzzi, B. (1997). Social structure and competition in interfirm networks: The paradox of embeddedness. *Administrative Science Quarterly*, **42**: 35–67.
Van de Ven, A.H. (1993). The development of an infrastructure for entrepreneurship. *Journal of Business Venturing*, **8**(3): 211–30.
Von Hippel, E. (1988). *The Sources of Innovation*. New York: Oxford University Press.
Williamson, O.E. (1975). *Markets and Hierarchies*. New York: Free Press.
Yli-Renko, H., Autio, E. and Sapienza, H.J. (2001). Social capital, knowledge acquisition, and knowledge exploitation in young technology-based firms. *Strategic Management Journal*, **22**: 587–613.
Zahra, S.A., Ireland, R.D. and Hitt, M.A. (2000). International expansion by new venture firms: international diversity, mode of market entry, technological learning and performance. *Academy of Management Journal*, **43**: 925–50.

4. The evolution of firms created by the Swedish science and technology labour force, 1990–2000

Frédéric Delmar, Karin Hellerstedt and Karl Wennberg

INTRODUCTION

The purpose of this chapter is to explore the entrepreneurial activities of the science and technology labour force (STLF) in Sweden. We are interested in understanding the magnitude of their entrepreneurial efforts and how it is related to economic growth. By entrepreneurial activities we here mean the establishment, growth and exit of independent firms. This topic is interesting because the entrepreneurial activities of this group are recognized to be of potentially great economic value as it has been proposed as the link between the production of new technological knowledge and its commercialization (Acs, 2002; Baumol, 2002; Carlsson and Eliasson, 2003). However, there is still a lack of empirical evidence to support this claim. By studying the entrepreneurial activities of the STLF we hope to reach a better understanding of how new technological knowledge is converted into economic growth.

The science and technology labour force is important for several reasons. First, it is the labour force that has the highest probability to be part of the research and development sector producing new knowledge. The relative size of the STLF is thus essential because they represent the accumulated technological knowledge in the economy. Second, the STLF can be seen as carriers of knowledge from one firm to another as they move between employers, acting as agents of technology dissemination and knowledge spillovers (Almeida and Kogut, 1999). Third, as they have access to new information they are the most likely to discover potentially valuable opportunities (Hayek, 1945).

If the entrepreneurial activities of this labour group are of importance, then we can conclude that Sweden has a framework that encourages entrepreneurial initiatives based on the commercial exploitation of new knowledge. Entrepreneurship in the form of new firms has become an important substitute to large and old firms, since new entrepreneurial firms are more able to create new jobs and effectively use new technological knowledge for commercial purposes (Aldrich, 1999; Audretsch, 1991; Audretsch and Mahmood, 1995).

In earlier work we have focused on the involvement of this labour group in self-employment (Delmar et al., 2003). In the present work, we will specifically examine how this self-employment translates into different firm-level activities. Knowledge about these activities is still scarce. For example, we do not know how many firms this group creates, and whether or not these firms create any substantial economic growth. We want to know how new knowledge is used to establish and to expand firms, and how often such firms exit from the market. To achieve our goals we have created a specific population of firms that are managed and owned by self-employed people with an education in the natural sciences, medicine or technology. We follow this population of firms between 1990 and 2000. These types of analyses have previously been impossible due to data limitations. With the help of experts[1] from Statistics Sweden, we have been able to mitigate this problem and match individual-level data with firm-level data. This enables us to follow the evolution of both entrepreneurs, and the firms that they found. This chapter includes a description of:

- the extent of independent firms owned and managed by entrepreneurs from the science and technology labour force;
- the entries and exits of firms owned and managed by entrepreneurs from the science and technology labour force;
- the growth and survival of these firms;

The descriptions are broken down by industry, size class and legal form. The report is structured as follows. In the next section we present the theoretical framework, followed by the method. We discuss the strengths and limitations of the present design. In the third section, we present the results from the analyses. We then discuss in detail how these firms come into existence, if they grow, and in which industries and legal form. To end, we put forward our conclusions and discuss the implications of this study for research and for policy purposes.

THEORY

New Knowledge and Entrepreneurship

Endogenous growth theory distinguishes itself from neoclassical growth theory by emphasizing that economic growth is an endogenous outcome of an economic system and not the result of forces that impinge from the outside (Romer, 1990, 1994). Technological change leads to a change in the output per hour worked, and thus leads to increased growth. The reason that technological change plays such a central role is due to the basic characteristics that technology or technological discoveries have. Technological discoveries differ from other inputs in the sense that many people can use them at the same time.

Consequently, the creation and commercial use of new knowledge plays an important role in economic growth. This new knowledge comes from things that people do. They create new knowledge because they think they may be able to achieve market power and earn rents. An interesting question that follows is: who are the agents most likely to create new knowledge and introduce it to the market for commercial ends, and why do they do this? Research suggests that certain agents in the economy such as entrepreneurs are more likely to use new knowledge commercially than others.

New knowledge is non-rival[2] and under some circumstances even free to use, but only by those who actually have knowledge of its existence. In line with Hayek (1945), we argue that knowledge about the existence of this knowledge is not equally distributed across all individuals in an economy. A central quality of a market economy is the division of knowledge among individuals, such that no two individuals share the same knowledge or information about the economy. Only a few will know about a new way of organizing, a new way to produce, new products or services or new raw materials that are not being put to best use. Such knowledge is personal because it is acquired through each individual's own situation, including present and previous occupation, education, social position and daily life. The unequal distribution of information among individuals who consequently do not have access to the same interpretations, experiences or observations has implications for entrepreneurship (Acs, 2002).

Entrepreneurship is possible because people do not have the same access to information, and therefore they differ in what they believe to be a valuable opportunity to exploit. It is this unequal distribution of information that creates opportunities in the first place. The same unequal distribution of information creates obstacles for exploiting the opportunity profitably, because there is no current market for these future goods and services. Entrepreneurial processes are thus a function of the uncertainty of an opportunity's real value, in combination with asymmetric information. Despite not knowing its actual value, some people will still choose to invest their time, talent and resources to exploit what they believe is a valuable opportunity.

Our framework is based on an Austrian-economic (Kirzner, 1997; Schumpeter, 1934) perspective of entrepreneurship which identifies the historically and culturally determined framework conditions affecting entrepreneurship and the idiosyncratic prior experiences of enterprising – and potentially enterprising – individuals (Shane and Venkataraman, 2000; Venkataraman, 1997). By 'framework conditions' we refer to general conditions defining the context in which entrepreneurship occurs. Examples of such conditions are the stock of knowledge, of financial and of human capital in the economy, the institutions, the history and the culture of the economy. Such conditions determine what opportunities are identified and how entrepreneurs will exploit them (Baumol, 1993). The framework assumes that changes in technology create opportunities that are not equally obvious to everyone, but are discovered and exploited because some individuals have an advantage in discovering specific opportunities. This advantage is provided by these individuals' access to idiosyncratic information and resources that are generated by their prior experiences and their position in social networks. Entrepreneurial opportunities are not equally obvious to everyone, but they are equally available to anyone with the experiences and the knowledge of discovering them.

The science and technology labour force represents the educational groups that have the highest return in terms of income growth for educational investment. Hence, there exists a tension between the ability to discover and the willingness to exploit in this labour group. While they frequently have access to new knowledge and technology and therefore have a higher probability of finding valuable opportunitics, thcy will also demand a high value of their utility to exploit opportunities because they have high incomes and good career opportunities. They might identify a number of opportunities that might be valuable for others, but choose not to exploit them because the perceived gap between the expected utility of exploiting the opportunity and alternative uses of their time is too small.

Industrial Organization and Firm Behaviour

Our framework suggests that entrepreneurship – here defined as the establishment of new firms and their development – represent an important mechanism in transforming new technological knowledge into economic activities. In this section we review earlier empirical research on new firm formation and development (growth and exit). Empirical research supports our theoretical framework, but research also points heavily towards the fact that far from all new firms have a substantial impact on the market. Only a few of the firms started can be expected to have any effect on the market; however, put together their volume has a substantial impact on how industries and economies develop. We will focus on research dealing with industrial organization (Caves, 1998; Geroski, 2001), but also to some extent on organizational ecology (Carroll and Hannan, 2000; Hannan and Freeman, 1984).

Firm entry, exit (or the birth and death of firms) and growth are intimately related. This intimacy seems to be related to two mechanisms. First, the survival rate among most entrants is low, especially during the early years. Second, even successful entrants may take more than a decade before they reach a size comparable to the average firm size in the industry (Dunne et al., 1988; Geroski, 1995). Firm growth takes time and most firms never grow (Aldrich, 1979; Reynolds and White, 1997; Storey, 1994). While young firms have a higher probability of failure, we also observe that younger firms grow more and faster than older firms.[3] Moreover, new firms in young industries are particularly likely to grow (Bottazzi et al., 2002; Bottazzi et al., 2001; Dunne et al., 1988).

New firm entry is common. Large number of firms enter most industries in most years. Most new entrants are small, even if there is substantial variation within and between industries. In other words, firms enter industries at different initial sizes, and the entrant's size distribution varies from industry to industry. This pattern is aligned with the structure of the entered industry, which is often called barriers to entry (Mata and Portugal, 1994; Mata and Machado, 1996) and also affects the probability of survival of the firms. Larger entry barriers in an industry mean a large initial size on average for entrants, but most entrants remain very small. Audretsch and Mahmood (1995) studying a US population, and Wagner (1994) studying a German population, both found that the survival rate of firms increased with their initial size. Firms in industries with high entry rates grow more than firms in more stable industries (Barnett and Sorensen, 2002; Carroll and Hannan, 2000). A dynamic environment is thus favourable for the growth of firms.

These patterns should not necessarily be interpreted as that small firms fail to survive or grow just because they lack resources or ability. On a macro scale, most new firms seem to act quite rationally and to limit their initial investment in accordance with a real option approach. This approach explains that since firm founders cannot *a priori* know the value of their opportunity, less confident firm founders start out small, incurring a unit-cost penalty but limiting their sunk cost investment while they gather evidence of the value of the opportunity. If the feedback is positive, firm founders can increase their investments; if the feedback is negative they can exit at a minimum loss. Smaller entrants would therefore be expected to show higher exit rates. They may therefore start small because there are large risks of failure, and consequently want to limit their investment (Caves, 1998; Jovanovic, 1982).

Summary

The empirical findings on industry dynamics have been linked to a more abstract discussion linking economic growth, the production of new technological knowledge and entrepreneurship (defined as the establishment and evolution of new independent firms). We have argued that the production and commercialization of new technological knowledge is a key to economic growth. Entrepreneurial activities by individuals represent the mechanism by which new knowledge is transformed into economic activities. Entrepreneurial activities by the science and technology labour force may be particularly important to economic growth. If it is important and there is a supportive environment for such activities we should expect to see high entry rates (and exit rates) coupled with high-growth firms producing economic growth such as employment.

METHOD

Data Sources

This study relies on register data from Statistics Sweden. We have closely cooperated with register experts from Statistics Sweden in order to create a solid data set. By combining data from various registers we have developed a unique data set that allows us to analyse the development of the firms owned and managed by individuals educated in engineering, the natural sciences and medicine from 1990 to 2000. We combine data on the individual level with firm-level data to identify what firms are owned and managed by persons included in the STLF. We focus solely on full-time entrepreneurs. A person is defined as being full-time self-employed when they receive the majority of their income from a firm in which they are owner or part owner.

This design enables us to study the dynamics and development over time of the population. We can follow firms that are already in the population (that is, firms being owned and managed by the STLF prior to 1990), firms that enter the population during the studied period, as well as firms exiting the population. This allows us to examine both changes in the population (all active members) and the progression of cohorts (firms becoming owned and managed by the STLF after 1990). We can therefore control for age and cohort effects.

Population

The primary unit of analysis is the firm, that is, STLF firms. The data set comprises all independent firms that are owned and managed full-time by the STLF between 1990 and 2000. With respect to these categories of firms, it is therefore a census study. There are 22 312 such firms in the population;

11 077 (49.6 per cent) of those entered the population during the studied period between 1991 and 2000. A description of self-employment among the science and technology labour force at the individual level can be found in Delmar et al. (2003).

Table 4.1 depicts how many firms are included in the population for each year, that is, the total stock of STLF firms each year. As can be seen, the number of firms is rather stable during the observation period. There is a slight drop in the number of firms during 1991, 1992 and 1993. In 1994 the number starts to increase and it does so during the remainder of the period. In 1999 it is back to the same level as in 1990 and the highest observed number can be found in 2000, when there are 9348 firms that are owned and managed by the STLF. The number of full-time self-employed (FTSE) follows the same trend as the total number of firms. The reason for the figures being higher for FTSE than number of firms is that some firms are owned and managed by more than one individual from the STLF.

Table 4.2 displays the stock of firms owned by STLF entrepreneurs and the stock of firms that are included in this group during at least one year. As we match ownership and firm status, we have to remember that a firm's status is independent of ownership, that is, a firm can have many different owners over its lifespan. This means that a firm might have a life prior to and after it has left our population of study. A firm can enter our population in two ways: (1) as created by an STLF entrepreneur; or (2) an STLF entrepreneur becomes owner or part-owner of an already active firm. Therefore, for every year we can also observe a number of firms that are active and present in our data set but not included in our population until they fulfill the selection criteria. The number of these firms varies between 2523 in 1990 and 4780 in 1996.

To be included in our analyses a firm has to have at least one owner who has a three-year or longer university degree in engineering, the natural sciences or medicine (nursing school excluded) (Delmar et al., 2003). As indicated previously, there are two ways in which a firm can enter the population. Table 4.2 displays the dynamics of this specific population when it comes to entry and exit. In the first case, a person with the relevant education starts a firm. Those cases are labelled '*De novo* STLF' in Table 4.2. In the second case, persons not having any of the relevant educations have established a firm and this firm becomes owned or partly owned by a person from the STLF at a later time. Those cases are labelled 'Acquired firms' in Table 4.2.[4] In this case the firm becomes part of the population when the change of ownership takes place and it becomes fully or partly owned by a person from the STLF. Similar to entry, firms can exit the population in two ways. In the first case, a firm exits the population because it is terminated. Those cases are labelled 'Exiting firms STLF' in Table 4.2.

Table 4.1 Number of firms operated by STLF self-employed 1990–2000

	1990	1991	1992	1993	1994	1995	1996	1997	1998	1999	2000	CHANGE 1990–2000
Number of firms	8610	7191	7069	7073	7422	7670	7602	8124	8240	8687	9348	738 (8.6%)
FTSE	9244	7815	7673	7637	7969	8181	8041	8553	8650	9079	9743	499 (5.4%)
Stlf/firm	1.07	1.09	1.09	1.08	1.07	1.07	1.06	1.05	1.05	1.05	1.04	−0.03 (−2.8%)

Table 4.2 The stock, entry and exit of firms owned by STLF entrepreneurs 1990–2000

	1990	1991	1992	1993	1994	1995	1996	1997	1998	1999	2000
New firms											
De novo STLF		838	525	559	760	676	732	950	859	904	913
Acquired firms		934	890	769	862	1048	874	1011	762	859	1192
Exiting firms											
Exiting firms STLF	1671	538	644	471	564	617	628	678	733	1000	
Sold firms	1513	1000	803	699	947	1079	811	805	671	521	
FTSE with firm level data	8596	7186	7063	6944	7396	7609	7519	8041	8179	8538	9123
FTSE identifed	8610	7191	7069	7073	7422	7670	7602	8124	8240	8687	9348
Diff	14	5	6	129	26	61	83	83	61	149	225
Active firms but not part of population this year	2523	3656	4004	4215	4408	4499	4780	4489	4374	3892	2740
Total firms	11 119	10 842	11 067	11 159	11 804	12 108	12 299	12 530	12 553	12 430	11 863

Note: Because we are matching individual-level data and firm-level data, which are not totally compatible, we get a number of cases at the individual level that are indicated as individuals with firms, but there is no data at the firm level. Those cases are indicated in the row 'Diff'. The cases are kept in the analyses for sake of clarity. The absolute majority of these cases are single individual firms.

In the second case, a firm exits the population because the owner sells all ownership of the firm to persons with other educational backgrounds that are not part of the STLF. In this case, the firm can continue to be active but is no longer part of our population. Those cases are labelled 'Sold firms' in Table 4.2.

An important technical detail is that over our period of observation we have 7716 *de novo* entries and 9201 'acquired firms' accumulated over the years. This represents in total 16 917 firms entering. This is a figure that is higher than the 11 077 firms mentioned previously. The difference is that the latter represent unique entries, whereas the former figure counts the same firm each time it makes a transition back into the population. Firms exit from our population when an STLF entrepreneur does not receive their primary income from that firm or is no longer the firm's owner.

Descriptor Variables

Five different variables were used to break down the analysis into sub-categories: survival, firm growth, industry (18 industries), legal form and initial firm size (with different size classes). We analyse our data by cross-tabulating our descriptor variables by the years in our observation period.

Survival

Firm survival is central to our topic since it varies substantially between firms (Audretsch and Mahmood, 1995; Carroll and Hannan, 2000). Survival is measured as the number of years a firm is active. A firm is active as long as there is any economic activity, independent of whether or not the original founders are still active in that same firm.[5]

Since we need to know when a firm is started, we only calculate the survival of firms established in 1991 or later.

Firm growth

An important indicator of a well-functioning economy is that newly established firms are able to grow. This is especially important for this group of firms, as some of them have probably acted on opportunities with substantial value. We measure the absolute growth in employment for each cohort of newly started firms. Other possible measures include sales, assets and market shares. The advantages of employment are that it is commonly used and easy to compare across studies, it is insensitive to inflation and has a direct inference to economic growth in terms of employment creation (Delmar, 1996). We measure growth on a yearly basis. Measuring growth only for the cohorts has important advantages as we control for the effect of age and size (Bottazzi et al., 2002; Dunne and Hughes, 1996).

Industry
Industry differences are known to have an important impact on the growth and survival of new firms (Carroll and Hannan, 2000; Klepper and Graddy, 1990). Following and expanding on previous work in this area (Davidsson and Delmar, 2003; Davidsson et al., 1994) we use an industry classification where firms are grouped into 18 categories based on their Swedish industry standard code (SNI92): High-tech manufacturing, Wood, Manufacturing, Mining, Other manufacturing, Technology services, Knowledge industries-intensive services (consulting etc.), Finance, Trade, Hotel and restaurants, Communications (including logistics), Education, Other services, Land, forestry and fishery, Public sector etc., Research and development, and finally, Healthcare. This classification enables us to study in which industries STLF entrepreneurship takes place and if it changes over time.[6]

Legal form
We differentiate between legal form since it is associated with the development of the firm. For example, we know that sole proprietorships are more likely to be terminated than incorporations. We have three different legal forms: sole proprietorship, partnership and incorporation. Legal form is a time-variant variable that can change between years.

Initial size
Initial firm size was chosen based on its supposed importance to growth and employment creation (Dunne and Hughes, 1996; Storey, 1994; Wagner, 1992). We investigate the total population of firms based on their initial size. The variable does not change with time.

RESULTS

The results section first describes the population of firms which provide the primary income of and are owned by STLF entrepreneurs. Secondly, patterns of entry and exit are examined with analyses broken down according to industry affiliation, legal form, size distribution, survival and growth. The analyses covers the period from 1990 to 2000.

The Population of Firms Owned by STLF Entrepreneurs

Size distribution and job creation
Table 4.3 displays the mean and maximum size among the firms which are owned by and constitute the primary income for STLF entrepreneurs, as well as what kind of people these firms tend to employ. This is the total

Table 4.3 Size distributions of firms owned by STLF entrepreneurs

	1990	1991	1992	1993	1994	1995	1996	1997	1998	1999	2000
Average size	4	4.5	4	3.9	3.8	3.6	3.2	2.9	3	2.9	3.2
Maximum size	710	820	506	507	514	514	498	517	984	1103	498
Number ST no research degree	10934	9679	9125	8439	9217	9233	8375	8751	8953	9404	8375
Number ST with research degree	924	685	686	669	766	750	759	781	860	884	759
Total ST	11858	10364	9811	9108	9983	9983	9134	9532	9813	10288	9134
Total number of employees	34432	31868	27812	25948	27681	27046	23680	22455	23829	24499	26237
Total number of firms	8610	7191	7069	7073	7422	7670	7602	8124	8240	8687	9348

stock of firms in our population. The number of firms varies between a minimum of 7073 firms in 1993 and a maximum of 9348 firms in 2000. It is thus a growing firm population.

With respect to the size of the firms and their ability to generate employment, the conclusion is the opposite. The ability of these firms to generate employment diminished dramatically over the observation period. The absolute majority of all firms, 84.9 per cent, are in the size bracket 1–4 employees.[7] Despite some yearly variation, there is no dramatic change over years. With a few exceptions, all firms have less than 50 employees. We are dealing with a population of very small firms, with almost no medium-sized firms. Two additional analyses confirm this image. The average size varies between 4 employees and 2.9 employees. Over time we observe that the average firm size actually decreases. Table 4.3 also displays the size of the largest single firm in the population for each year. This maximum size varies quite dramatically over time. The maximum size peaks in 1991 with a firm having 820 employees, to hit the bottom in 1997 with a firm having 498 employees. Thereafter, the maximum size peaks once more quite dramatically in 1998 and 1999 with firms having 984 and 1103 employees respectively. Apart from the years 1998 and 1999 which represent an economic boom in Sweden, especially in the ICT sector, the maximum firm size has decreased over the period 1990–2000.

A closer look at the kind of jobs created by this group reveals a slight increase in the share of STLF employed relative to other categories. However, we note dramatic and negative changes when the total number of jobs created are analysed. In 1990 34 432 individuals worked in these firms, in 2000 only 26 237 individuals worked in these firms. This represents a net drop of 23.8 per cent over 11 years. It is obvious that the ability of this population to generate jobs diminishes over time.

The loss in job creation ability becomes even more accentuated in Table 4.4 where we investigate the ability of this group to hire other individuals from the STLF relative to other organizations. As indicated previously, the STLF has grown substantially over the period. In 1990 there were 134 230 individuals with a degree in science, technology or medicine active on the labour market. In 1999, the number is 191 920, which corresponds to an increase of 43 per cent.[8] During the same period, the share of STLF employed by our population of firms diminished from 9.3 per cent in 1990 to 5.6 per cent in 1999. That corresponds to an actual loss of 39.8 per cent in our population's ability to generate employment for their own labour group.

The critical reader would probably argue that these are not necessarily true changes, because the way we have constructed our population means we create a 'non-growth' bias. Firms that grow substantially and go public or are acquired by other firms become excluded from our population

Table 4.4 The share of science and technology (ST) employment held by STLF entrepreneurs compared to other employers

	1990	1991	1992	1993	1994	1995	1996	1997	1998	1999	2000
Percentage employed in STLF Firms no research	9.3%	8.0%	7.6%	7.0%	7.3%	7.0%	6.1%	6.0%	5.7%	5.6%	3.3%
Number of ST no research degree	117 571	120 506	120 177	119 996	126 283	131 996	137 599	145 057	155 732	167 041	253 251
Percentage employed in STLF Firms with research	5.5%	3.9%	3.9%	3.7%	3.9%	3.7%	3.5%	3.5%	3.7%	3.6%	2.9%
Number of ST with research degree	16 659	17 445	17 658	18 039	19 410	20 502	21 386	22 311	23 515	24 879	26 399
Percentage employed in STLF Firms	8.8%	7.5%	7.1%	6.6%	6.9%	6.5%	5.7%	5.7%	5.5%	5.4%	3.3%
Total number ST	134 230	137 951	137 835	138 035	145 693	152 498	158 985	167 368	179 247	191 920	279 650

Note: In 2000 the education codes are changed and the number of educations that are defined as part of the STLF increase, and hence the number of people part of that population.

because they are publicly traded. In the later analyses when we follow the cohorts of newly established firms we investigate this possibility by following the firm through its whole life independent of changes in ownership. The results shown here do not change substantially. Only a very few firms go public. Many firms are acquired, but they do not show any substantial growth before they are bought up. Hence the result still stands. This population has dramatically lost its power to generate jobs both for their own labour group and in general. This is a population of firms where the number of firms that grow and their ability to generate jobs diminishes on average and in total.

The dominant legal forms are sole proprietorship and incorporations. Partnership represents on average only 3.2 per cent. The proportion of sole proprietorship has grown from 28.9 per cent in 1992 to 51.2 per cent in 2000. The share of incorporations has diminished steadily over time, from 59.6 per cent in 1991 to 37.1 per cent in 2000. Also note that on average 8.6 per cent of all firms do not have any legal form indicated. Our own analyses combined with consultation with data experts from Statistics Sweden indicate that new firms and firms that later on are categorized as sole proprietorship are over-represented here. Most of these firms exist only for one year.

The number of employees in STLF firms also differs greatly between industries. Two industries, healthcare and technology services, account for 47.1 per cent of all employees. A difference between the industry classification by firms and the industry classification by employment is that a significant fraction of the total number of employees (21 per cent) is employed by firms in the manufacturing sector, but these firms only comprise 4.5 per cent of the total number of STLF firms. Firms in the manufacturing sector are generally larger than firms in the service sector. The majority of the new firms, however, belong to the service sector. In that respect, this population of firms follows the general trend in industry dynamics: the average size of firms goes down, and the number of firms in the service sector increases relative to the manufacturing sector. The changes in number of employees are thus less accentuated than changes in number of firms. This is also in line with previous research suggesting that the dynamics of entry and exit have relatively little effect in terms of employment in an industry (Geroski, 1995). However, as we will see in the following section, entry and exit have an important effect on the structure of the population as a whole.

Entry and Exit from the STLF Firm Population

The numbers of entries and exits are presented in Table 4.5. *De novo* entries are defined as new firms from which an individual belonging to the STLF

Table 4.5 De novo *entry and exiting firms in the STLF firm population*

Year	1990	1991	1992	1993	1994	1995	1996	1997	1998	1999	2000
Number of firms	8610	7191	7069	7073	7422	7670	7602	8124	8240	8687	9348
Number of *de novo* entries		838	525	559	760	676	732	950	859	904	913
Number of STLF exits	1671	538	644	471	564	617	628	678	733	1000	
Percentage *de novo* entries		11.7%	7.4%	7.9%	10.2%	8.8%	9.6%	11.7%	10.4%	10.4%	9.8%
Percentage STLF exits	19.4%	7.5%	9.1%	6.7%	7.6%	8.0%	8.3%	8.3%	8.9%	11.5%	

receives their main salary, is part-owner or owner, and was present from the beginning. Exits are defined as the firm being terminated. We first examine the development of *de novo* entries over time. The column 'Percentage *de novo* entries' illustrates what proportion of the current year's number of firms was created in the same year. This proportion is roughly the same at the beginning and the end of the period. The column 'Percentage STLF exits' illustrates what proportion of firms in one year exit during the next year. Similar to entries (with the exception of 1991) there does not seem to be any upward or downward trends for exits: around 8.5 per cent of the firms seem to exit annually. Comparing this figure to the average annual entry rate of 10 per cent indicates that there is a slow but consistent increase in the number of firms run by the STLF. This should not be attributed to a general increase in entrepreneurship frequency among this labour force but is due to a general increase in the number of individuals with the relevant education (cf. Delmar et al., 2003).

Entry and exit rates are clearly related to each other. When the entry rate is high, so is the exit rate. Two exceptions exist. If we go back to the exit rate in the year 1991, almost 20 per cent of the population of firms active in 1990 exited, leading to a sharp decrease in the total number of firms. This is a consequence of the severe recession that Sweden experienced in the early 1990s. The second exception is the development during the years 1993–94, where the number of entries in 1994 is relatively high, but the number of exits in 1993 is the lowest in all years during the period. The low number of exits is probably attributable to an upturn in the economy after the recession in the early 1990s.

The relationship between entry and exit rates has been noted in earlier research (Geroski, 1995; Picot and Dupuy, 1998). The phenomenon can be explained as entry and exit rates being parts of a larger process of change where a large number of new firms displace a large numbers of older firms without significantly changing the gross number of firms in operation at any given time. This concept is known as 'churning' and is positively associated with times of economic booms (Birch, 1979). By looking at the gross flows in and out of the population (that is, entries and exits) we can determine the structural stability of the group. The more stable the group is (the less entries and exits), the longer is the average lifespan of firms, and the less dynamics can be observed. This 'dynamics', measured as the gross flows of entries and exits of firms, more important than the number of net entries (entries minus exits) as a sign of economic vitality (Audretsch, 1995). For the individual firm, a low number of entries and exits could very well be positive since those firms that are eventually started have higher probability of survival. It is, however, negative on a societal level, since inadequate competition does not drive economic development effectively. More entries and exits can therefore indicate that more people actually become entrepreneurs at one or several points during their working life, and that it is possible to start new firms easily and close these at an early stage if the firm does not provide enough earnings. Before we can determine if the churning of STLF is an indication of much or little competition, we need to look at the average lifespan and characteristics of the firms being started.

Industry

A large proportion, 20.8 per cent, of the new STLF firms are started in the technology services industry. Examples of businesses included in this sector are computer software companies, technical testing and analysis, and firms providing services to the construction industry. We can also observe a large number of firms, 7.6 per cent, being started in the related industry of 'other knowledge-intensive services'. Examples of such businesses include business and management consultancies, as well as firms providing services related to patents and intellectual property rights. Relatively many firms, 9.9 per cent, are also founded in the healthcare sector. This can be explained by the entrepreneurial activities of a certain group within the science and technology labour force, namely those with an education in medicine. As could be seen in Table 4.1, this sub-group is the one most frequently starting new firms, often as a way to establish their own medical practices.

The literature offers three, partly compatible, explanations to these findings. First, people are likely to discover and exploit opportunities that are related to their prior knowledge (Shane, 2000), which is based on prior experience and education (Casson, 1982). A large proportion of the STFL has experience in the healthcare and technological services sectors, which would explain a large number of start-ups in these sectors. Second, conditions for business survival differ across industries. For example, few entries are noted in sectors such as mining or wood, paper and pulp where initial capital investments are substantial. Third, technological regimes are likely to be different across industries (Audretsch, 1991). Some sectors are characterized by a routinized regime whereas other sectors are structured according to an entrepreneurial regime, the latter a more favourable environment for new and innovative firms.

Few firms, about 0.4 per cent, are started within the high-tech manufacturing sector. However, Swedish studies using the same industry classification as we do here have found that approximately 1 per cent of all new firms started belong to this sector (Dahlqvist et al., 2000). As our population consists of individuals likely to discover opportunities relevant to high-tech companies, we would expect a proportion higher than 1 per cent, rather than the opposite. Given the large financial investments needed, we suspect that the low propensity of STLF start-ups might be attributed to these individuals considering the opportunity costs to be too large. An alternative explanation may be that more entrepreneurial individuals with other educational backgrounds start within the high-tech manufacturing sector firms and subsequently employ individuals with relevant knowledge, such as the STLF.

The distribution of *de novo* start-ups in general mirrors the distribution of the population they enter. Technological services and healthcare represent the most important industries with 30.7 per cent of all started firms. They both represent growing industries, but other industries also grow in terms of a yearly increase of new start-ups. Most important are the following industries: knowledge-intensive firms, communication, education and other services. Hence, while traditional industries still dominate heavily, we can see that other industries have increased their relative importance. Similarly, we can see that the manufacturing sector becomes less and less prevalent for this category of start-ups.

Initial size

The average size of firms started by the STLF is 1.2 employees without substantial variation over time. In other words, in most cases only the founder is employed in the newly established firm. The vast majority are to be found among single firms with the owner-manager as the sole employee. On average during the period, 89 per cent of the new firms had only one employee, and 8.4 per cent of the firms started with two to four employees.

Legal form

Start-up costs vary considerably depending on what legal form is chosen. The financial and legal requirements are substantial for incorporated companies where a share capital of 100 000 SEK is needed in addition to formal registration costs with the Swedish patent office (PRV). Since incorporation provides the owners with limited liability, it is likely associated with riskier adventures and greater initial commitment. Sole proprietorships, on the other hand, require virtually no initial investment. In Sweden it is sufficient to fill out a form at the local tax office to start this type of firm.

The vast majority of firms are founded as sole proprietorships: 82 per cent of all firms started during the period of observation started as sole proprietorships compared to 14 per cent for incorporations and 4 per cent for limited partnerships. The distribution of legal forms among *de novo* entries differs from the distribution in the population, where incorporations are more frequent. As we will see later this does not reflect an ongoing change towards other legal forms. Rather, it is associated to the survival and performance structure that relates to different legal forms. It should be kept in mind that the firms in this study are not operated as sidelines to regular employment but should be considered as 'real firms' operated by an entrepreneur on a full-time basis. This indicates that most STLF firms are, at least initially, started as marginal operations. A theoretical explanation is provided by the real options view (Caves, 1998, p. 1961) where entrepreneurs, in order to manage the uncertainty related to the value of their opportunities, make low initial investments until they have received feedback from the market.

Survival of *De Novo* Entries

The specific conditions under which a firm is founded can have long-term effects on its future development (Brüderl and Schussler, 1990; Fichman and Levinthal, 1991). Such conditions can partly be macro-level factors such as economic development and industry affiliation, and micro-level factors such as initial size and legal form. Given that Sweden underwent a dramatic recession during the first years of the 1990s followed by an upswing, it is possible that these changes affect firms' chances of survival. Some firms were established during the 1997–99 period when financial capital was abundant. Other firms were started during the 1991–93 period when resources were scarce. In addition, 1994 represents a unique year with important legal changes as well as regulatory changes on the labour market. We could therefore expect a cohort effect based on when the firm was established.

Table 4.6 shows the survival rate of the different cohorts started between 1991 and 2000. The table clearly shows that the liability of newness (Baum, 1986) is very large during the first year and gradually diminishes. On average 21 per cent of the firms started exited during the following year. Survival during the first year was lowest for firms started in 1992 and 1999. The cohort started in 1992 appears to be strongly effected by the recession that Sweden experienced at the time, but the effect wears off in subsequent years. The cohort of 1999 also suffers from the downturn that began to affect Sweden in 2000. Survival during the first year was highest for 1991, 1994 and 1997. For the cohorts of 1994 and 1997 it is clear that they were able to take advantage of the changes in the legal structure and the economic boom respectively. These survival rates are in line with results from other countries. Geroski (2001) investigated the survival rates among entries into the US market. He found that 60 per cent of all entrant firms exited within five years of entry, and 80 per cent exited within ten years of entry. The estimates for these firms are 53 per cent exited within five years of entry and 65 per cent exited within ten years of entry. This would indicate that this group on average consists of firms with a somewhat higher probability of survival.

Table 4.6 Percentage survival by cohorts of de novo *entries*

No. of years	% 1991	% 1992	% 1993	% 1994	% 1995	% 1996	% 1997	% 1998	% 1999	% 2000	Mean survival between cohorts for no. of year, respectively (%)
1	100	100	100	100	100	100	100	100	100	100	100
2	81	75	79	81	79	79	82	79	72		79
3	68	65	68	69	66	69	71	63			67
4	64	57	61	59	57	59	58				59
5	58	50	55	53	48	50					53
6	53	46	51	45	42						47
7	47	42	45	38							43
8	43	38	39								40
9	39	33									36
10	35										35

It is important to note that while there are differences in survival between the different cohorts they are not large, but persistent over time (see Table 4.6). The cohorts with the highest survival rates during the first year also have the highest rate of survival after three years. However, the effect fades out over time and there seems to be a regression towards the mean.

Industry

As indicated in the theoretical framework we can expect significant differences among industries in terms of survival. Industry differences are associated with entry barriers. In industries with high entry barriers we can expect the firms to survive longer since entry barriers are overcome by a larger initial investment and a larger size.

We find that firms started in the manufacturing industry have a significantly higher survival rate than the other industries. By the end of the period 57.1 per cent of the firms started in manufacturing are still active, compared to 35.1 per cent for all types of firms. This is in line with the effect of entry barriers (Geroski, 1995). However, manufacturing does only differ from other categories after the second year. It is possible that the effects of different technological regimes as suggested by Audretsch and colleagues only have an effect once firms have been able to establish themselves. The industry with the second-highest survival rates is healthcare. After ten years 46.9 per cent of the firms are still active.

Initial size

We examine the effect of initial size on survival rates for each cohort over the years. The results show that a larger initial size strongly affects the survival of new firms for all of the first seven years. After year seven the effect seems to wear off. Nevertheless, size has a significant impact on survival and the impact is long-lasting. In year seven, only 41.5 per cent of the firms that started with only one employee remained, compared to 72.9 per cent for the firms that started with 5–9 employees.

Legal form

There are large differences in survival of firms based on legal forms. Partnerships are more quickly disbanded than the other legal forms: more than 80 per cent disappear during the period of study compared to 64 per cent for sole proprietorships and 53 per cent for incorporations. An explanation is that partnership is an organizational form with mutual liability; it may be therefore difficult to maintain a good relationship in such organizations for many years. Incorporated firms clearly have higher survival rates than the other legal forms during any year of existence. This is in accordance with the theoretical arguments of higher capital reserves and thus indirectly a higher commitment to the firm's business idea.

Growth of *De Novo* Entries

Firm growth among young firms is one of the most important indicators of industry renewal and economic growth (Davidsson and Delmar, 2003). Growth among young firms is known to be an important contributor to new jobs, and also a strong indicator of the possibility to exploit opportunities successfully. The lack of growing firms can be interpreted as an important indicator that a country's institutional framework does not support growth and entrepreneurship.

The 7716 *de novo* entry firms created 11 879 jobs of which 6604 jobs still remained in 2000 (55.6 per cent). Of the 11 879 created jobs, 79.2 per cent were created the same year the firms were established. The remaining 20.8 per cent of the jobs created came from subsequent growth. The jobs still remaining in 2000 represent 25.2 per cent of all jobs held by the population of STLF firms.

Three results stand out. First, as expected, firms have grown on average but the growth pace is modest. After four years, the average size of the firms in the seven cohorts that we follow for at least four years have increased with a factor of 1.34. This might be impressive but one has to remember that they have also started very small (Size year 1: mean 1.21, st.d. 1.19; size year 4 mean 1.60, st.d. 2.53). Moreover, there is substantial variation across the cohorts. The cohort of 1996 and 1997 are especially impressive since they achieve an average growth by factors of 1.47 and 1.65 respectively. The cohorts of 1991 and 1992 are less impressive, and achieve only an average growth by factors of 1.20 and 1.19 respectively. It is clear that the economic situation when firms are started has an important impact on the growth of the cohort. Firms established during an economic boom enjoy much higher growth than firms created during a recession. Second, the standard deviation increases over time. This indicates that a subset of firms achieve the lion's share of growth. Third, it is important to note that none of the cohorts are close to reaching the average size of incumbent firms. In 2000, the mean for the population of STLF firms was 3.2 employees. Previous studies mention the time for new firms to reach the average size of incumbents to vary between five to ten years (Caves, 1998; Geroski, 1995). In this study none of the cohorts had achieved the average size of the incumbent firms of the population. This is a serious indication that growth is difficult to achieve for this group of firms in Sweden.

As growth tends to be concentrated to a small share of firms (Davidsson and Delmar, 2003; Storey, 1995), we get a firm size distribution where most firms cluster around the smallest size classes and only a few firms cluster in the larger size classes. In the respective cohorts, it is therefore of interest to examine the maximum size achieved by any firm. Not a single firm achieves a size above 100 employees. The largest is a firm created in 1998 that increased to 94 employees in 1999. Otherwise the maximum size is concentrated in a bracket of 30–40 employees.

Industry

No large industry effects pertaining to growth are apparent. There are size differences among the industries but those can be attributed to initial size rather than to subsequent growth. Firms in the manufacturing sector and from the technology service industry have a tendency to grow quicker. Four years after entry, firms in the manufacturing sector have grown 1.84 times, whereas firms in the technology service industry have grown 1.55 times. This can be compared to the average four-year growth for other technology services (1.15) and healthcare (1.13). An interesting remark is that the 1994 cohort in the manufacturing sector showed an exceptional development in size, a development that influenced the average for the industry.

Initial size

In all size classes and cohorts, both the average size of firms and their standard deviation increase with firm age. However, we do not observe a linear relationship between initial size and growth. Rather, the relationship seems to be curvilinear. The probability of achieving growth increases with the initial size of the firm, but the effect is lower for firms that start out with six or more employees. Four years after entry, firms with 4–5 initial employees have on average grown 1.65 times, firms with 2–3 initial employees have on average grown 1.19 times, and firms with only one initial employee have on average grown 1.16 times. For firms with six or more initial employees, we see that growth is less pronounced than for firms with 4–5 employees. Four years after entry, firms in the size class of six or more employees have on average grown 1.21 times. The reason seems to be that it is hard for these firms to keep the initial size during the first subsequent years.

Legal form

Similarly to survival, legal form is strongly associated with growth. Incorporated firms have on average a much higher growth than the two other forms. Four years after entry, incorporated firms have grown 1.65 times, whereas sole proprietorships and partnerships have grown 1.10 and 1.15 times respectively. We have also witnessed an important shift over time where the growth for incorporations increases rapidly for the 1996, 1997 and 1998 cohorts. It is possible that firms based on more valuable opportunities were started as incorporations where the financial arrangements relative to venture capital are most easily made.

DISCUSSION

In this chapter we have explored the entrepreneurial activities of the science and technology labour force in Sweden, outlining the magnitude of their entrepreneurial efforts and how it is related to economic growth. We investigated all 22 312 firms that have been partly or fully owned by a member of the STLF between 1990 and 2000. 7716 of these firms were *de novo* entries, that is, firms that were established between 1991 and 2000 by at least one person of the STLF. We have analysed the entry, survival and growth of the *de novo* firms.

We can conclude that this group does not represent a population of entrepreneurs in the Schumpeterian sense. It is quite the contrary; the economic contribution of this group of firms is minimal and seems to be diminishing. We have observed a group of firms that as a population have become less able to generate employment over the period investigated.

The total population of STLF firms has augmented from 7073 in 1993 to 9348 in 2000, but the average size of the incumbent firms has diminished. In 2000 the average firm employed 3.2 persons, and in 1991, 4.5 persons, so we are dealing with a population of rather small firms. Furthermore, the total number of people employed by this group has diminished by 23.8 per cent from 34 432 in 1990 to 26 237 in 2000. The effect is even stronger for this group's ability to generate work for their own labour market group. The share of individuals in the STLF employed by these STLF-run firms decreases from 9.3 per cent in 1990 to 5.6 per cent in 1999. This corresponds to a loss of 39.8 per cent in our population's ability to generate employment for their own labour group.

We have focused on *de novo* entries since theoretical work indicates that such firms can represent a strong force to rejuvenate a population of firms. We find that about 10 per cent of the population at any given year is made up of newly established firms. A somewhat lower share of firms is terminated on a yearly basis. In total, 7716 firms were established in ten different yearly cohorts. Most entries are found in technology services, healthcare, and in other knowledge-intensive industries. They are generally very small (89 per cent have one employee, that is, the founder).

Examining the survival and employee growth for these firms shows that 53 per cent of the firms exit within five years of entry; 65 per cent exit within ten years of entry. This indicates a somewhat higher probability of survival than the general population of new Swedish firm (c.f. Davidsson et al., 1994).

In terms of employment growth, not even the firms in the oldest cohort are able to achieve the average firm size of their industry. Of the 11 879 created jobs, 79.2 per cent were created the year the firms were established. The remaining 20.8 per cent of the jobs created came from subsequent growth. Very few firms actually grow, and the ones that do grow do not grow substantially. Not a single firm reached past 100 employees, demonstrating that growth is difficult to achieve for this group of firms in Sweden.

Theoretical Implications

This study informs three strands of theory; endogenous growth theory, entrepreneurship theory and industrial organization theory. It informs endogenous growth theory because it is a unique attempt to test the impact of one of the important mechanisms in converting new knowledge into commercial activities. We have here closely examined the entrepreneurial activities of the science and technology labour force. We have suggested that this labour force is the labour force having the most access to new and emerging technologies. Therefore, they represent the individuals that have the highest probability to discover and pursuit entrepreneurial opportunities based on new technological knowledge. We did not find any support for this connection.

There are several possible interpretations beside the fact that entrepreneurship does not seem to work as a mechanism of commercialization of new knowledge. One reason is that there is an important lack of an environment that supports entrepreneurship (that is, high entry barriers, administrative burden and limited access to venture capital). It is also possible that other mechanisms of knowledge spillovers are more efficient for economic growth than entrepreneurship. An example of such a mechanism is the mobility of highly educated employees that move between firms. Such an explanation, however, has limited applicability to Sweden since mobility patterns are low compared to other industrialized countries (Henrekson and Rosenberg, 2001). There is a strong Swedish tradition of large industrial companies producing most of the research, development and innovation, and by tradition people relatively seldom switch employers (cf. Granstrand and Alänge, 1995). In other words, there is a strong routinized technological regime in most, if not all, industries in Sweden (Nelson and Winter, 1982, p. 258). Most likely, the Swedish STLF does have the ability to discover entrepreneurial opportunities, but for the most part, these opportunities are exploited within the framework of the organizations where they work. Hence, innovations inside large corporations can compensate for the lack of entrepreneurs. Therefore, endogenous growth theory would still be valid, but other mechanisms than entrepreneurship in the form of new independent firms are more important. While endogenous growth theory offers an interesting explanation as to how growth is achieved, there is little empirical support for it. More research is needed to operationalize the different factors of the model and employ them to empirical testing.

For example, more research is needed on how innovations are discovered and exploited both within and outside existing firms. Entrepreneurship theory would suggest that new firms discover other types of innovations than do established firms. Established firms are mainly involved in routinized upgrading of technology that already exists, while start-up firms are the ones credited for path-breaking non-routine innovations (Baumol, 2002). Research on how new knowledge is created and exploited in the economy as a whole is important to understand the balance in an economy between an entrepreneurial-driven economy and a large corporation-driven one.

This study informs entrepreneurship research because it is able to mitigate a number of methodological problems such as survival bias, heterogonous samples, reliance on small samples and reliance of cross-sectional data. By examining a large population of firms and following the establishment of the firms from the very beginning we have been able to gather evidence supporting a model about the behaviour of entrepreneurs. This behavioural theory lends support to work in industrial organization theory (Caves, 1998; Jovanovic, 1982). The results clearly support a real option strategy from the perspective of entrepreneurs (Folta and O'Brien, 2004). Because firm founders cannot *a priori* know the value of their opportunity, less confident firm founders start out small, incurring a unit-cost penalty but limiting their sunk cost investment while they gather evidence of the value of the opportunity. If the feedback is positive, firm founders can increase their investment, and if the feedback is negative they can exit at a minimum loss. Initially smaller entrants would therefore be expected to show higher exit rates. Hence, they may start small because they expect to have a high probability of failure, and consequently want to limit their investment. More confident firm founders would then start larger in order to achieve an optimal size more rapidly (Caves, 1998; Jovanovic, 1982). This argument is based on the observation that the smallest initial investments on the market are the first to disappear. We have seen that initial conditions such as initial size and choice of legal form have a long-term effect on firm survival, salary development and growth. Multivariate analyses where we can better control for the influence of other variables might reveal stronger support for this behavioural model.

This study also adds to the accumulated knowledge we have about industry dynamics. To a large degree the examined population follows the patterns found in other studies. However, this study represents an important departure from previous studies that have focused on new firms. We have here focused on the nature of founders and owners and thereby added an extra dimension in explaining firm behaviour. Firms are composed of people that act for different reasons. One of the major determinants of their behaviour is their education and experience. We have seen that taking this into account gives somewhat different results, but perhaps most importantly offers new avenues to understand better how firms evolve by offering multilevel analyses. Also, our use of longitudinal data has underlined the long-lasting effects of initial conditions on subsequent firm development.

Practical Implications

It appears that starting an independent firm is not a very attractive option for most members of the STLF. Given the lack of growth achieved and the industries they chose to enter, we are bound to suspect that several of those starting businesses in fact do so because they are unable to find suitable employment opportunities. While this is a common situation for the labour force at large, it is surprising that it also applies to the STLF. Consequently, the opportunities exploited by those of the STLF starting their own businesses are probably not the most promising ones. A first implication is that more research is needed to understand how the STLF functions both as employed and as entrepreneurs. With better knowledge about the uniqueness of this group, specific policy implications or measures can be developed. Such research is needed considering that several policy measures (cf. Henrekson and Rosenberg, 2001) have been initiated during the period of investigation to support entrepreneurship among members of this labour group. Our results show no evidence that these measures so far have had any positive impact.

Acs (2002) suggests that in a society where little knowledge is produced, this can be compensated for by a large degree of entrepreneurial activity. In Sweden there is substantial knowledge creation in terms of large expenditure on R&D. However, this knowledge creation only to a small extent transforms into economic growth. In this report we tap into one of the important reasons why this is the case. Our empirical results suggest that there is too little entrepreneurial activity in the economy for new knowledge to be transformed into new viable economic activity. The relative loss in employment creation by STLF firms indicates that it might even be in a downward spiral. Sweden appears to be in a situation where there is an imbalance between knowledge creation and entrepreneurial action, the latter being insufficient.

Baumol (1990, p. 894) stated that 'how the entrepreneur acts at a given time and place depends heavily on . . . the reward structure in the economy . . . [or] the prevailing rules of the game that govern the payoff' to entrepreneurship. The policy implications of this study are primarily that initiatives should be taken to increase the number of firms being started, with special emphasis on increasing the number of start-ups by the STLF, but also to facilitate their ability to grow. The problem is both the lack of start-ups and the scarcity of growth in new as well as established firms. Probably, initiatives need to be taken both at national and regional levels to support this kind of entrepreneurship (Henrekson and Rosenberg, 2001).

Examples of more regional or local initiatives are science parks (Jacobsson and Lindholm Dahlstrand, 2001) and entrepreneurship education. The role of education in entrepreneurship should not be underestimated. Our results lead us to believe that many of those who have the highest chances of discovering and exploiting entrepreneurs through independent entrepreneurial activities do not choose to do so. A major reason for this is probably that they never consider entrepreneurship as a viable career option. In order to change this, it is necessary that the STLF gets exposed to entrepreneurship as a career option during their education.

Limitations and Future Research

This study also has limitations that provide opportunities for future research. Three important limitations are worth mentioning: first, we have not done any analyses at the regional level. Modern cluster theory and developments of endogenous growth theory, as well as entrepreneurship research (Baumol, 1993; Davidsson et al., 1994), suggest that this is an important level of analysis. However, we have done regional analyses on the individual level (Delmar et al., 2003). Considering that most firms that we have tracked are one-person firms we do not expect the results to differ at the firm level.

Second, as we do not have any control group, it is difficult to assess precisely the exact levels of performance of this particular labour group relative to other labour groups. Even though the STLF represent a relatively homogenous labour force, there still remains an important variation in the quality of education depending on where degrees have been obtained. Universities tend to vary substantially in their ability to provide high-quality education. Future work directed at establishing more detailed comparisons in order to develop policy implications should look at more detailed levels of education, and also make use of designs that allow group comparisons. Even if we have taken precautions to minimize heterogeneity in our sample, there is still work to do.

Third, it seems that this group does not represent a population of entrepreneurs in the Schumpeterian sense that entrepreneurial action will have an impact on the market. The traditional way to observe this impact has been to examine the economic impact of firms by examining their individual growth, and the overall number of firms. The connection between entrepreneurial behaviour and entrepreneurial outcome on the micro level is important because we believe that an important incentive for individuals to act entrepreneurially is the possibility to appropriate the rents of their entrepreneurial opportunities. That is, some – but not all – entrepreneurs must succeed, and their joint contribution must lead to a net increase in economic growth. However, we cannot observe this pattern when examining this specific population. On the contrary, their ability to generate jobs seems to be very small. Nevertheless, we cannot conclude that this group is unimportant for economic growth, because the possibility that they bring innovations to the market still remains. Even if these firms enjoy limited success, their contribution might be to bring new technologies to the markets (McGrath, 1999). For example, the large proportion of all e-commerce firms established in the late 1990s failed, but a couple of years after the dotcom bust we can see that the surviving firms have established themselves based on business models that have been shown to work. So if the individual development of STLF firms and their contribution to new jobs are not large, they may still play an important role as carriers of new technology to the market. Such a possibility must be examined using techniques that allow us to track technological knowledge. However, in the long run we would expect that the willingness to commercialize new knowledge should be related to personal gains in order to take place.

CONCLUSIONS

The purpose of this chapter has been to explore the entrepreneurial activities of the science and technology labour force in Sweden from the perspective of endogenous growth theory. We argued that an important mechanism to explain how new technological knowledge is converted to economic growth is the economic behaviour of the science and technology labour force, and especially the entrepreneurial activities of that group. However, we have found little evidence supporting this statement. Entrepreneurship plays a marginal role, and firms once started seldom manage to achieve any substantial growth. Furthermore, the population of firms owned by the STLF has over time become less and less able to generate employment growth.

ACKNOWLEDGEMENTS

Handelsbanken Research Foundations, the Swedish Agency for Innovation Systems (Vinnova), the Swedish Foundation for Small Business Research (FSF), the Swedish National Board for Industrial and Technological Development (NUTEK) and the Swedish Institute for Growth Policy Studies (ITPS) financed the study. Their support is gratefully acknowledged.

NOTES

1. We would especially acknowledge the valuable support and work offered by Jan Andersson, Statistics Sweden.
2. Non-rival means that the use of a particular piece of knowledge by an individual or a firm in no way limits its use by others.
3. Most of the failures of new entrants occur during the first year and then survival rates increase steadily. The survival rates for entrants reported from various countries are quite similar.
4. It is worth noting that the terms 'acquired firms' and 'sold firms' do not exactly mean that an ownership has been transferred. It could also mean that the STLF entrepreneur no longer has ownership *and* receives their primary income from that firm.
5. It is important to note that we here depart from our analyses displayed in Table 4.2 where a firm exits when none of the owners are part of the STLF. We choose the present definition because it is the best indicator of the true value of the firm founded by the STLF entrepreneurs.
6. It is important to note that this variable is a self-reported variable. This is a weakness since some firms tend to fill out many industry codes while some are missing codes completely. Firms with missing industry codes are highly over-represented among sole proprietorships that only exist for one or a few years.
7. Due to how we define the population as firms that provide their STLF owner with their primary income, we should not have any firms with no employees. However, as mentioned in the method section we have a number of cases where the individual file indicates a person as full-time self-employed, but all data except the firm's identity number in the firm file are missing. Those are the firms indicated as having no employees.
8. We exclude year 2000 from this analysis as the educational codes were changed that year which leads to an artificial increase in our estimates.

REFERENCES

Acs, Z.J. (2002). *Innovations and the Growth of Cities*. Cheltenham, UK and Northampton, MA, USA: Edward Elgar.

Aldrich, H. (1979). *Organizations and Environments*. Englewoods Cliffs, NJ: Prentice-Hall.

Aldrich, H. (1999). *Organizations Evolving*. London: Sage Publications.

Almeida, P. and Kogut, P. (1999). Localization of knowledge and the mobility of engineers in regional networks. *Management Science*, **45**(7): 905–17.

Audretsch, D.B. (1991). New-firm survival and the technological regime. *Review of Economics and Statistics*, **73**(3): 441–50.

Audretsch, D.B. (1995). Innovation and industry evolution. Cambridge, MA: MIT Press.
Audretsch, D.B. and Mahmood, T. (1995). New firm survival: New results using a hazard function. *Review of Economics and Statistics*, **77**(1): 97–103.
Barnett, W.P. and Sorensen, O. (2002). The Red Queen in organizational creation and development. *Industrial and Corporate Change*, **11**(2): 289–325.
Baum, J.A. (1996). Organizational ecology. In Clegg, S.R., Hardy, C. and Nord, W.R. (eds). *Handbook of Organization Studies* London: Sage, pp. 77–114.
Baumol, W.J. (1990). Entrepreneurship: Productive, unproductive, and destructive. *Journal of Political Economy*, **98**: 893–921.
Baumol, W.J. (1993). *Entrepreneurship, Management, and the Structure of Payoffs*. Cambridge, MA: MIT Press.
Baumol, W.J. (2002). *The Free-market Innovation Machine: Analyzing the Growth Miracle of Capitalism*. Princeton, NJ: Princeton University Press.
Birch, D.L. (1979). *The Job Generation Process*. Cambridge, MA: MIT Program on Neighborhood and Regional Change.
Bottazzi, G., Cefis, E. and Dosi, G. (2002). Corporate growth and industrial structures: Some evidence from the Italian manufacturing industry. *Industrial and Corporate Change*, **11**(4): 705–23.
Bottazzi, G., Dosi, G., Lippi, M., Pammolli, F. and Riccaboni, M. (2001). Innovation and corporate growth in the evolution of the drug industry. *International Journal of Industrial Organization*, **19**(7): 1161.
Brüderl, J. and Schussler, R. (1990). Organizational mortality: The liabilities of newness and adolescence. *Administrative Science Quarterly*, **35**(3): 530–48.
Carlsson, B. and Eliasson, G. (2003). Industrial dynamics and endogenous growth. *Industry and Innovation*, **10**(4): 435–55.
Carroll, G.R. and Hannan, M.T. (2000). *The Demography of Corporations and Industries*. Princeton, NJ: Princeton University Press.
Casson, M. (1982). The entrepreneur: An economic theory. Oxford: Martin Robertson.
Caves, R.E. (1998). Industrial organization and new findings on the turnover and mobility of firms. *Journal of Economic Literature*, **36**: 1947–82.
Dahlqvist, J., Davidsson, P. and Wiklund, J. (2000). Initial conditions as predictors of new venture performance: a replication and extension of the Cooper et al. study. *Enterprise and Innovation Management Studies*, **1**(1): 1–17.
Davidsson, P. and Delmar, F. (2003). Hunting for new employment: The role of high growth firms. In Kirby, D.A. and Watson, A. (eds), *Small Firms and Economic Development in Developed and Transition Economies: A Reader*. Aldershot, UK: Ashgate Publishing, pp. 7–19.
Davidsson, P., Lindmark, L. and Olofsson, C. (1994). *Dynamiken i svenkt näringsliv (The dynamics of the Swedish business sector)*. Lund, Sweden: Studentlitteratur.
Delmar, F. (1996). Measuring growth: Methological considerations and empirical results. Paper presented at the RENT X, Research on Entrepreneurship, Brussels.
Delmar, F., Sjöberg, K. and Wiklund, J. (2003). *The Involvement in Self-employment among the Swedish Science and Technology Labour Force between 1990 and 2000*. Stockholm: ITPS.
Dunne, P. and Hughes, A. (1996). Age, size, growth and survival: UK companies in the 1980s. *Journal of Industrial Economics*, **42**(2): 115–40.
Dunne, T., Roberts, M. J. and Samuelson, L. (1988). Patterns of firm entry and exit in US manufacturing firms. *RAND Economic Journal*, **19**(4): 495–515.

Fichman, M. and Levinthal, D.A. (1991). Honeymoons and the liability of adolescence: A new perspective on duration dependence in social and organizational relationships. *Academy of Management Review*, **18**(2): 442–68.

Folta, T.B. and O'Brien, J.P. (2004). Entry in the presence of dueling options. *Strategic Management Journal*, **25**(2): 121–38.

Geroski, P.A. (1995). What do we know about entry? *International Journal of Industrial Organization*, **13**: 421–40.

Geroski, P.A. (2001). Exploring the niche overlaps between organizational ecology and industrial economics. *Industrial and Corporate Change*, **10**(2): 507–40.

Granstrand, O. and Alänge, S. (1995). The evolution of corporate entrepreneurship in Swedish industry: Was Schumpeter wrong? *Journal of Evolutionary Economics*, **5**: 133–56.

Hannan, M.T. and Freeman, M.T. (1984). Structural inertia and organizational change. *American Sociological Review*, **49**: 149–64.

Hayek, F.A. (1945). The use of knowledge in society. *American Economic Review*, **35**(4): 519–30.

Henrekson, M. and Rosenberg, N. (2001). Designing efficient institutions for science-based entrepreneurship: lesson from the US and Sweden. *Journal of Technology Transfer*, **26**(3): 207–31.

Jacobsson, S. and Lindholm Dahlstrand, Å. (2001). Nya teknikbaserade företag och industriell tillväxt. (New technology-based firms and industrial growth.) In Davidsson, P. Delmar, F. and Wiklund, J. (eds), *Tillväxtföretagen i Sverige*, Stockholm: SNS, pp. 116–43.

Jovanovic, B. (1982). Selection and the evolution of industry. *Econometrica*, **50**(3): 649–70.

Kirzner, I.M. (1997). Entrepreneurial discovery and the competitive market process: An Austrian approach. *Journal of Economic Literature*, **35**(1): 60–85.

Klepper, S. and Graddy, E. (1990). The evolution of new industries and the determinants of market structure. *RAND Journal of Economics*, **21**(1): 27–44.

Mata, J. and Portugal, P. (1994). Life duration of new firms. *Journal of Industrial Economics*, **42**(3): 227.

Mata, J.M. and Machado, J.A. (1996). Firm start-up size: A conditional quantile approach. *European Economic Review*, **40**(6): 1305.

McGrath, R.G. (1999). Falling forward: Real options reasoning and entrepreneurial failure. *Academy of Management Review*, **24**(1): 13–30.

Nelson, R. and Winter, S. (1982). *An Evolutionary Theory of Economic Change*. Cambridge, MA: Belknap Press.

Picot, G. and Dupuy, R. (1998). Job creation by company size class: The magnitude, concentration and persistence of job gains and losses in Canada. *Small Business Economics*, **10**: 117–39.

Reynolds, P.D. and White, S.B. (1997). *The Entrepreneurial Process: Economic Growth, Men, Women, and Minorities*. Westport, CT: Quorum Books.

Romer, P.M. (1990). Endogenous technological change. *Journal of Political Economy*, **98**(5): S71–S102.

Romer, P.M. (1994). The origins of endogenous growth. *Journal of Economic Perspectives*, **8**(1): 3–22.

Schumpeter, J.A. (2000) (1934). Entrepreneurship as innovation. In Swedberg, R. (ed.), *Entrepreneurship: The Social Science View*. Oxford: Oxford University Press.

Shane, S. (2000). Prior knowledge and the discovery of entrepreneurial opportunities. *Organization Science*, **11**(4): 448–69.

Shane, S. and Venkataraman, S. (2000). The promise of entrepreneurship as a field of research. *Academy of Management Review*, **25**(1): 217–66.
Storey, D.J. (1994). *Understanding the Small Business Sector*. London: Routledge.
Storey, D.J. (1995). Symposium on Harrison's 'Lean and mean': A job generation perspective. *Small Business Economics*, **7**(5): 5–8.
Wagner, J. (1992). Firm size, firm growth and persistence of chance. Testing GIBRAT's law with establishment data from lower Saxony, 1978–1989. *Small Business Economics*, **4**: 125–31.
Wagner, J. (1994). The post-entry performance of new small firms in German manufacturing industries. *Journal of Industrial Economics*, **42**(2): 141–54.
Venkataraman, S. (1997). The distinctive domain of entrepreneurship research: An editor's perspective. In Katz, J. and Brockhaus, R.H.S. (eds), *Advances in Entrepreneurship, Firm Emergence, and Growth*, vol. 3, Greenwich, CT: JAI Press, pp. 119–38.

5. Innovation and the characteristics of cooperating and non-cooperating small firms

Mark Freel

INTRODUCTION

There can be little doubt that the dominant network theory of innovation, in its various incarnations (cf. Håkansson, 1987; Maillat, 1995; Florida, 1995; Baptista and Swann, 1998; Cooke and Morgan, 1998; Oughton and Whittam, 1997; Lundvall, 1995; Hagedoorn, 1993), has had considerable influence upon academic fashion and industrial policy. In the latter case, this has been clearly manifest in a preference for policies which aim at promoting interfirm cooperation, rather than providing direct financial assistance to individual firms – at least within OECD economies (Bougrain and Haudeville, 2002).

Underpinning this *Zeitgeist* is a widespread belief that, on the one hand, increasing uncertainty (associated with changing technology and global competition) has encouraged many firms to concentrate on fewer activities and competencies as a way of generating specialization economies (Demsetz, 1991; Simmie et al., 2002; Krugman, 1991) and, on the other, a common conviction that the sorts of information relevant for innovation cannot be easily traded on neoclasssical 'spot markets' (Geroski, 1995). In other words, the seeming incompatibility between an increasing division of labour and the associated specialization pressures, which appear to characterize many industries, and apparent difficulties in market contracting for innovation assets (Quintana-García and Benavides-Velasco, 2004). Certainly, there appears to be general agreement that innovation activity is 'becoming increasingly distributed, as fewer firms are able to "go it alone" in technological development' (Tether, 2002, p. 947). As firms concentrate on a narrower range of activities, it is inevitable that many innovation tasks will require complementary resources (including knowledge and information) drawn from outside the boundaries of the firm and, given the nature of such assets, their acquisition may require the framework of a cooperative relationship (Fritsch and Lukas, 2001).

Since at least the early 1990s there have been a growing number of empirical studies which have sought to demonstrate, or test, the importance of cooperation or networking for innovation (see for example Rothwell, 1991; Oerlemans et al., 1998; Love and Roper, 1999; Sternberg, 2000; Freel, 2003). By and large, though with important provisos, the results have been confirmatory. That is, interfirm and firm–institution collaboration does appear to effect innovation activities positively. Or, in other words, a firm's capacity for innovation seems to be enhanced by the extended knowledge base and cost and risk sharing offered through extensive cooperative linkages with external agencies. Where conditions apply, they commonly relate to the relationship between the type of innovation partner (for example customer, supplier, competitor, university and so on) and the scope of innovation (novel or incremental, product or process) (Freel, 2003). However, notwithstanding any conditions, the conclusion one is generally asked to reach is that 'cooperation is good, more cooperation is better' – at least where innovation activities are concerned. The implied collaboration imperatives, which inevitably draw from such a proposition, have been directed at the small firm sector with particular vigour. MacPherson (1997, p. 127), for instance, suggests that 'there is little doubt that few SMFs [small and medium-sized firms] can successfully introduce new products without resorting to some form of external collaboration'. Whilst one may conceive of large firms undertaking most innovation activities internally, small firms, with limited internal resources, are unlikely to be so self-sufficient (Bayona et al., 2001).

However, whilst numerous studies testify to the importance of innovation networks, our understanding of 'who co-operates for innovation and why' (Tether, 2002) is notably less well developed. In other words, 'in contrast to its importance for innovation activities, our knowledge about the determinants and effects of [innovation] cooperation is rather limited' (Fritsch and Lukas, 2001, p. 297). This is clearly a concern. If we are to counsel firms to engage in innovation networks, we must have a clearer understanding of the 'who' and 'why' of cooperation – which sorts of firms, pursuing which sorts of strategies, are likely to benefit from collaboration with which sorts of partners? Certainly, the effective design and targeting of policy cannot proceed without better recognition of the characteristics and motivations of potential users. To this end, the aim of this chapter is to contribute to an improved awareness of the characteristics of cooperative innovators – in terms of both their resources and their strategic intent. The chapter draws upon data from a large-scale survey of northern British SMEs and, rather than treating innovation-related cooperation as an explanatory variable which influences innovativeness (as is commonly the case), reverses the standard equation and tries to 'explain' the propensity to cooperate. Importantly, the chapter is able to distinguish between various potential cooperative partners (customers, suppliers, service providers, competitors, universities, local economic development actors and government departments) and to assess the extent to which the factors that influence cooperation vary.

Before progressing any further, a point of clarification seems in order. As Huggins (2001, p. 443) notes, 'there is a danger that the term 'network' will slip directly from obscurity to meaninglessness without an interesting period of coherence'. Certainly, the tendency to use the terms 'networks', 'linkages', 'cooperation' and 'collaboration' interchangeably, with little attempt at definition, creates unwanted and unwarranted ambiguity. Here, the concern is with innovation cooperation (and the specificity this implies) and not, less precisely, with 'networks' of informal information sharing, social networks or tacit links between firms in a local area: 'The concern is thus with formal innovation networks, but which fall short of full-scale merger or any other form of equity sharing arrangement; specifically, the focus is on collaborative . . . relationships between [firms and organizations] unrelated by ownership' (Love, 1999, p. 3).

THE CHARACTERISTICS OF COOPERATIVE INNOVATORS

Whilst it is true to say that our understanding of the factors which influence innovation-related cooperation, or of the characteristics of cooperative firms, is disappointingly limited, it would be wrong to suggest that we are wholly ignorant. Indeed, in one journal alone (*Research Policy*) there has been a steady flow of recent articles dedicated to investigating the characteristics of firms engaged in cooperative innovation (for example Kleinknecht and Reijnen, 1992; Fritsch and Lukas, 2001; Bayona et al., 2001; Tether, 2002; Miotti and Sachwald, 2003). However, such studies have almost exclusively been concerned with R&D collaboration. Even where they have been nominally concerned, more broadly, with cooperation for innovation, there has been a tendency to privilege R&D (for example Tether, 2002).[1] Unfortunately, the generalizability of any findings is limited for two reasons: Firstly, the tendency to privilege formal R&D in studies of innovation activity may capture only a small proportion of technical change activities (Patel and Pavitt, 1994). As early as the 1970s, the innovation-related literature was stressing that R&D, narrowly defined, accounted for only a fraction of total innovation costs (Sterlacchini, 1999). Indeed, the bulk of new theoretical and empirical research on innovation emphasizes that the critical and creative aspects of innovation and competitiveness 'are *not* dependent upon frontier research, doctoral graduates, gross expenditures and so on, but on spillovers, linkages, networks, interdependencies, synergies, etc.' (de la Mothe and Paquet, 1998, p. 106). Moreoever, there is substantial evidence that the majority of commercially significant innovations are technologically incremental, rather than radical (Audretsch, 1995). In other words, '[t]he first step in recognizing innovation as a ubiquitous phenomenon is to focus upon its gradual and cumulative aspects . . . Almost all innovations reflect already existing knowledge, combined in new ways' (Lundvall, 1995, p. 8) – with undoubted implications for the need to collaborate and the nature of any collaborations. Secondly, there are longstanding concerns over small firms' ability to adequately discriminate R&D spending (Roper, 1998). Many small firms do not possess formal R&D departments and R&D in small firms tends, largely, to have a developmental rather than fundamental research focus (Kleinknecht, 1989; Santarelli and Sterlacchini, 1990), with development work often carried out on an *ad hoc* basis. Given the context of the current research and the urgency with which policy prescriptions are applied to the sector, this latter issue is of particular concern.

Further, whilst studies of R&D cooperation often distinguish between potential partners on the basis of either ownership or geography (for example Kleinknecht and Reijnen, 1992), very few have systematically discriminated between customers, suppliers, competitors, universities, government and so on. Yet, by way of illustration, the relationship between customer cooperation and product innovation on the one hand, and between supplier cooperation and process innovation on the other, have long been recognized (Freel, 2000). Intuitively, one would think that who firms cooperate with will influence (and be influenced by) not only innovation outcomes and motivations, but also the characteristics of innovators.

However, notwithstanding these considerations, the recent literature on the characteristics of R&D collaborators has, on the whole, been methodologically robust and systematic in its exploration of broadly the same themes. As such, it provides a valuable platform for the development of general propositions in the current context – a context which draws on a broader conception of innovation and a narrower sub-set of firms than many of these studies. These propositions serve to structure the discussion and clarify *a priori* expectations.

To this end, a common preliminary observation is to note that 'firms must have resources to get resources' (Eisenhardt and Schoonhaven, 1996, p. 1497). Rothwell and Dodgson (1991, p. 131), for instance, suggest that 'the most important factors determining a SMEs propensity and ability to access external sources of technology are *internal* to the firm'. This is often framed in terms of the 'absorptive capacity' thesis (classically Cohen and

Levinthal, 1989 and 1990). That is, a firm's ability to evaluate and utilize external knowledge is, to a greater extent, a function of the level of its prior related knowledge – that is, its 'absorptive capacity'. Arguing from this, it is often suggested that a highly developed absorptive capacity is a precondition for innovation-related cooperation (Koschatzky and Sternberg, 2000). The key ingredient of a firm's absorptive capacity is thought to be its accumulated R&D. In studies of cooperative innovation, this has led, in turn, to the common hypothesizing – explicitly or otherwise – of a positive association between R&D intensity and cooperation (Kleinknecht and Reijnen, 1992; Fritsch and Lukas, 2001; Bayona et al., 2001; Tether, 2002). However, the empirical evidence has been far from unequivocal in endorsing this proposed relationship. On the one hand, a number of studies have found either no relationship, or indeed a negative relationship, between R&D intensity and the propensity to cooperate (for example Oerlemans and Meeus, 2001; Keinknecht and Reijnen, 1992) – with Love and Roper (1999) going as far as to suggest that networking may, in fact, substitute for internal R&D activities. In contrast, Tether (2002), Bayona et al. (2001) and Fritsch and Lukas (2001) all identify a positive relationship between firm-level R&D (variously measured) and the propensity to cooperate. Persuasively, Tether (2002, p. 954) rationalizes this link in terms of complexity or novelty, as well as in terms of absorptive capacity:

> If the greater intensity of R&D activities relates to the development of more complex or novel (i.e. higher level) innovations, which are more likely to require close interactions between the innovator, its suppliers, customers and possibly other innovation partners, then we would expect that not only will the conduct of R&D impact positively on participation in cooperative arrangements for innovation, but the propensity to engage in these will also increase with the intensity of R&D activities.

Indeed, notwithstanding the empirical ambivalence, it is this latter view – that R&D intensity and cooperation are positively correlated – that enjoys greatest currency. Accordingly, the following proposition is suggested:

Proposition 1: The likelihood of engaging in innovation-related cooperative ventures is positively associated with firm-level R&D expenditure.

However, R&D is not the only constituent of a firm's absorptive capacity. Importantly, a sufficient supply of suitably qualified personnel is also thought to influence the firm's propensity to engage in innovation-related cooperative ventures. Rothwell and Dodgson (1991, p. 135), for instance, observe that 'one of the prime stimuli to collaboration has been shown to be the employment of in-house QSEs [qualified scientists and engineers]'.

For less complex forms of innovation, or in less technology-intensive sectors, it seems reasonable to conjecture that technicians, rather than technologists, will be important (Freel, 2003). Moreover, 'critical knowledge does not simply include substantive, technical knowledge; it also includes awareness of where useful complementary expertise resides within and outside the organisation' (Cohen and Levinthal, 1990, p. 133). This sort of knowledge may often be characterized as managerial knowledge. Indeed, Beesley and Rothwell (1987) note the importance of the 'outward lookingness' of management in determining an SME's propensity to engage with external sources of technology, while Freel (2000), drawing upon a sample of 230 small manufacturers, observes that almost a third of firms perceived problems of management as important or crucial barriers to innovation-related cooperation. In light of this, the following propositions are suggested:

Proposition 2: The propensity to cooperate for innovation will be positively associated with the employment of QSEs.

Proposition 3: The propensity to cooperate for innovation will be positively associated with the employment of technicians.

Proposition 4: The propensity to cooperate for innovation will be positively associated with the employment of managers.

Whilst having resources is generally thought to be an important influence on the propensity to cooperate (and, indeed, the rate of return to cooperation), perceived resource constraints must also be a prerequisite for collaboration. The view that, particularly, small firms cooperate with a wide range of partners in order to alleviate internal resource deficiencies is commonplace in the literature (Freel, 2000). Importantly, it is managerial perception which matters (Penrose, 1995). If firms perceive resource constraints they are liable to act in such a way as to minimize these – whether or not they have any objective basis in reality. Moreover, such constraints are unlikely to be limited to human or intellectual capital, broadly defined. Rather, perceived financial constraints are frequently cited as a spur to innovation-related cooperation (Bayona et al., 2001). Indeed, the increasing costliness of innovation is often implied as a first principle underpinning industry's desire to leverage external knowledge (Tether, 2002). From this, the following propositions are suggested:

Proposition 5: Perceptions of skills and knowledge constraints will be positively associated with the propensity to cooperate for innovation.

Proposition 6: Perceptions of financial constraints will be positively associated with the propensity to cooperate for innovation.

Turning from the hypothesized influence of a firm's resources, to its activities and environment: the relationship between complexity and the propensity to cooperate, touched upon above, is often developed with reference to the novelty of innovation activities and to the technological intensity of the industry. In the former instance, Tether (2002) and Fritsch and Lukas (2001) both posit a positive relationship between the novelty of innovations and the need for obtaining external know-how through cooperation. For Tether (2002), drawing on the second Community Innovation Survey (CIS-2), 'novelty' is a function of 'newness to market'; 'new to the market' innovations 'are likely to require greater inputs and/or greater novelty of inputs, and involve greater market uncertainty' (Tether, 2002, p. 954) – frequently requiring, in turn, external networking. Importantly, both studies recognize that novelty may be a consequence, rather than a cause, of collaborations. However, both also view the introduction of novel innovations as a signal of 'the strategic intent to innovate at a higher level' (Tether, 2002) or of 'relatively higher aspiration levels' (Fritsch and Lukas, 2001), associated, in turn, with greater motivation to seek external partners. Of course, one would anticipate some variation in the likely profile of innovation partners depending upon the type of innovation under development. For instance, working with UK CIS-3 data, Swann (2002) noted that companies involved in process innovations (new to their markets) were more likely to have cooperated with universities, whilst those involved in product innovations (new to their markets) were more likely to have cooperated with competitors and consultants – over and above the expected supplier and customer relationships (see, for example, Sako, 1994; von Hippel, 1978). However, for simplicity, the suggested proposition merely holds that:

Proposition 7: Firms that are engaged in relatively novel innovation activities exhibit a greater propensity to cooperate.

With regards to sector of activity, it is commonly thought that firms located in high-technology industries have a greater incentive and higher propensity to engage in cooperative innovation (Miotti and Sachwald, 2003). Lundvall (1990) rationalized this in terms of transaction costs. The more complex the existing technology, the less efficient is the market as a mechanism of technology transfer – due to, *inter alia*, contractual complexity and high information asymmetries between buyers and sellers (Bayona et al., 2001). From a resource-based perspective, it may simply be that 'the need for rapid new product development often precludes internal development of critical technologies' (Quintana-García and Benavides-Velasco, 2004, p. 1). In contrast, firms belonging to mature and traditional sectors are thought to have only a minor need to be integrated in networks (Koschatzky and Sternberg, 2000) – most of their external technological requirements being available off the shelf. Whilst there has been some empirical ambivalence (cf. Kleinknecht and Reijnen, 1992; Oerlemans and Meeus, 2001), the positive relationship between industry technology intensity and the propensity to collaborate has acquired the status of 'stylized fact'. Accordingly, the following proposition is suggested:

Proposition 8: Firms located in sectors characterized by higher technology intensities are likely to have a higher propensity to be engaged in innovation-related cooperation.

Two further factors, indicative of activities and environment, which commonly feature in studies of cooperative behaviour, are the export orientation of firms and their degree of customer dependency. In the former instance, Kleinknecht and Reijnen (1992, p. 354) comment upon 'the generalizing statement that firms operating in global markets . . . have a higher propensity to engage in R&D cooperation'.[2] In the latter, it is suggested that 'close and stable relationships with customers are positively associated with (a) supplier relations, (b) product innovation, and (c) process innovation' (Bengtsson and Sölvell, 2004, p. 232). The degree of customer dependency (that is, the extent to which a limited number of customers account for a large proportion of total sales) may reasonably proxy this closeness and stability. Hence, the following propositions are tentatively suggested:

Proposition 9: The extent to which firms operate in global markets will be positively correlated with the propensity to cooperate.

Proposition 10: The degree of customer dependency will be positively correlated with the propensity to cooperate (especially with customers).

In terms of motivations, one would anticipate that a firm's motivation for innovation would, in turn, influence its propensity to cooperate and the nature of that cooperation. Firms collaborate, not only to access technological knowledge, but also gain access to sales abilities, market information or new markets (Teece, 1992). To this end, Bayona et al. (2001, p. 1293) conjecture that 'firms which seek to improve their knowledge of the market and their access to the same through extending their range of products or increasing their domestic or foreign market share will have a higher propensity for cooperative R&D' (see also Hagedoorn, 1993). Indeed, these authors report tentative evidence that cooperating firms place greater emphasis upon increasing market share as an objective of innovation. In contrast, one might suppose that more reactive forms of innovation, in response to changing legislation and standardization or to maintain market share, for example, would correlate negatively with the propensity to engage in innovation-related cooperation. In very general terms, the following proposition is suggested:

Proposition 11: Firms which innovate to increase revenues, enter new markets or diversify their products are more likely to engage in innovation-related cooperative arrangements.

Finally, in this section, the influence of firm size is considered. Firm size is a classic variable in innovation studies. Indeed, the relationship between firm size and innovation has given rise to the second-largest corpus of empirical literature in the field of industrial organization (Cohen, 1995) – though with no very definite conclusions. Certainly, it features prominently in all the empirical studies of innovation-related collaboration discussed here. The general presupposition, if not the consistent finding (cf. Miotti and Sachwald, 2003; Kleinknecht and Reijnen, 1992), is that firm size will positively correlate with the propensity to collaborate. However, there is considerably less agreement regarding the underlying 'causes'. Fristch and Lukas (2001, p. 300), for instance, argue that if 'there exists a given probability for cooperation per unit of economic activity . . . large enterprises, which, by definition, are characterised by a relatively large amount of economic activity, will be more likely to cooperate than smaller enterprises'. Koschatzky and Sternberg (2000), see it as an issue of accumulated and developed competencies, positively effecting the absorptive capacity of the firm (see also Le Bars et al., 1998). By way of contrast, Tether (2002, p. 955) suggests that 'firm size itself gives little guidance as to whether or not firms might engage in cooperative arrangements for innovation'. Rather, it is the role of market power, for which firm size is a common proxy, which actually matters. Regardless of both the occasional empirical disagreement and the variety of causal explanations, the general tendency is to hold that:

Proposition 12: Firm size is positively associated with the propensity to cooperate for innovation. In other words, the larger the firm the greater the likelihood of cooperating.

DATA

The data presented here were collected as part of a wide-ranging survey of enterprise in northern Britain.[3] This project drew heavily, in style and substance, upon the successful Cambridge studies (see SBRC, 1992; CBR, 1996, 1998, 2000, 2003). The rationale for undertaking the project emanated from concerns over coverage in these earlier (and ongoing) studies of UK SMEs. For instance, data from the 1997 Cambridge survey included only 146 Scottish firms. Notwithstanding this, the success of the work carried out at Cambridge provides a suitable exemplar from which to build. Accordingly, in common with the Cambridge studies a postal questionnaire was employed, which covered a number of issues, including business advice, training, ICT and finance. This chapter is based principally upon the sections concerned with innovation and general business characteristics.

Again, in common with the Cambridge studies, the sample frame used in constructing the database was the Dun and Bradstreet UK Marketing Database (D&B). This database has its origins in the credit-rating business and, as such, it is likely that it over-represents expanding firms in search of finance. Moreover, the database is known to under-represent single-person self-employed, sole proprietors and partnerships in comparison to the overall enterprise sector (Bullock and Hughes, 2000). Accordingly, one obvious consequence of using this database is the likely under-representation of the smallest firms, relative to the UK business stock. However, studies of firm-level innovation processes (such as the CIS), as a result of concerns over data adequacy, response rates and issue relevance, invariably under-survey micro-firms. Whilst there is some evidence to counter these presuppositions (Cosh et al., 1998), custom and practice, and indeed commonsense, continues to underwrite their veracity. In the context of this chapter, the principal consequence of this skew is likely to be an over-estimate of population levels of innovation, R&D, workforce skills and so on. However, when this caveat is borne in mind (that is, that the survey did not seek to represent, in any isomorphic manner, the national population), then the legitimacy of the subsequent analyses should not be compromised.

Consistent with the Cambridge studies, the sample design adopted a size-stratified approach (though our weightings and size bands differ, given the differing populations). We sought to obtain a manufacturing sample split in the ratio 30:60:10 across the employment bands 1–9, 10–99 and 100–499. For business services we sought a 75:20:5 ratio. The difference in ratios reflects the lower number of service firms in the larger size bands, within both the D&B database and the stock of firms. In addition to the size stratification, the sample frame was split between manufacturing and business services on a 40:60 basis. Again, this over-represents manufacturing firms relative to the population. However, this weighting was deemed appropriate in light of industrial policy objectives.

At the sub-sectoral level, weightings were also employed. Within manufacturing, for instance, textile and clothing firms and firms involved in the manufacture of wood and paper products (SIC (92) Divisions 17–19 and 20–21 respectively), were over-surveyed relative to the population. By contrast, printing and publishing firms and manufacturing firms were under-represented in the sample (SIC (92) Divisions 22 and 36–37 respectively). In all other manufacturing SIC (92) divisions, the sample reasonably represents the population – though in the case of food and beverages, not the UK. The decision to over-survey firms in the identified sectors was made with reference to recognized regional industrial clusters (DTI, 2001). Over-representation of some sectors necessarily leads to under-representation of others. Accordingly, the decision was made to under-survey printing and publishing firms – since many of these are *de facto* business service providers – and manufacturing firms 'not elsewhere specified', as a result of the inherent ambiguity.

Similarly, the services sample is dominated by 'other business activities' (SIC (92) division 74). This seemingly ambiguous division includes the management consultancy, financial and legal service firms which, as knowledge-intensive business services, were our primary target (they account for 65 per cent of our service firms). Thereafter, computer and related activities (division 72), renting of machinery and equipment (division 71), post and telecommunications (division 64), and those elements of recreational, cultural and sporting activities (division 92) concerned with the media complete the services sample. Whilst stratification of the sample in this manner will inevitably distort aggregate observations, one does not anticipate that the legitimacy of the analysis presented below will be greatly compromised.

The survey was conducted during April and May of 2001. Mailings were followed up with telephone prompts to initial non-respondents, though limited resources permitted only *ad hoc* re-mailing. This latter failing is likely to have, at least in part, contributed to the disappointing response rate: of the 5200 manufacturing firms surveyed, 597 provided useable responses (an 11.5 per cent response rate); for service firms the figures are 7472 and 748, respectively (a 10 per cent response rate). On the whole, however, the sample appears reasonable reliable, statistically. For instance, from a SME (that is, less than 500 full-time employees (FTEs)) manufacturing population of approximately 15 180 firms, the 597 responses represent a 3.9 per cent sampling error at the 95 per cent confidence level. For services, give an approximate SME population of 40 555 firms (SIC (92) divisions 52.7, 64, 72–74, 92.1 and 93 only), the 750 responses represent a 3.5 per cent sampling error at the 95 per cent confidence level. In most survey research, error levels typically lie between 2 and 6 per cent with 95 per cent confidence limits (Oerlemans et al., 2001).

A BRIEF DESCRIPTIVE ANALYSIS

Following Kleinknecht and Reijnen (1992), it seems appropriate to outline some general patterns in the data, prior to the more formal multivariate analysis. To this end, Figures 5.1–5.4 illustrate the distributions of cooperative relationships by degree and type of innovation (novel and incremental, product and process), by broad industrial sector and by potential partner. In general terms, the figures would appear to offer support to those who would proffer networking imperatives, generally, and to policy instruments designed to encourage innovation-related cooperation, specifically. Indeed, in all instances, excepting process innovation and cooperation with competitors (for both manufacturing and service sector firms), universities, and the local economic development network (LEDN) (for service firms only) and government (manufacturing only), the observed differences in Figures 5.1–5.4 are statistically significant (based on simple χ^2 tests). That is, with few exceptions, the propensity to cooperate seems to be positively associated with 'innovativeness' – this is true for both product innovation and, a little less so, for process innovation; for manufacturers and, again a little less so, service firms. Moreover, there is also tentative support for the idea that the propensity to innovate increases with the novelty of innovation (Tether, 2002), where novelty is a function of newness to the firm and market.

However, a couple of further points warrant elaboration. Firstly, it seems clear from the proportions of novel innovators reporting no innovation-related collaborations, that networking (as implied here) cannot be regarded as either sufficient or even necessary for innovation. In all instances, over 30 per cent of novel innovators record no cooperative ventures (almost 40 per cent in the case of manufacturers). Though the issue is beyond the remit of this chapter, this should undoubtedly sound a note of caution to those with universalizing tendencies (Freel, 2003). Secondly, the distribution of cooperative ventures, across partners, exhibits a fairly standard pattern: value chain linkages dominate by some considerable margin. In other words, irrespective of whether the firm is engaged in product or process innovation, whether it is in services or manufacturing, customers are the most common partners, followed by suppliers. This finding is hardly remarkable. If one considers collaboration to be facilitated by cognitive (Nooteboom, 1999a), institutional and organizational (Kirat and Lung, 1999) proximities, and by trust-creating mechanisms (such as frequency of contact, competence and disinterestedness) (Nooteboom, 1999b), then one is bound to anticipate just

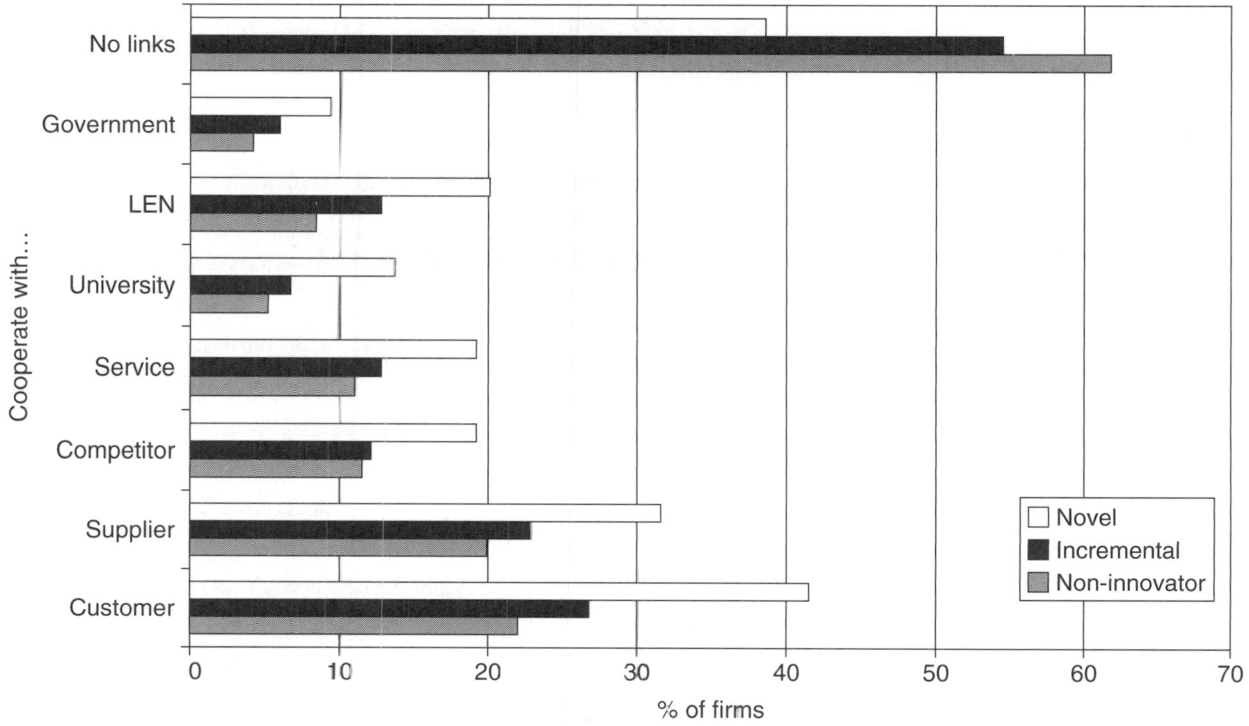

Figure 5.1 Product innovation and cooperation (manufacturing)

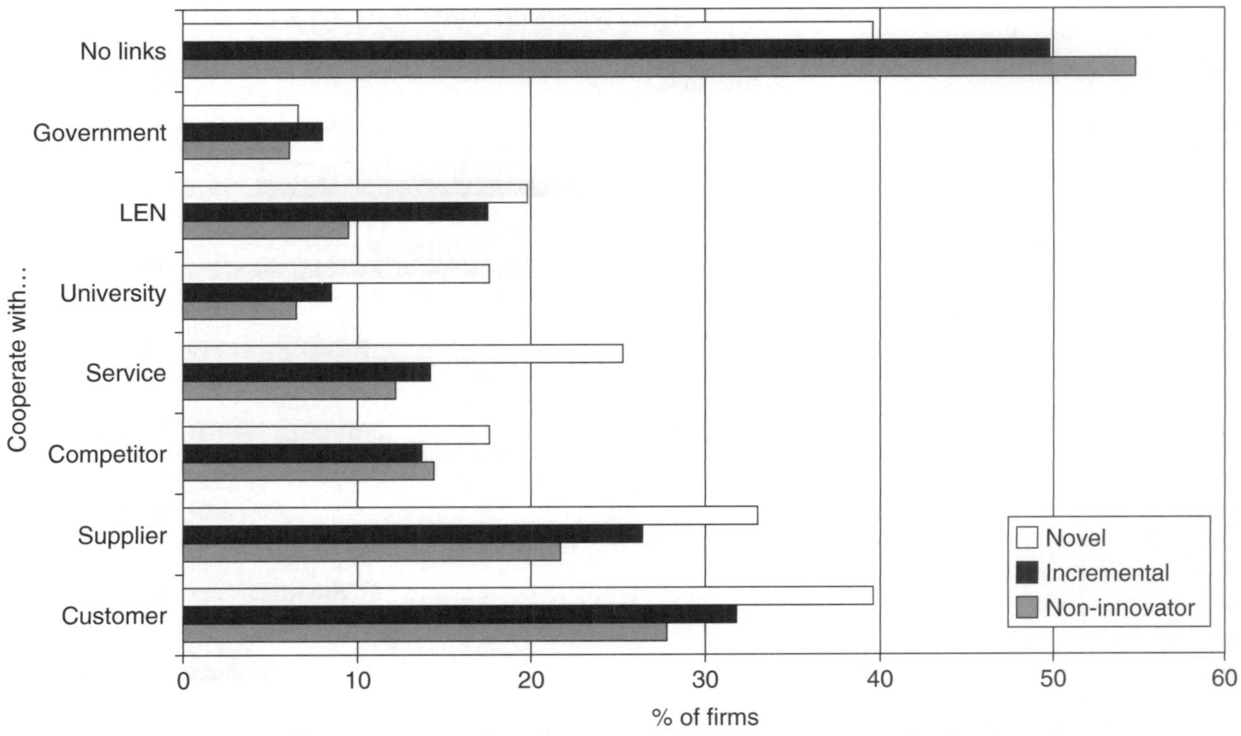

Figure 5.2 Process innovation and cooperation (manufacturing)

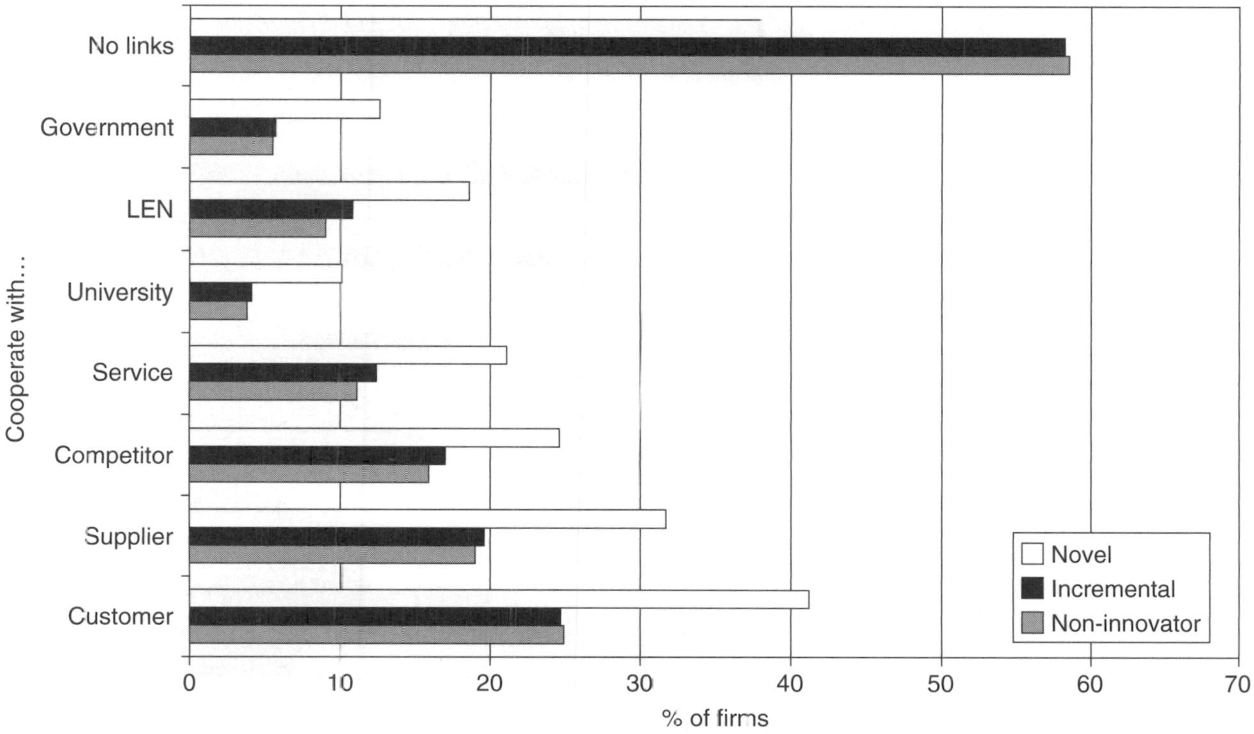

Figure 5.3 Product innovation and cooperation (services)

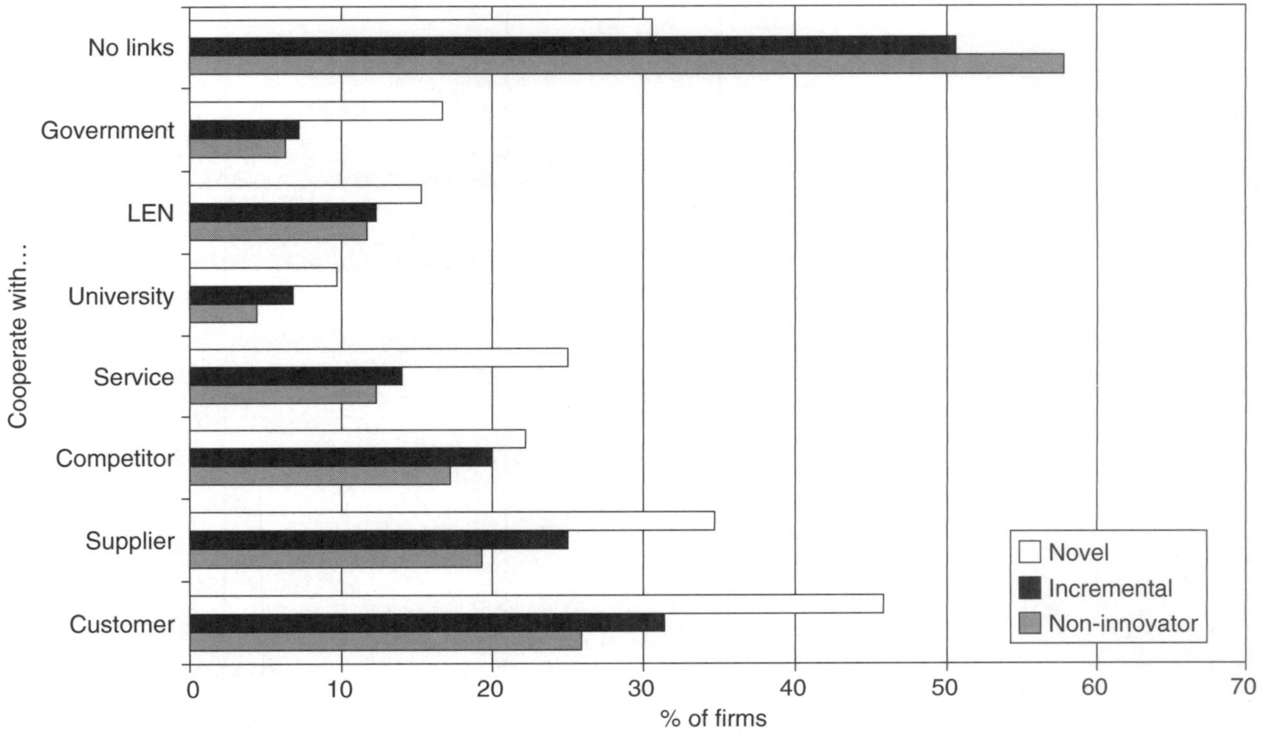

Figure 5.4 Process innovation and cooperation (services)

Table 5.1 Proportion of firms with cooperative arrangements by size class and partner

	Customers	Suppliers	Competitors	Service	University	LEN	Govt
Size classes							
			Manufacturing				
0–9	23.7	20.5	9.6	7.7	1.9	9.6	6.4
10–19	24.8	20.4	12.4	11.7	5.8	10.9	5.1
20–49	37.9	28.6	17.1	17.1	11.4	16.4	7.9
50–99	30.3	29.2	14.6	18.0	13.5	15.7	6.7
100+	42.1[a]	35.5[b]	23.7[b]	27.6[a]	19.7[a]	23.7[b]	6.6
			Services				
0–9	29.5	24.7	19.2	13.1	4.8	11.2	7.6
10–19	33.3	20.0	14.7	15.3	10.0	16.0	8.7
20–49	32.4	21.3	23.1	18.5	7.4	14.8	8.3
50–99	24.4	17.8	13.3	15.6	4.4	20.7	2.2
100+	21.7	21.7	30.4	13.0	0	17.4	8.7

Notes: Based on simple χ^2 tests; [a] significant at 1% level; [b] significant at 5% level; [c] significant at 10% level.

Table 5.2 Proportion of firms with cooperative arrangements by technology intensity of sector

	Customers	Suppliers	Competitors	Service	University	LEN	Govt
Sector							
HT	33.3	29.2	8.3	16.7	16.7	20.8	8.3
MHT	28.4	24.1	12.9	17.2	12.9	17.2	6.9
Non-HT	31.0	25.8	15.3	14.2	7.6	13.1	6.3
T-KIBS	32.2	23.5	20.1	18.6	6.1	14.8	8.7
P-KIBS	28.4	23.7	18.1	12.0	6.4	11.4	7.0
Non-KIBS	29.7	19.8	18.7	12.6	5.5[c]	14.3	7.1

Notes: Based on simple χ^2 tests; [a] significant at 1% level; [b] significant at 5% level; [c] significant at 10% level.

such a pattern of innovation networking. Indeed, there is plenty of empirical precedent (Kaufmann and Todtling, 2000; Freel, 2002). However, once again, it should give pause for thought.

Turning next to those classic variables of innovation studies, size and sector; Tables 5.1 and 5.2 contain data on the proportions of firms with cooperative arrangements by size class and by technology intensity of sector, respectively. The most striking feature of these tables, at least to the author, is the extent to which the observations tally with those of Kleinknecht and Reijnen (1992) – who undertook a similar exercise prior to multivariate analysis. Whilst these earlier authors were expressly concerned with R&D cooperation and the current concern is, more generally, with innovation-related cooperation, both data sets appear to suggest a positive relationship between firm size and the propensity to cooperate, for manufacturing firms, and little difference in the levels of cooperation between manufacturing and service firms. The former observation is, more or less, in line with expectations. However, that there is little difference in the propensity to cooperate between manufacturing and services is perhaps more remarkable. Indeed, casual reading of the data may be thought to indicate a greater propensity to cooperate amongst the smallest service firms, relative to their manufacturing peers, and vice versa. This may say something about the relative size of minimum efficient scales, in manufacturing and services, or about the general tendency to underplay the role of service firms in innovation (Tether and Hipp, 2002). Either way, the observation is intriguing.

With regards to the influence of the technology, or knowledge, intensity of the industry; the data in Table 5.2 are disaggregated along lines proposed by the OECD (see Jagger and Perryman, 1997; Nählinder and Hommen, 2002). In this way, manufacturing firms are classed as 'higher tech' (HT), 'medium-high tech' (MHT) and 'non-high tech' (Non-HT). Service firms are classed as technology-based knowledge-intensive business services (T-KIBS), professionally-based knowledge-intensive business services (P-KIBS) or non-KIBS. Counter to expectations, no clear pattern emerges. Again, this echoes Kleinknecht and Reijnen (1992, p. 350):

> It is interesting to note from the raw data that R&D cooperation does not seem to be concentrated in sectors which cover high-tech activities . . . [rather] . . . there seem to exist equally high or even above average rates of R&D cooperation in typical medium and low-tech sectors.

The one exception, from the current data, involves cooperation with universities. There is tentative evidence that technology intensity in manufacturing is positively associated with the likelihood of engaging in collaborations with universities. More intriguingly, though not significantly, the data appear to suggest a negative relationship between technology intensity (again, in manufacturing) and the propensity to cooperate with competitors – perhaps suggesting concerns over appropriability.

Though the above section serves a valuable purpose in describing the data and offers one or two interesting observations, there are obvious limitations to such simple analyses. Again, turning to Kleinknecht and Reijnen (1992): 'we have to warn against attributing the differences in [the tables] to various sectors and size classes as we have no control over a number of other factors'. A more comprehensive multivariate analysis is required and it is to this that the chapter now turns.

MULTIVARIATE ANALYSIS

Estimation of the multivariate models suggested by the various propositions takes the form of seven logit equations (Table 5.4). Given the binary nature of the dependent variables (that is, firms either cooperated or did not) logits are suggested. Logit equations allow one to compare those firms which cooperate for innovation with those that do not, and to estimate which of the measured independent variables (Table 5.3) exhibit a systematic influence on the propensity to cooperate with a given type of partner. On the whole, the models seem to have a number of satisfactory properties. For instance, tests for multicollinearity (using correlation matrices and multiway frequency analysis – Tabachnik and Fidell, 2001) give no cause for concern. Moreover, as the data in Table 5.4 indicate, the models appear reasonable predictors of the propensity to cooperate – significantly improving upon constant only prediction at the 1 per cent level.

Turning to the results of the logit equations (Table 5.4), it is clear that there is considerable variation in the extent to which the independent variables influence the propensity to cooperate with different partners. Perceptions of skill constraints to innovation are the nearest one comes to a consistent influence, irrespective of partner. That is, firms that perceive limitations in skill to be a serious barrier to innovation are significantly more likely to have collaborated with all but customers and the local economic development network (LEDN) – though here too there are positive signs on the coefficients. This should not be too surprising. If collaboration is driven by the logic of strategic resource needs (Angel, 2002), then one should anticipate a relationship between perceived resource constraints on the one hand, and the propensity to cooperate on the other. This is likely to be particularly true where constraints relate to skills (given issues of acquisition, mobility, context and tacitness). It is also most likely to apply to the small firm sector, where concerns over firms' ability to recruit, train and retain highly qualified and competent employees are longstanding (Rothwell, 1983, 1987; Oakey, 1997).

However, this single observation aside, perhaps the most striking feature of the data in Table 5.4 is the lack of observed systematic influences relating to the variables most commonly thought to effect the propensity to

Table 5.3 Variables used in regression equations

Age	In years (2001)
Size	Number of full-time employees (2001)
Technicians	Proportion of staff classed as technicians
QSEs	Proportion of staff classed as scientists or engineers
Managers	Proportion of staff classed as managers or professionals
R&D	Series of binary variables identifying expenditure on R&D as a proportion of turnover. No R&D expenditure is the reference group
Novel product	Binary dummy indicating the introduction of at least one 'new to the market' product
Incremental product	Binary dummy indicating the introduction of at least one 'new to the firm' product and no 'new to the industry' products
Novel process	Binary dummy indicating the introduction of at least one 'new to the market' process
Incremental process	Binary dummy indicating the introduction of at least one 'new to the firm' process and no 'new to the industry' processes
Skills barrier	Factor score from 10 item question detailing 'factors hindering innovative activity' (see appendix 1)
Finance barrier	Factor score from 10 item question detailing 'factors hindering innovative activity' (see appendix 1)
Legislation	Variable measuring the extent to which 'to comply with legislation/regulation' was a reason for innovating
Competition	Variable measuring the extent to which 'to respond to competition' was a reason for innovating
Customer request	Variable measuring the extent to which 'to meet a specific customer request' was a reason for innovating
New market	Variable measuring the extent to which 'to enter a new market' was a reason for innovating
Diversify	Variable measuring the extent to which 'to diversify the business' was a reason for innovating
Maintain revenue	Variable measuring the extent to which 'to maintain sales revenue/market share' was a reason for innovating
Increase revenue	Variable measuring the extent to which 'to increase sales revenue/market share' was a reason for innovating
Standardization	Variable measuring the extent to which 'as a result of standardization' was a reason for innovating

Table 5.3 (continued)

Sector	Series of binary variables identifying technology/knowledge intensity of sector. Non-HT and non-KIBS are the references
Customer dependency	Dummy customer dependency variable; >49% of turnover from largest 5 customer = 1, otherwise = 0
Overseas competitors	Number of identified overseas competitors as a proportion of total identified competitors

cooperate – namely, firm size, technology intensity of sector and R&D expenditure. Firm size, for instance, appears only statistically significantly associated with the likelihood of cooperating with a university.[4] Whilst this finds an echo in Kleinknecht and Reijnen's (1992) observation that, barring cooperation with research institutions (see also Diez, 2002), firm size does not seem to have a significant influence on cooperation, it stands in contrast to most other similarly motivated studies (Miotti and Sachwald, 2003; Tether, 2002; Fritsch and Lukas, 2001; Bayona et al., 2001). In the case of sectoral technology intensity, there is no evidence of an increasing propensity to cooperate in sectors characterized as 'high-technology' or 'knowledge-intensive'. Indeed, there is some tentative evidence that lower-technology manufacturing firms are more likely to have cooperated with customers and competitors. Again, these observations are not without empirical precedent. Miotti and Sachwald (2003), for instance, find that cooperation along the value chain is relatively more frequent in the low-tech sector, whilst both Kleinknecht and Reijnen (1992) and Oerlemans and Meeus (2001, p. 89) find 'no evidence for the assumption that . . . cooperation occurs mainly in high tech firms'. However, by and large, these studies are exceptions to the rule (cf. Koschatzky and Sternberg, 2000). Finally, with regards R&D intensity, statistically significant results were noted only with respect to competitor and public sector cooperation. In contrast, Tether (2002, p. 958) captures the gist of most of the studies reviewed here,[5] noting that 'quite simply, those that engaged in R&D were more likely to have cooperative arrangements for innovation than those that did not undertake R&D'.

Rationalization of these divergent findings undoubtedly starts with differences in the conception of innovation cooperation assumed. In the current study, firms were asked if they had cooperated 'with firms or organisations for innovation related activity (including marketing and training) and/or technology transfer during the last three years'. This certainly suggests a more encompassing view of innovation and innovation cooperation

Table 5.4 Logit models of the probability of cooperating for innovation

	Customers	Suppliers	Competitors	Services	Universities	LEDN	Government
Age	−0.100 (1.297)	−0.094 (1.059)	0.052 (0.238)	−0.015 (0.020)	0.046 (0.106)	−0.089 (0.652)	0.122 (0.639)
Size	0.032 (0.158)	0.016 (0.039)	0.045 (0.214)	0.155 (2.382)	**0.375 (7.172)**	0.158 (2.384)	−0.091 (0.412)
Technicians	0.010 (0.000)	−0.711 (1.735)	−0.784 (1.466)	−0.083 (0.019)	0.587 (0.498)	−0.212 (0.114)	−1.134 (1.295)
QSEs	0.155 (0.080)	−0.297 (0.249)	−0.601 (0.688)	−0.081 (0.013)	0.271 (0.079)	−0.814 (1.042)	0.035 (0.001)
Managers	−0.307 (0.978)	−0.491 (2.321)	0.240 (0.411)	−0.110 (0.076)	**1.112 (3.848)**	−0.145 (0.125)	−0.357 (0.411)
R&D >20%	−0.137 (0.078)	−0.055 (0.011)	**1.058 (4.461)**	0.461 (0.677)	0.049 (0.004)	**0.925 (2.946)**	−0.140 (0.028)
R&D11–20%	−0.383 (0.707)	−0.892 (2.374)	0.779 (2.424)	0.421 (0.702)	0.842 (2.177)	**0.962 (3.830)**	0.328 (0.215)
R&D 6–10%	−0.144 (0.220)	0.326 (1.129)	**0.575 (2.594)**	0.040 (0.011)	−0.130 (0.079)	0.261 (0.477)	**0.742 (2.883)**
R&D 1–5%	−0.085 (0.219)	0.156 (0.674)	**0.447 (3.822)**	0.123 (0.291)	−0.488 (2.280)	0.238 (0.999)	−0.052 (0.025)
Novel product	**0.543 (6.974)**	0.325 (2.243)	0.229 (0.844)	0.183 (0.520)	0.588 (2.492)	**0.688 (6.408)**	**0.924 (5.771)**
Incremental product	−0.258 (1.390)	−0.153 (0.460)	−0.418 (2.358)	−0.389 (1.929)	0.006 (0.000)	0.051 (0.031)	0.067 (0.025)
Novel process	**0.465 (3.570)**	**0.628 (6.077)**	0.0169 (0.330)	**0.621 (4.707)**	**0.732 (3.578)**	0.312 (0.990)	−0.009 (0.000)
Incremental process	0.268 (2.216)	**0.405 (4.661)**	0.035 (0.024)	0.193 (0.724)	**0.595 (3.510)**	**0.642 (7.908)**	**0.511 (2.717)**
Skills barrier	0.129 (2.469)	**0.158 (3.420)**	**0.247 (6.331)**	**0.277 (7.717)**	**0.290 (4.634)**	0.104 (0.978)	**0.278 (4.009)**
Finance barrier	0.084 (1.099)	0.083 (0.997)	0.015 (0.022)	0.011 (0.011)	−0.054 (0.152)	−0.034 (0.110)	0.112 (0.689)
Legislation	0.008 (0.014)	**0.138 (3.779)**	0.037 (0.200)	0.125 (2.197)	−0.087 (0.480)	−0.007 (0.005)	−0.092 (0.502)
Competition	−0.077 (1.109)	−0.101 (1.827)	−0.023 (0.071)	0.049 (0.301)	0.014 (0.014)	0.021 (0.051)	−0.112 (0.841)
Customer request	**0.099 (3.168)**	0.032 (1.430)	0.033 (1.436)	−0.022 (0.163)	−0.004 (0.005)	−0.043 (0.402)	−0.023 (0.057)
New market	−0.041 (0.325)	0.020 (0.072)	−0.024 (0.075)	0.015 (0.028)	−0.034 (0.074)	0.060 (0.404)	0.187 (2.007)
Diversify	**0.122 (3.006)**	0.104 (1.996)	**0.165 (3.668)**	**0.196 (4.878)**	0.089 (0.555)	0.037 (0.175)	−0.141 (1.369)
Maintain revenue	0.081 (1.326)	−0.019 (0.152)	−0.019 (0.098)	0.071 (1.221)	−0.028 (0.168)	0.081 (1.661)	0.087 (1.857)
Increase revenue	0.013 (0.029)	0.063 (0.687)	0.005 (0.003)	−0.058 (0.409)	0.025 (0.042)	−0.090 (0.955)	−0.061 (0.242)

Standardization	−0.066 (0.483)	−0.043 (0.193)	0.079 (0.506)	−0.012 (0.012)	0.176 (1.239)	**0.237 (4.420)**	**0.323 (4.454)**
High-tech	−0.646 (0.892)	0.157 (0.062)	−0.105 (0.017)	−0.105 (0.016)	−0.240 (0.047)	−0.332 (0.160)	0.652 (0.553)
Medium high-tech	**−0.521 (2.857)**	−0.342 (1.128)	**−0.819 (3.465)**	−0.232 (0.394)	0.224 (0.275)	−0.164 (0.180)	0.070 (0.021)
T-KIBS	0.060 (0.068)	0.119 (0.234)	0.170 (0.364)	0.289 (1.002)	−0.105 (0.059)	0.046 (0.021)	0.494 (1.492)
P-KIBS	−0.244 (1.130)	−0.038 (0.026)	0.056 (0.042)	−0.161 (0.301)	−0.127 (0.103)	−0.042 (0.020)	−0.177 (0.183)
Customer dependency	0.200 (1.194)	0.052 (0.092)	0.119 (0.359)	**−0.384 (3.405)**	−0.001 (0.000)	**−0.382 (3.120)**	−0.235 (0.648)
Overseas competitors	**0.551 (3.148)**	−0.064 (0.036)	−0.404 (0.952)	−0.028 (0.005)	**0.953 (5.203)**	−0.659 (2.401)	0.557 (1.290)
Constant	**−2.573 (6.625)**	**−1.645 (2.807)**	**−3.440(7.928)**	**−3.704 (8.981)**	**−5.303 (9.883)**	**−3.797 (9.109)**	**−2.624 (3.024)**
Nagelkerke R^2	0.117	0.087	0.90	0.114	0.157	0.114	0.131
−2 Log-likelihood	938.635	881.613	697.195	675.124	405.849	643.522	397.717
$^d\chi^2$	70.933	49.662	44.894	57.326	57.627	55.627	46.171
N	817	817	817	817	817	817	817

Notes: Figures in parenthesis are Wald χ^2 test statistics; [a] significant at 1% level; [b] significant at 5% level; [c] significant at 10% level; [d] full model *versus* constant only model.

than a narrow focus upon R&D. However, just such an inclusive approach sits comfortably with the tenor of policy – most especially that which has drawn on theoretical developments and empirical exemplars from the 'new industrial districts' literature (Brusco 1982; Becattini 1978 and 1990; Bianchi 1990; Camagni and Rabellotti, 1992). From this perspective, one might consider the lesser roles accorded to R&D expenditure and technology intensity to be unremarkable. Importantly, however, the findings do imply that innovation-related cooperation is a considerably more widely distributed phenomenon than casual reading of the literature might suggest. Networking for innovation is emphatically not the sole province of high-tech, knowledge-intensive firms, nor does it inevitably require the accumulated resources or developed competence frequently conflated with firm size.

In terms of the specific observations: one may reasonably rationalize the relationship between firm size and university cooperation in terms of search costs and/or processes and perceptions of 'ivory-towerism', at least from a demand perspective.[6] That is, whilst repeated contact with customers, suppliers and service providers and the determined, and proactive, marketing of government and quasi-government support services are likely to result in a relatively high degree of visibility for these potential partners, finding out what universities do and can do for the firm is likely to be less straightforward and more costly. To this end, the positive statistical associations noted between the propensity to collaborate with a university and the proportionate employment of managers, and between university cooperation and overseas competition, may both speak of more sophisticated and extended managerial search processes – rather in the manner of Beesely and Rothwell's (1989) 'outward lookingness'. Indeed, the extent to which search processes are constrained is likely to be a function of not only managerial resource, but of managerial perceptions. Certainly, the view that there exists 'an inherent, intractable mismatch between the essentially long-term research interests and focus of most HEIs [higher education institutions] and the short-term, near-to-market needs of most SMEs' (Hoffman et al., 1998, p. 48), prevails. This is well illustrated by the UK case, where universities have come under increasing government pressure 'to move closer to industry . . . [and] . . . undertake more industrially relevant research, in order to assist competitiveness' (Tether, 2002, p. 952). However, as the data in Table 5.4 imply, there is a positive relationship between the propensity to cooperate with universities and firm-level process innovation (both novel and incremental), whilst there does not appear to be an equivalent relationship involving product innovation (see also Swann, 2002). It is difficult to see how these observations can be taken as indicative of anything other than the sorts of 'closeness' or 'industrial relevance' university research is often accused of lacking. Surely, if the standard critique of universities were entirely warranted, one would anticipate, if anything, a greater marginal contribution to product, rather than process, innovation. This is clearly and (given the absolute levels of cooperation) emphatically not the case.

With regards to the tentative evidence of a greater likelihood of customer cooperation in lower-technology (manufacturing) sectors, one may see this as either an issue of appropriability or, more likely, of customers' familiarity with technological possibilities. Classically, von Hippel (1988) proposed a greater role for customers in the development of innovations in circumstances where customer needs were overt. This in turn is likely to be a function of technological maturity and the technological sophistication of customers. This view is buttressed by the positive association between the propensity to cooperate and 'to meet a specific customer request' as an important motivation for innovation Other factors associated with customer cooperation include, more or less as expected, the introduction of 'novel' products, diversification as a stimulus to innovation, and a greater proportion of overseas competitors. Perhaps a little surprisingly, the probability of engaging in customer cooperation is also positively associated with the introduction of at least one 'novel' process innovation. However, to the extent that genuinely new products often require new ways of producing them, this may be less remarkable than it first seems. All in all, a tentative picture emerges of the sorts of firms that are more likely to engage in innovation-related customer cooperation. As caricature, these firms operate in lower-technology sectors, but international markets, introduce products and processes which are new to their markets and are stimulated to innovate by either a specific customer requests or by the desire to diversify into other areas. That is not to say that only firms with these characteristics will engage in customer cooperation. It is simply that having these characteristics significantly increases the likelihood.

The issue of appropriability concerns may better explain the apparent negative relationship noted between higher-technology manufacturing and the propensity to engage in competitor collaboration (Freel, 2000; Quintana-García and Benavides-Velasco, 2004) – at least in medium- to high-tech sectors. Moreover, remarkably, there is no evidence that competitor cooperation is associated with either product or process innovation (regardless of 'novelty' considerations). Indeed, competitors are the only group to which this observation applies. In all other instances there is at least one positive relationship between the propensity to cooperate and some form of innovation output. However, uniquely, almost any amount of R&D expenditure is positively associated with the likelihood of engaging in innovation-related cooperative ventures with competitors. Given that firms were asked to record cooperative relationships engaged in between 1998–2001, and a similar timescale was specified for new product and process introductions, one may reasonably conjecture that innovation-related cooperative ventures, involving competitors, are frequently concerned with more strategic, longer-term projects. That is, projects in which the measured research input is greater and the anticipated outcomes take longer to realize. This seems a more plausible explanation than simply noting that 'competitor cooperation doesn't work'. Other factors associated with competitor collaboration include, as elsewhere, perceptions of skill constraints and diversification as an important motive for innovation.

The pictures which emerge of firms engaged in cooperative innovation with either suppliers or service firms are possibly the least remarkable. In both instances, the introduction of 'novel' process innovations is positively associated with the propensity to cooperate – as are perceptions of skill constraints. These are as anticipated (Sako, 1994; MacPherson, 1997). The key difference, however, lies in the motivations for innovation. In the case of supplier cooperation, 'responding to changing legislation or regulations' is positively associated with cooperation, whilst, for service firms, it is diversification which appears to matter more. Whilst the former suggests greater reactivity and passivity (and, here, the observed association with 'incremental' innovation may be germane), the latter hints at a more proactive and, perhaps, aggressive motivation. Here too, the issue of customer dependency may be pertinent. That is, firms cooperating with service firms are less likely to be dependent on a small number of customers for a relatively large proportion of sales.

The final two potential innovation partners considered represent, to a greater extent, the 'public sector': the local economic development network (LEDN) and government.[7] Unsurprisingly, the data in Table 5.4 show similar patterns of association for cooperation with LEDN and government. In both cases the probability of cooperating is significantly associated with 'novel' product, but 'incremental' process, innovation and with R&D expenditure, but also the importance of standardization (for example ISO 9000) as a stimulus to innovation. Initially, at least, this seems a somewhat muddled picture. However, it may suggest that the public sector is disproportionately engaging with two very different types of firms, occupying different ends of the innovation spectrum. On the one hand, there are relatively R&D-intensive firms, engaged in the development of 'new to the market' products – and casual attention to public sector pronouncements attests to the concern with these. On the other hand, and less dramatically, there are firms seeking assistance in complying with standards, which inevitably lead to improvements in processes. It may be that if one were better able to discriminate between the specific possible partners covered by the broad umbrellas of 'LEDN' and 'government' then the patterns of association would be more transparent. Nevertheless, understood in this way, the observations fit comfortably with likely *a priori* expectations.

Finally, in addition to commenting upon the various statistically significant associations observed, it is worth briefly remarking upon those variables where no such associations were noted. To this end, the proportionate employment of both technicians and QSEs and the perception of finance as a barrier to innovation stand out. In the former case, one is tempted to refer to the almost universal importance of perceptions of skill constraints in predicting cooperation. When deciding whether or not to cooperate, having a given stock of skilled labour does not appear to matter quite so much as perceiving those skills to be adequate. With respect to perceived financial constraints, the notion that access to capital acts as a significant barrier to innovation is one of the more popular 'stylized facts' in the literature. North et al. (2001), for instance, find problems in accessing finance to be a persistent policy theme across Europe. From this perspective, cooperation with other firms could be 'a solution to the problems of sharing costs and obtaining finance' (Bayona et al., 2001, p. 1293). Unfortunately, for both the basic problem (finance as a barrier to innovation) and the proposed solution (financial constraints stimulating cooperation), the empirical evidence is far from unequivocal (see Freel, 1999 and Hoffman et al., 1998 on the general issue; and Kleinknecht and Reijnen, 1992; Tether, 2002 and Miotti and Sachwald, 2003 on the specific). In the current sample, there is simply no evidence that perceived financial constraints spur innovation-related cooperation within any of the potential partners considered.

CONCLUDING REMARKS

'There is a broad belief among local economic development policy-makers that the number and the quality of intraregional innovation networks can be increased by means of policy instruments' (Koschatzky and Sternberg, 2000, p. 494). Yet, whilst the utility of innovation networking has been the subject of numerous (generally confirmatory) studies, policy development has proceeded with a more limited understanding of who cooperates for innovation and why. One might suggest that, though we know cooperation for innovation is often 'good', we are less knowledgeable about for whom it is 'good' and under what circumstances it might represent a preferred strategy – given the many successful innovators who do not appear to network in any substantive sense. As Maskell and Malmberg (1999, p. 20) observe, 'there is a great discrepancy between, on the one hand, a general agreement that innovation should be understood as an interactive process and, on the other, very limited knowledge about the purpose and nature of this interaction and why it matters so much'. If one admits this lacuna, policy prescriptions appear precipitate.

Drawing upon data from a sample of 1345 small firms, this chapter was concerned with contributing to a better understanding of the 'who' and 'why' of innovation networking. That is, with identifying the characteristics and motivations of firms engaged in innovation-related cooperation, with a variety of partners. Importantly, the definition of innovation-related cooperation adopted was far broader than commonly appears in similarly motivated studies. That is, the interest was with innovation-related activity (including marketing and training) and/or technology transfer and not, narrowly, with R&D. The more encompassing view of innovation that this implies sits comfortably with the bulk of recent academic literature, which recognizes the essentially cumulative and incremental nature of most technological innovations.

The implications of adopting this broader definition of innovation are quite stark. Whilst firm size, R&D intensity and 'high-techedness' are generally thought to positively influence the propensity to engage in R&D cooperation, their influence over innovation-related cooperation is far more restricted. Firm size, for instance, appears positively associated with the propensity to engage in cooperative ventures with universities only. The influence of R&D is limited to competitors and the public sector. And, there appear no systematic patterns in the distribution of cooperation by sectoral technology intensity. In other words, innovation-related cooperation is a far more widely distributed phenomenon than a casual reading of the literature might lead one to suppose. From the perspective of policy, this should be read encouragingly. Though, importantly, 'widely distributed' should not be confused with widespread, in the sense of commonly occurring. Any discussion has to carry the caveat that cooperating is not a majority activity.

Beyond this, and in very general terms, the results point to considerable variation in the factors associated with the propensity to cooperate with the assorted potential partners. The factors which associate with competitor cooperation, for instance, vary sharply from those associated with customer cooperation, which vary, in turn, from those associated with supplier cooperation, and so on. Without reference to the particulars, this general observation should, nonetheless, caution against the sorts of blanket networking and cooperation imperatives which seem so tempting. Any encouragement to cooperate should begin with an understanding of the relationships between the resources of the firm, its competitive environment, its innovation objectives (in terms of both the type of innovation and the motivation to innovate) and the sorts of networking which might prove most appropriate. Hopefully, this chapter makes a modest contribution to achieving this objective, and in so doing, sheds the narrow R&D bias common to similarly motivated studies and much policy rhetoric.

NOTES

1. In his paper 'Who cooperates for innovation and why?', Tether (2002, p. 949) takes innovation cooperation to mean 'participation in joint R&D and other technological innovation projects'.
2. Though these authors, in fact, find limited support for such a proposition.
3. For the present purposes 'northern Britain' encompasses Scotland and the northern English counties of Northumberland, County Durham, Tyne and Wear, Teesside and Cumbria.
4. This is not what one might expect, given the data in Table 5.1. However, it is likely that the results in Tables 5.1 and 5.2 'are to a considerable degree pseudo correlations which result from the lack of control of other variables' (Kleinknecht and Reijnen, 1992, p. 351).
5. Oerlemans and Meeus (2001) is a notable exception.
6. Alternatively, one might equally argue, from the supply-side, such that, universities' needs may be best served by fewer links with larger firms, rather than a larger number of links with smaller firms, with universities driving the observed firm size–/cooperation relationship.
7. The local economic development network includes such actors as Scottish Enterprise, Business Links, LECs and so on. 'Government' includes the central government departments of the Department for Trade and Industry, Ministry for Agriculture, Farming and Fishing (as was), the Ministry of Defence, and so on.

REFERENCES

Angel, D. (2002). Inter-firm collaboration and technological development partnerships within US manufacturing industries. *Regional Studies*, **36**: 333–44.

Audretsch, D. (1995). *Innovation and Industry Evolution*, Cambridge, MA: MIT Press.

Baptista, R. and Swann, P. (1998). Do firms in clusters innovate more? *Research Policy*, **27**: 525–40.

Bayona, C., García-Marco, T. and Huerta, E. (2001). Firms' motivations for cooperative R&D: An empirical analysis of Spanish firms. *Research Policy*, **30**: 1289–1308.

Becattini, G. (1978). The development of light industry in Tuscany. *Economic Notes*, **2–3**: 53–78.

Becattini, G. (1990). The Marshallian industrial district as a socio-economic notion. In Pyke, F., Beccatini, G. and Sengenberger, W. (eds). *Industrial Districts and Inter-Firm Cooperation in Italy*. Geneva: International Institute for Labour Studies, pp. 37–51.

Beesley, M. and Rothwell, R. (1987). Small firm linkages in the United Kingdom. In Rothwell, R. and Bessant, J. (eds). *Innovation, Adaptation and Growth*. Amsterdam: Elsevier, pp. 189–201.

Bengtsson, M. and Sölvell, Ö. (2004). Climate of cooperation, clusters and innovative performance. *Scandinavian Journal of Management*, **20**: 225–44.

Bianchi, G. (1990). Innovating in the local system of small-medium sized enterprises. *Entrepreneurship and Regional Development*, **2**: 57–69.

Bougrain, F. and Haudeville, B. (2002). Innovation, collaboration and SMEs' internal research capacities. *Research Policy*, **31**: 735–48.
Brusco, S. (1982). The Emilian model: Productive decentralisation and social integration. *Cambridge Journal of Economics*, **6**: 63–82.
Bullock, A. and Hughes, A. (2000). The survey method, the SME panel database and sample attrition. In CBR (ed.). *British Enterprise in Transition*. Cambridge: ESRC Centre for Business Research, University of Cambridge.
Camagni, R. and Rabellotti, R. (1992). Technology and organisation in the Italian textile-clothing industry. *Entrepreneurship and Regional Development*, **4**: 271–85.
CBR (1996). *The Changing State of British Enterprise*. Cambridge: ESRC Centre for Business Research, University of Cambridge.
CBR (1998). *Enterprise Britain*. Cambridge: ESRC Centre for Business Research, University of Cambridge.
CBR (2000). *British Enterprise in Transition*. Cambridge: ESRC Centre for Business Research, University of Cambridge.
CBR (2003). *Enterprise Challenged*. Department of Applied Economics, Cambridge: Centre for Business Research, University of Cambridge.
Cohen, W. (1995). Empirical studies of innovative activity. In Stoneman, P. (ed.). *Handbook of the Economics of Innovation and Technological Change*, Oxford: Blackwell, pp. 182–264.
Cohen, W. and Levinthal, D. (1989). Innovation and learning: The two faces of R&D, *Economic Journal*, **99**: 569–96.
Cohen, W. and Levinthal, D. (1990). Absorptive capacity: A new perspective on learning and innovation, *Administrative Science Quarterly*, **35**: 128–52.
Cooke, P. and Morgan, K. (1998). *The Associational Economy: Firms, Regions and Innovation*. Oxford: Oxford University Press.
Cosh, A., Hughes, A. and Woods, E. (1998). Innovation surveys and very small enterprises. WP89, ESRC Centre for Business Research, University of Cambridge.
de la Mothe, J. and Paquet, G. (1998). National innovation systems, 'real economies' and instituted process. *Small Business Economics*, **11**: 101–11.
Demsetz, H. (1991). The theory of the firm revisited. In Williamson, O. and Winter, S. (eds). *The Nature of the Firm*. New York: Oxford University Press, pp. 159–78.
Diez, J.D. (2002). Metropolitan innovation systems: a comparison between Barcelona, Stockholm and Vienna. *International Regional Science Review*, **25**: 63–85.
DTI (Department of Trade and Industry) (2001). *Business Clusters in the UK – A First Assessment*. London: DTI.
Eisenhardt, K. and Schoonhaven, C. (1996). Resource-based view of strategic alliance formation: Strategic and social effects in entrepreneurial firms. *Organization Science*, **7**: 136–50.
Florida, R. (1995). Towards the learning region. *Futures*, **27**: 527–36.
Freel, M. (1999). The financing of small firm product innovation within the UK. *Technovation*, **19**: 707–19.
Freel, M. (2000). External linkages and product innovation in small manufacturing firms. *Entrepreneurship and Regional Development*, **12**: 245–66.
Freel, M. (2002). On regional innovation systems: Illustrations from the West Midlands. *Environment and Planning C: Government and Policy*, **20**: 633–54.
Freel, M. (2003). Sectoral patterns of small firm innovation, networking and proximity. *Research Policy*, **32**: 751–70.
Fritsch, M. and Lukas, R. (2001). Who cooperates on R&D? *Research Policy*, **30**: 297–312.

Geroski, P. (1995). Markets for technology: Knowledge, innovation and appropriability. In Stoneman, P. (ed.). *Handbook of the Economics of Innovation and Technological Change*. Oxford: Blackwell. pp. 90–131.

Hagedoorn, J. (1993). Understanding the rationale of strategic technology partnering: interorganizational modes of cooperation and sectoral differences. *Strategic Management Journal*, **14**: 371–85.

Håkansson, H. (1987). Product development in networks. In Håkansson, H. (ed.). *Industrial Technological Development: A Network Approach*. London: Crook-Helm, 84–127.

Hoffman, K., Milady, P., Bessant, J. and Perren, L. (1998). Small firms, R&D, technology and innovation in the UK: a literature review. *Technovation*, **18**: 39–55.

Huggins, R. (2001). Inter-firm network policies and firm performance: evaluating the impact of initiatives in the United Kingdom. *Research Policy*, **30**: 443–58.

Jagger, N. and Perryman, S. (1997). Measurement of employment in high technology sectors at the regional level, Institute for Employment Studies Report 318, IES Brighton.

Kaufmann, A. and Todtling, F. (2000). Systems of innovation in traditional industrial regions: the case of Styria in comparative perspective. *Regional Studies*, **34**: 29–40.

Kirat, T. and Lung, Y. (1999). Innovation and proximity: Territories as loci of collective learning. *European Urban and Regional Studies*, **6**: 27–38.

Kleinknecht, A. (1989). Firm size and innovation. *Small Business Economics*, **1**: 215–22.

Kleinknecht, A. and Reijnen, J. (1992). Why do firms cooperate on R&D? An empirical study. *Research Policy*, **21**: 347–60.

Koschatzky, K. and Sternberg, R. (2000). R&D cooperation in innovation systems: some lessons from the European Regional Innovation Survey (ERIS). *European Planning Studies*, **8**: 487–501.

Krugman, P. (1991). *Geography and Trade*. Cambridge, MA: MIT Press.

Le Bars, A., Mangematin, V. and Nesta, L. (1998). Innovation in SMEs: The missing link. Paper presented at the 6th annual High-Technology Small Firms Conference, University of Twente.

Love, J. (1999). Patterns of networking in the innovation process: A comparative study of the UK, Germany and Ireland, RP9913, Aston Business School, Aston University, Birmingham.

Love, J. and Roper, S. (1999). The determinants of innovation: R&D, technology transfer and networking effects. *Review of Industrial Organisation*, **15**: 43–64.

Lundvall, B.-Å. (1990). Explaining inter-firm cooperation and innovation – limits of the transaction cost approach. Socioeconomics of Interfirm Cooperation Workshop. Berlin: Wissen Schafetzentrum, 11–13 June.

Lundvall, B.-Å. (1995). *National Systems of Innovation: Towards a Theory of Innovation and Interactive Learning*. London: Pinter. (First published in 1992.)

MacPherson, A. (1997). The contribution of external service inputs to the product development efforts of small manufacturing firms. *R&D Management*, **27**: 127–45.

Maillat, D. (1995). Territorial dynamic, innovative milieus and regional policy. *Entrepreneurship and Regional Development*, **7**: 157–65.

Maskell, P. and Malmberg, A. (1999). The competitiveness of firms and regions. *European Urban and Regional Studies*, **6**: 9–25.

Miotti, L. and Sachwald, F. (2003). Co-operative R&D: Why and with whom? An integrated framework of analysis. *Research Policy*, **32**: 1481–1500.

Nählinder, J. and Hommen, L. (2002). Employment and innovation in services: Knowledge intensive business services in Sweden. Report prepared for the final meeting and conference of AITEG, Clore Management Centre, Birbeck College.
Nooteboom, B. (1999a). Innovation, learning and industrial organisation. *Cambridge Journal of Economics*, **23**: 127–50.
Nooteboom, B. (1999b). Innovation and inter-firm linkages: New implications for policy. *Research Policy*. **28**: 793–805.
North, D., Smallbone, D. and Vickers, I. (2001). Public sector support for innovating SMEs: The effectiveness of support measures in London's Lee Valley region. *Small Business Economics*, **16**: 303–17.
Oakey, R. (1997). A review of policy and practice relating to high technology small firms in the United Kingdom. WP. 359, Manchester Business School, University of Manchester.
Oerlemans, L., Buys, A. and Pretorius, M. (2001). Research design for the South African Innovation Survey 2001. ECIS, WP 01.02, Technical University of Eindhoven.
Oerlemans, L. and Meeus, M. (2001). R&D cooperation in a transaction cost perspective. *Review of Industrial Organisation*, **18**: 77–90.
Oerlemans, L., Meeus, M. and Boekema, F. (1998). Do networks matter for innovation? The usefulness of the economic network approach to analysing innovation. *Tijdschrift voor Economische en Sociale Geografie*, **89**: 298–309.
Oughton, C. and Whittam, G. (1997). Competition and cooperation in the small firm sector. *Scottish Journal of Political Economy*, **44**: 1–30.
Patel, P. and Pavitt, K. (1994). The continuing, widespread (and neglected) importance of improvements in mechanical technologies. *Research Policy*, **23**: 533–45.
Penrose, E. (1995). *The Theory of the Growth of the Firm*. Oxford: OUP. (First published 1959.)
Quintana-García, C. and Benavides-Velasco, C. (2004). Cooperation, competition, and innovative capability: A panel data of European dedicated biotechnology firms. *Technovation*, **24**: 927–38.
Roper, S. (1998). Under-reporting of R&D in small firms: The impact on international R&D comparisons. *Small Business Economics*, **12**: 131–5.
Rothwell, R. (1983). Innovation and firm size: A case of dynamic complementarity. *Journal of General Management*, **8**: 5–25.
Rothwell, R. (1987). Small firms, innovation and industrial change. *Small Business Economics*, **1**: 51–64.
Rothwell, R. (1991). External networking and innovation in small and medium-sized manufacturing firms. *Technovation*, **11**: 93–112.
Rothwell, R. and Dodgson, M. (1991). External linkages and innovation in small and medium-sized enterprises. *R&D Management*, **21**: 125–37.
Sako, M. (1994). Supplier relations and innovation. In Dodgson, M. and Rothwell, R. (eds). *The Handbook of Industrial Innovation*. Cheltenham, UK and Northampton, MA, USA: Edward Elgar, pp. 268–74.
Santarelli, E., and Sterlacchini, A. (1990). Innovation, formal vs. informal R&D, and firm size: Some evidence from Italian manufacturing firms. *Small Business Economics*, **2**: 223–8.
SBRC (1992). *The State of British Enterprise*. Department of Applied Economics, Cambridge: ESRC Centre for Business Research, University of Cambridge.
Simmie, J., Sennet, J., Wood, P. and Hart, D. (2002). Innovation in Europe: A tale of networks, knowledge and trade in five cities. *Regional Studies*, **36**: 47–64.

Sterlacchini, A. (1999). Do innovative activites matter to small firms in no-R&D intensive industries? An application to export performance. *Research Policy*, **28**: 819–32.
Sternberg, R. (2000). Innovation networks and regional development – evidence from the European Regional Innovation Survey (ERIS): Theoretical concepts, methodological approach, empirical basis and introduction to the theme issue, *European Planning Studies*, **8**: 389–407.
Swann, G.M.P. (2002). *Innovative business and the science and technology base: An analysis using CIS3 data*, report for the Department of Trade and Industry, London, available at http://www.dti.gov.uk/iese/cisreportpdf.
Tabachnik, B. and Fidell, L. (2001). *Using Multivariate Statistics*, 4th edn. Needham Heights, MA: Pearson.
Teece, D. (1992). Competition, cooperation and innovation. *Journal of Economic Behaviour and Organization*, **18**: 1–25.
Tether, B. (2002). Who cooperates for innovation and why? An empirical analysis. *Research Policy*, **31**: 947–68.
Tether, B. and Hipp, C. (2002). Knowledge intensive, technical and other services: Patterns of competitiveness and innovation. *Technology Analysis and Strategic Management*, **14**: 163–82.
von Hippel, E. (1978). Successful industrial products from customer ideas. *Journal of Marketing*, **42**: 39–49.
von Hippel, E. (1988). *The Sources of Innovation*. Oxford: Oxford University Press.

6. Complex explanations of order creation, emergence and sustainability as situated entrepreneurship

Ted Fuller and Lorraine Warren

INTRODUCTION

This chapter is towards a theory of entrepreneurial mechanisms, that is, those which create novel patterns of economic activity such as new ventures. It takes a realist perspective of entrepreneurship as a structural cause of emergent properties, grounded in a Schumpeterian account of entrepreneurship, developing theoretical explanations of the phenomenon Schumpeter described and putting this into a constructionist context – that is, that entrepreneurship is inherently a social act that produces specific types of social structure.

The theory is far from esoteric; it resonates with the experiences of owner-managers, and is grounded in their accounts of those experiences. The theory is salient to an understanding of such policy and practice phenomena as business start-ups, spin-outs, growth and survival and also helps the articulation of 'entrepreneurship' in different contexts.

The link between complexity science and entrepreneurship as an order-creating activity is made via notions of causation from interacting agents. The emergent properties of such interactions are conceptualized as hierarchical and multilevel models. It is the relationships between the agents and between the layers of these models that becomes the focus of the study of entrepreneurship in context.

Following this theoretical discussion, two analyses are produced; the first from a study of the sustainability of an enterprise over a period of 15 years in a fast-changing environment. This analysis leads to the articulation of four related processes that produce emergent properties and lead to temporary order. The processes are dynamic, continual and socially embedded. The model which articulates these processes (EROS) is then applied to a second enterprise, in this case a start-up venture from a university spin-out. The same processes of emergence appear to be resonant with the second case.

What is significant in these cases is the situatedness of the EROS processes. They cannot be explained without reference to the social context of the performances. We thus introduce the notion of a 'Community of Practice' to articulate the nature of the social context that accounts for the emergence of order at different levels in the model through the EROS processes.

COMPLEXITY SCIENCE AND ENTREPRENEURSHIP

The starting point for this theory-building narrative is with complexity science. The salience of complexity science to understanding small business and entrepreneurship is becoming recognized (for example Fuller and Moran, 2000; Fuller and Moran, 2001; Lichtenstein, 2000; McKelvey, 2004). McKelvey (2004) proposes that complexity science provides the potential for understanding the dynamics of entrepreneurship as Schumpeter defined it. A complex adaptive system is one that is far from equilibrium, self-organizing and co-evolving from the interaction between heterogeneous agents. Such interrelationships are, in McKelvey's words, 'pre-equilibrium', characterized by constant change and mutual dependence, and behaving in non-proportional ways (Lichtenstein, 2000). Their emergent systems and structures are not analytically reducible to the constituent parts. The activity of a complex adaptive system is order-creating. There is significant consonance between the Schumpeterian conception of entrepreneurship, the observed empirical phenomenon of entrepreneurial firms, and the behaviour of 'agents' in a complex adaptive system. In short, the innovative creation of new ventures or enterprises is an order-creating activity.

The Schumpeterian notion of 'creative destruction' is probably the most well established in modern discourse on entrepreneurship (Schumpeter, 1934). That is, entrepreneurial acts develop 'new combinations' which change the dominant patterns of behaviour. One limitation of modern interpretations of Schumpeter is the sense in which entrepreneurship is an individualistic activity, and the creation of order arising from entrepreneurship has no other explanation than a linear causal relationship between the existence of the innovation and its subsequent pattern creation. We argue, from the perspectives of both complex adaptive systems and social constructionism, that the ontology of the entrepreneurial domain includes multiple agents and an emergent hierarchy of structures, and again analytically irreducible to individual agents. Explanations for the emergence, existence and sustainability of particular patterns (firms, networks, industries) should, we argue, be grounded in an understanding of the dynamics operating between heterogeneous agents through multiple levels.

MULTILEVEL MODELS AND EMERGENCE

A key concept in complexity science is emergence (Holland, 1998), as it is in the modern discourse of entrepreneurship, and in particular the emergence of new enterprise, for example (Busenitz et al., 2003; Fischer et al., 1997; Gartner, 1993; Lichtenstein, 2000). The notion of emergence is that ontological properties are formed by the interactions of a historically situated ontology: that is, the next moment is connected to the previous one. As Low and Macmillan pointed out (1988), to understand entrepreneurship, one needs to understand process, context and outcomes. Writing ten years later, Aldrich and Martinez (2001) and Davidsson and Wiklund (2001) conclude that understanding the links between these and the fitness of the firm continues to be a nascent activity.

Social science utilizes multilevel models for connecting 'units of analysis' to their wider environment in recognition, or expectation, of causal relationships between macro and micro, agent and structure, or process and context – where these bipolar constructs (for example agent–structure) are socially constructed through abstraction and claims of salience. Various methodological strategies are used for this as outlined for example by DiPrete and Forristal (1994). One contribution to multilevel modelling in the field of entrepreneurship, which is further developed in this chapter, comes from Fuller and Moran (2001). The contribution suggests that rather than each layer being seen as an independent ontology for study, it is the interrelationships between layers and in particular the mechanisms underlying those relationships that should be studied. One outcome of an approach that considers the mechanisms rather than the empirical outcomes is likely to be the re-conceptualization of the emergent properties of entrepreneurship. An axiomatic description of the outcome of entrepreneurship as 'the creation of a new enterprise' (Low and MacMillan, 1988) may be negatively limiting as well as positively normative. For example such an axiom would omit the unwanted consequences of entrepreneurship and also tends to deny the creation of new enterprise as in some way a by-product of more enduring human and social qualities. Clearly, however, studies of entrepreneurship need definitional boundaries.

Notwithstanding the inherent rhetorical flaw (that a study of emergent structures starts with extant socially constructed structures), Fuller and Moran have suggested that one starting point for understanding emergent structures in the field of entrepreneurship is implicit in the cannon of entrepreneurship literature (for example Bygrave, 1989; Moore, 1986). That is, the disciplinary domains suggest corresponding models of ontological structures (individuals: values and motivation; business organizations: functions, models, relationships, networks; environment: networks, sectors,

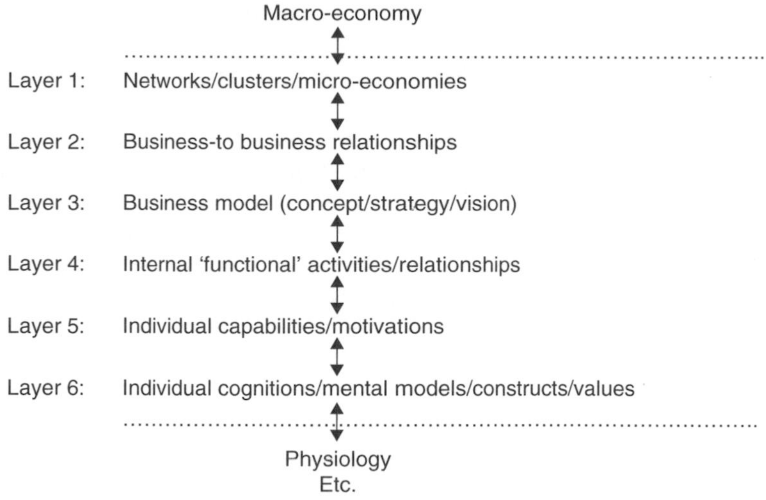

Source. Fuller and Moran (2001), Figure 1, p. 54.

Figure 6.1 An ontologically layered model of the small firm domain

economies and so on). The framework is shown Figure 6.1. Following Harvey and Reed (1996), Fuller and Moran suggest that such ontological structures are hierarchically emergent, that is, they are produced from the interactions of their substructures, behave differently from the substructures, but are interdependent on their substructures. Furthermore, the emergent properties are unpredictable from any analytical reductionism of their substructures. This position legitimates single-layer models for their descriptive and analytical power (that is, that substructure behaviour is characterized independently from their individual constituents). However, it also renders incomplete any theoretical explanation of the cause of such characteristics and behaviour which is based on a single-level model (see for example Davidsson and Wiklund, 2001), because the properties are emergent from substructures, that is, from other layers.

SOCIALLY SITUATED ENTREPRENEURSHIP

In our exploration of the relationships between ontological 'layers' of the entrepreneurial domain, we acknowledge the salience of social structures. Indeed it would, in our view, be impossible to operationalize a methodology that was not inherently sociological in order to understand socio-economic processes and phenomena. The tension between social constructionism and the realist paradigm inherent in complexity science cannot easily be addressed. However, Sayer (2000) provides some insights with respect to critical realism in his discussion on (the inevitability of) epistemological relativism within a realist (absolute) perspective, that is, that in reaching theoretically generalizable accounts of causal mechanisms, one accepts that epistemic knowledge is socially constructed and fallible, as are the discourses that emerge with respect to observed empirical and implicit causal mechanisms.

From its early origins in the mathematics of chaos, complexity theory has been enriched by incorporation of social theory, as its application has extended into the social domain (Cilliers, 1998). If complexity theory is to account successfully for the entrepreneurial domain through a multi-layered model, then theoretical understandings of social contexts can deepen understanding of the layered framework and the interfaces between levels that lead to the emergence of new structures. We are encouraged in this sociological perspective by Thornton (1999) who suggests that multilevel models, amongst other sociological frameworks (embeddedness, ecological and institutional theories), help in the study of entrepreneurship as a class.

As we will show, in our explanatory framework of order creation, emergence and sustainability, we take cognisance of the situatedness of the entrepreneur and the (new) enterprise in the social domain. Our explanation rests on an assumption that social processes occur in the everyday practices of the entrepreneur and the firm. These social processes, such as inter-subjectivity, reflexivity, social capital (networks and relationships) and communities of practice are inherent in the account of the emergence of particular and specific properties.

THE EMERGENCE OF 'NEW ENTERPRISE': BECOMING ORDER

Our definition of 'new enterprise' for the purposes of this research is the establishment of novel practices within a particular context. This is consistent with the Schumpeterian notion of 'creative destruction' and with mainstream entrepreneurship theory. In empirical terms we have restricted the study to business economic activity. In that context, new enterprises or new ventures occur in pre-existing businesses and as new businesses. Considered as a complex adaptive system, a venture can exist in a variety of states of relative order. Our focus is on what McKelvey (2004) calls 'pre-equilibrium'. In this sense the outcome of entrepreneurship is some form of orderly, that is, recursive or repeated, pattern of activity – an established symmetry such as a 'business model' if you will. The process of entrepreneurship is one of creating new symmetries, and also one of breaking existing ones – whether by design or effect. The outcomes become manifest through the entrepreneurial processes. The fitness of these created symmetries in the environment is typically measured by their sustainability and by the rents created through that fitness. That is, by the value of the order creation relative to the overall landscape in which the enterprise is embedded.

From the perspective of multi-layered models, the creation of new symmetries in economic patterns has emergent effects on the landscape in which those activities are embedded. For example, an innovative service or product will change consumer demand and the supply chains that produce that product will be reconfigured, such as the introduction of low-price air travel into the European economy. In the analysis below we identify the processes involved in the production of new symmetries (creation of order) in two case studies.

ANALYSIS USING MULTILEVEL MODELS

In this particular analysis, we are locating three interconnected and hierarchical emergent properties: (1) the reflexive identity of the entrepreneur, represented through the language of mental models, motivations and everyday practice; (2) the recursive (regular, repeating or established) activities of the entrepreneur's firm; (3) the recursive activities in a network of firms (for instance a technological cluster, or particular industry) in which the entrepreneurial firm is engaged. (See Figure 6.2.)

The starting point for the analysis is the individual entrepreneurial firm and its relationships with the structures as conceived in Figure 6.1. In their research on the generation of new technological milieu, Garnsey et al. have steadfastly maintained the significance of individual voluntaristic entrepreneurial actions, as well as the individuality of local conditions (Druilhe and Garnsey, 2000; Garnsey, 1998; Miller and Garnsey, 2000). Similarly, from their studies of small business orientation to ICT and relationships, Fuller and Lewis (2003) propose that a firm's strategy and its relationships are closely bound. They suggest that innovative entrepreneurial actions are reflexively moderated by interaction with others, giving rise to certain emergent properties with respect to the firm and its stakeholders in response to a given set of interactions within the environment.

Reflexivity as a process links the cognitive domain of the individual to their experienced environment, which for the entrepreneur, includes the everyday practices of doing business with others. The meaning and identity of the entrepreneur are closely bound to the enterprise, such that personal

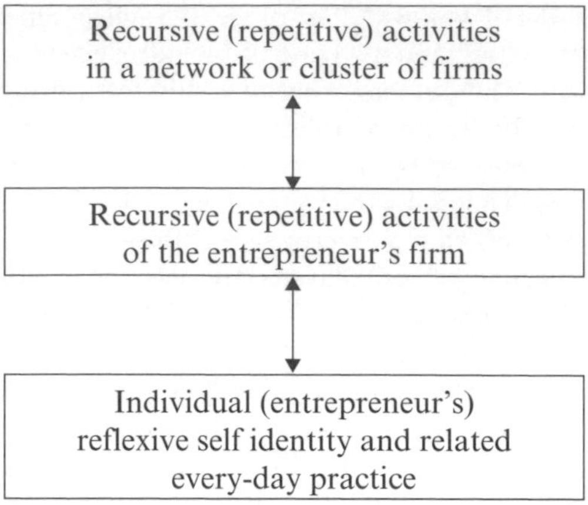

Figure 6.2 Multilevel model: the entrepreneur's reflexive engagement with 'their' own enterprise produces the emergent structures of that 'enterprise-in-context'

identity and the nature of the business are intertwined. Thus the identity of the business, what it does, how it does it and how it sustains itself through innovation are 'both the outcome and the medium' (Giddens, 1984, p. 25) of reflexivity. The entrepreneur, as shaper and decision-maker, in the context of their own 'business', in the context they engage with, appears to influence the emergent structures of the firm and the context. Their apparently idiosyncratic, voluntaristic acts are shaped by the nature of the coupling to the environment, that is, the everyday structures and their sense-making (Weick, 1995) of those structures.

EMERGENCE WITHIN AN ENTREPRENEUR-OWNED BUSINESS: THE CASE OF FLIGHT DIRECTORS LIMITED

To ground our analysis, we refer to a particular case study of sustainability and innovation in an entrepreneurial firm. We use the concepts identified above to explore empirically the question of emergence. This case study and the analysis that produced the conceptual model is described elsewhere (Fuller et al., 2004) and is consonant with the approach theoretical perspective taken in this paper.

The firm, Flight Directors Ltd, was established by two founders in 1984 to provide brokerage services in the air travel industry. In September 2001 with over 100 staff, it was chartering two 737 aircraft, brokering charter flights and running a multi-customer overspill ticketing call centre. A small business run by an entrepreneur, who innovates to remain 'fit' within the community of practice, has little power or influence. The effects of terrorist action on the demand for travel, the continued opening of trading regulations, direct internet bookings, were all features of the landscape outside the control of the individual firm. Fuller et al.'s (2004) analysis of the 'agility' and 'foresight' relating to the survival of that business produced a conceptual model of the creation of emergent properties. A development of this model from the original is shown below and in this chapter is called EROS.

The analysis suggested that the firm had no 'foresight' in the sense of anticipating its future through a well-constructed theory of its relationship to the environment. But rather the 'foresight' in the system was the entrepreneurial endeavours themselves. What the firm had become[1] emerged from: (1) the number and quality of experiments that anticipate the effects of 'weak signals' of opportunities; (2) the quality of reflexivity (the way that the dynamic internal model is able to transcend external systemic changes); (3) the capacity to restructure patterns of behaviour and self-image, that is the organizing domains; and (4) the sensitivity to changes in conditions. Thus the mnemonic 'EROS':

1. Experiments: operationalized as a range of diverse behaviours (projects) at any one time by the firm. Experiments in this case were projections from existing patterns or models which create new patterns. They were created because of an anticipated need from the close stakeholders, that is, they were co-evolutionary in their foundation. Some experiments worked and some did not; that is some enhanced the 'coupling' of the firm to its stakeholders, gaining rents or resources from these relationships, and some failed to do this.
2. Reflexive construction of identity: operationalized as motivations, learning processes and re-identification of behavioural imperatives. From a constructionist perspective the continuous reflection on the identity of the firm and the self-identity of its owner(s) through the discourses within the business and with stakeholders is central to the thesis of becoming. The inability to reshape identity puts the future at risk for the firm. This does not mean that firms are chameleon-like, and able or willing to change their more fundamental values. Paradoxically, it was the underlying strength and continuity of the basic values and self-identity of the founders that sustained Flight Directors Ltd.
3. Organizing domains: operationalized as the speed at which a change is constituted as consistent and sustainable (energy-attracting) patterns of behaviour. Fitness in most competitive landscapes requires efficient operations, and the speed at which new recursive structures can be put

into place, to increase efficiency of operations, contributes to the sustainability of the enterprise. The tension between innovative (symmetry-breaking) practices and recursive practices (new symmetries) requires managerial judgement, but is the manifestation of becoming, and is closely bound with the personal roles and identities of individuals and groups of people in the firm.

4. Sensitivity to conditions: operationalized in terms of: (a) the threshold of environmental change that triggers change in the agent; and (b) the length of time before change occurs. We suggest two salient perspectives on this. The first is a constructivist perspective – the cognitive capability to detect difference and the indicators used for this. The second is the relative imperative (motivation or incentive) to change, which we suggest may account for the threshold at which change is triggered and the rate at which it takes place.

SITUATED ENTREPRENEURSHIP AND EMERGENCE IN COMMUNITIES OF PRACTICE (COP)

We turn now to examining the dynamic between emergence at the firm level and its relationship with the emergent properties of its networks of stakeholders. For this purpose, we will utilize the concept of a Community of Practice (CoP). CoPs transcend individuals, individual firms and interfirm relationships. As we will show, they have a different ontology, but one which is resonant with our analysis of situated entrepreneurship, that is, that a salient perspective of the acts of entrepreneurship that create emergent properties is that they are situated in a Community of Practice.

If complexity theory is to account successfully for the entrepreneurial domain through multi-layered models, then theoretical understandings of social contexts can deepen understanding of the layered framework and the interfaces between levels that lead to the emergence of new structures. As noted earlier, entrepreneurial activity is processual, interconnected, reflexive and mediated through interaction with others. Although space precludes a full discussion of the literature pertaining to accounts of entrepreneurial networks, Nicolaou and Birley (2003) conclude that there is a gap in the literature concerning the understanding of dynamically evolving networks, and call for more studies in this area; in other words there is a gap concerning the temporal dimension essential to the notion of emergence. Here we argue that the notion of the CoP offers particular promise in that it is a discourse formulated around learning, innovation and change as a reflexive social process over time. The notion of the CoP is powerful, but has received little attention in the entrepreneurship literature so far. Specifically, we argue here that multi-membership of CoPs is a feeder source for change over time, plus an integral part of entrepreneurial understandings of pre-existing patterns, symmetries and structures.

Rationale

The notion of the CoP is rooted in social theories of learning and innovation. While their viewpoints have significant differences, the key proponents of CoP theory have argued for a community-based analysis, which seeks to support a unified view of learning and innovation: Brown and Duguid (1991), Lave and Wenger (1991) and Wenger (1998). Although they do not refer specifically to entrepreneurship, Lave and Wenger, and later Wenger, argue that developing a practice of any kind requires the formation of a community (however loosely defined) whose members can engage with one another and thus acknowledge and legitimize each other as participants; a process of becoming, not just encountering – the social process view, in other words. They expound further on the informal, non-canonical nature of such communities – that is, they are reflexive, socially constructed and emergent, existing outside formal organizational structures. For learners, a position on the periphery of practice is important, with access to formal and informal meetings, picking up 'know-how' – information, manner and technique – from being on the periphery of competent practitioners going about their business.

The linkage to entrepreneurship as a networked, processual dynamic activity is clear, and has been explored tentatively by Warren (2003, 2004) in the context, firstly, of spin-out firms in a UK university, and secondly, of women small business owners in a rural region of the UK. The linkage can be characterized as follows. Consider the position of an individual at the outset of an entrepreneurial career, the nascent entrepreneur. Typically, the nascent entrepreneur seeks to develop a new organization to carry out an area of activity associated with a potential opportunity. They must engage with the creation and management of a new network to carry out that activity; in doing so, the organization emerges as a set of new relations, that is, as a particular symmetry between members of the new organization, plus their wider set of business contacts, suppliers, customers and so on. Through the everyday practice of setting up a new organization, new contacts are made, new resources identified, and new knowledge assimilated and harnessed to the dynamically evolving network. In doing so, a process of sense-making occurs as a new CoP emerges around the primary task domain of the new organization: norms, values and vocabulary become accepted as 'the way we do things here'.

A learning process takes place as the organization develops; a new symmetry emerges as sets of relations are strengthened and become embedded within the context of the new organization. In other words a new CoP is developed at the level of the new organization, with the entrepreneur the most powerful influence in its development. Yet key players, including the initial entrepreneur, are not just involved with the newly emerged organizational CoP. Each individual in the organization brings their own range of existing CoP involvements with them, across a whole range of arenas, both business and social. Further, they will continue to identify and perhaps engage at the periphery with new social groupings and their associated resources (new CoPs in other words – not just other organizations). The cross-membership of CoPs and the multiple discourses involved are fertile grounds for the generation and exploration of potential futures, that is, the practice of entrepreneurial foresight.

The newly established organization is a dynamic, not a static entity. The task domain itself is dynamic, evolving in response to new business opportunities and challenges arising from the wider environment. A dynamic tension exists between the day-to-day experience of making the existing organization work and the continuous evaluation of different organizational futures.

Ideas for different organizational futures through novel structures or practices may well arise from the full range of CoPs with which the entrepreneur is involved. Let us now go beyond the CoP as a general source of ideas, to consider emergence as represented by the EROS model. A CoP may be a test bed for experiment. Evaluation of future opportunities could involve the playing out of 'experiments' within newly identified CoPs, where peripheral participation in a CoP is developed to an extent where a new business opportunity is explored. This goes beyond a thought experiment or a mental model – new contacts and resources are identified, new pathways, processes and discourses are familiarized with. In carrying out experiments, the entrepreneur would consider their own personal role, motivations and rewards. In other words, the potential for renegotiation of reflexive identity would be intrinsically linked with the experiment. Wenger (1998) places considerably more emphasis on self-identity than other CoP theorists. In particular, he highlights identity as a relation between the local and the global, which is significant in our proposal of a hierarchical, emergent dimension to the EROS model.

Organizing domains would also be considered. Experiments would be informed by insights into the strengths and weaknesses of existing symmetries, generating evaluations of what might potentially be viable new combinations across the old and the new, and what might not. At some point, if an experiment was deemed to be 'successful', the entrepreneur may break the symmetry, or at least re-pattern the old symmetry into a new form and a new CoP emerges. This could be a significant shift in the task domain of the existing entrepreneurial organization, or perhaps even the formation of a new organization. Finally, sensitivity to change, that is, awareness of environmental challenges and stakeholder imperatives, would inform a further refinement of whether an experiment was successful or not.

Theoretically, the above analysis could imply that the CoP approach is another means of examining the form and content of entrepreneurial networks, thereby adding to a considerable literature in that area. While the literature offers powerful insights, the CoP approach is based on much more than the consideration of networks as morphological or even dynamically evolving entities. The particular value of the CoP approach is that, in its emphasis on peripheral participation and the assimilation of new members into new areas of activity, it focuses directly on the processes of shift from one state – or symmetry – to another. In other words, a processual understanding of emergence from entrepreneurship results.

THE CASE OF HOTAIR

This case concerns the formation of HotAir, a university spin-out firm established by a design student at a UK university. The new company is seen to emerge through interactions of the CoPs dominant during the phases of company formation.

HotAir was formed around the development of a new product concept, the inflatable music speaker. The inflatable speaker was the brainchild of John Saxon, a final-year undergraduate student of design, class of 2000. The design concept was presented at John's degree show, an event where design projects were demonstrated in a public forum. Along with a small number of other projects that had been recognized within the Design Department as having significant commercial potential, the design was presented under a confidentiality agreement to protect any future intellectual property rights.

At this stage, although John felt his idea had potential, he was still seeking the security of employment by undergoing the rounds of large company interviews at the university. That changed when he met Alan Booth, a local venture capitalist, who was visiting the show to seek out innovative ideas with a view to funding their development to market. Alan persuaded John that there were attractions in setting up his own company and that he might be able to work with him to obtain equity funding for that purpose. For the next six months, although he still had not come to a final decision over his future, John, along with Alan, worked on the idea, carrying out patent searches, and due diligence procedures, and developing a business plan to analyse strategic, financial and market issues.

In February 2001, HotAir Sounds was registered as a company, receiving its first round of equity funding. The university also provided support to HotAir, its first student spin-out company, in the form of small pump-priming funds and intellectual property and public relations consultancy. Alan was instrumental in putting together the board of the company, which included himself as managing director, John as design director, two of Alan's business contacts (with financial backgrounds) and a representative of the university (from the technology transfer office). Other key appointments were made in the early stages of the company's existence to support the outsourced manufacturing operation in China and the aggressive international marketing strategy in the US and Japan.

Two further funding rounds have taken place since then and HotAir's products have made a successful impact on the market. In summary, in June 2000, John was a final-year student working on an individual project, interested mainly in getting a good degree and a job with a large company. By June 2002, he was a co-director of his own company, working in a team setting with the other directors who had considerable experience in their respective fields. He was operating on a global scale with widely dispersed manufacturing and marketing functions. He was also working in new fields from his original degree, involved in strategic decision-making over a range of key areas: marketing manufacture, finance, intellectual property and personnel. Clearly, John had undergone a steep learning curve in his transition from student to entrepreneur.

Turning now to the thesis of this chapter, we have used multi-membership of CoPs as a mechanism for the emergence of new patterns and symmetries which might take the form of new (or differently focused) firms in dynamically evolving networks. The HotAir experience is now used to illustrate this point. Initially, John is a member of a particular CoP concerned with obtaining his degree and getting a job – referred to here as the 'degree show domain' CoP (DSD). The DSD consisted of the staff and students working together to ensure the students developed projects in time for presentation at the show, and their assessment for the degree. As a result of peripheral participation with an alternative CoP, referred to here as the 'university spin-out domain' (USD), John did not get a job with a large company; instead, the HotAir organization emerged as a new set of relations (and its own CoP). The USD is a looser grouping consisting of university business support staff, academic staff with potential products, local professionals (lawyers, financiers, bankers) and regional support groupings (Regional Development Agencies – RDAs, Business Links).

Members of the USD sought to facilitate the process of establishing a spin-out company – a process that academic staff with good ideas for products were likely to be unfamiliar with.

Figure 6.3 seeks to identify the members, interactions and linkages of the three CoPs. In doing so, we note that there has been ambiguity and discussion over exactly what is meant by a CoP (Cox, 2004; Fox, 2000). A full review of this discussion is beyond the scope of this chapter, as it is a subtle concept and a well-informed debate from a variety of perspectives. Wenger (1998, pp. 125–6) provides a useful indicative list of characteristics. Although we do not detail the argument, we are satisfied that the domains identified here display the majority of Wenger's list of characteristics. Further we note Wenger et al.'s (2002, p. 42) later, and significant, identification of the distinctive purpose of CoPs, in relation to other groupings, that is 'to create and exchange knowledge, and *to develop individual capabilities*' (emphasis added). While learning is the basis of CoP theory, this seems particularly pronounced in a university setting.

Figure 6.3 depicts the key interaction that led to the emergence of HotAir. John Saxon was a member of the DSD, interacting with his tutors and other academic staff to put together a good project for his degree show and thereby contribute to his overall degree classification. Alan Booth was a director of a local venture capital company; he was very much a member of the USD in that he was chairman of the Enterprise Club, which was operated by the university's business support staff. He was also a peripheral member of the DSD, in that it was part of his annual calendar as a potential source of business opportunity.

Although John met Alan in June 2000, the company was not established until February 2001. During that time, John became a peripheral member of the USD, working with Alan and other members of the USD to carry out patent searches, negotiate with NXT, due diligence and develop a business plan – as well as continuing to work on his product. Interaction with the USD also enabled John to learn about the potential of becoming a director of his own company, rather than working for a larger company. In other words, he became familiar with the norms, values and vocabulary of the spin-out community in general. Following this phase, John made the critical decision to form HotAir: a new set of relations emerged as board and key staff were appointed around the primary task – the development, manufacture and sale of the speakers.

Processes of emergence are highly significant during this transitional phase, when the decision to go ahead with HotAir – or not – is under consideration. We can identify these through the EROS model. The key entrepreneurial actor in this part of the analysis is taken to be John, but clearly, a similar process could be undertaken for Alan. In brief:

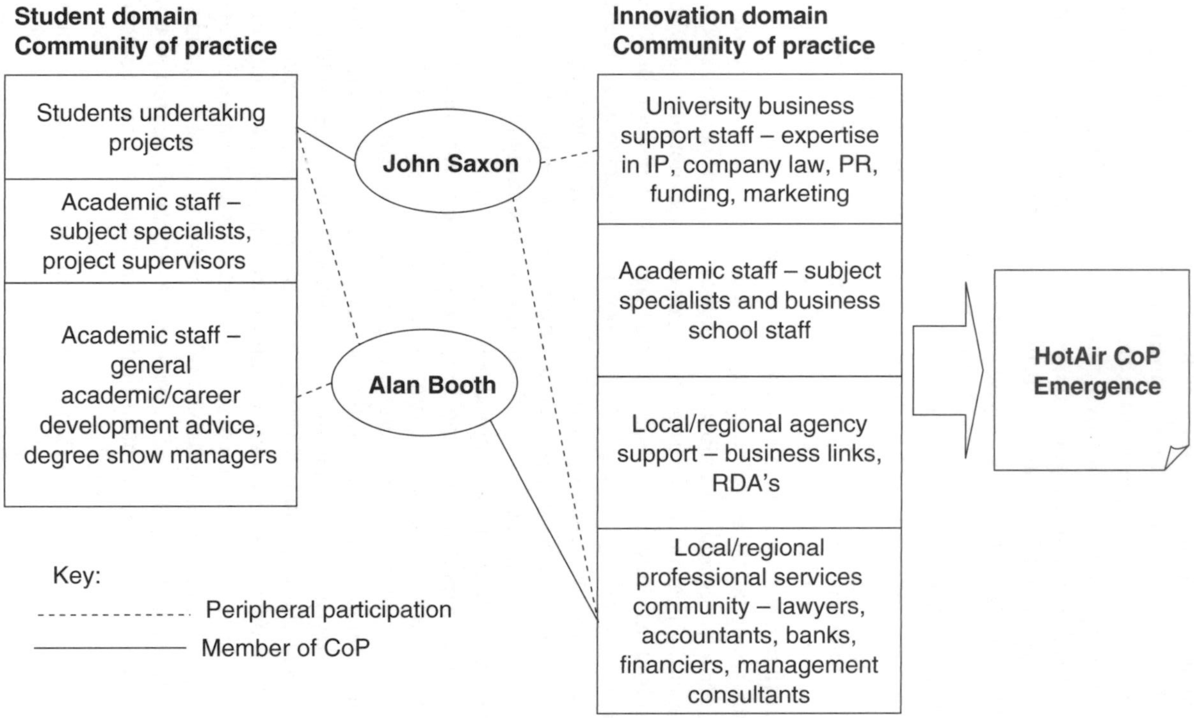

Figure 6.3 HotAir CoP membership and linkages

- Experiments were clearly taking place, in terms of concept formation and visioning, around both the potential new products and the nature of the new firm – what will work and what will not?
- Reflexive identity was also in transition as new career pathways were considered – do I have what it takes to become an entrepreneur?
- Organizing domains were restructured as working towards the degree show was replaced by developing the possibilities of the new business – will this new structure work for me?
- Sensitivity to change took place as possibilities and stakeholder imperatives were explored through new contacts – what are the environmental challenges I will have to face?

DISCUSSION

The underlying concept that this chapter illuminates is that of emergent properties. It depicts the new venture as an emergent property (or as having emergent properties), and the cluster or network or inter-venture relationships likewise. In each case the process of emergence is not one-way, but is reflexive, that is, constructed from the engagement between agents and between structures. The process of the creation of the emergence of a new venture, which is often referred to as entrepreneurship, is thus perceived from this perspective. We are thus not addressing the cause of entrepreneurship *per se*, but rather entrepreneurship as a cause – and therefore concerned with the type(s) of causes that exist within the field of entrepreneurship.

The emergent properties of a new venture are manifest as particular structures, that is, particular everyday and repeated practices, expectations and norms, in a particular context. The fitness of these structures gives rise to their sustainability. Part of the structures is the property of renewal, that is, the ability to respond reflexively to the tensions and powers exerted on the structure, in the form of competition, demands and so on. Thus we suggest that a study of entrepreneurship is a study of the reflexive shaping of recursive or repeating patterns, and patterns of new pattern formation.

This phenomenon is by definition non-equilibrium, or at the very least pre-equilibrium (McKelvey, 2004). Therefore, researching the nature of entrepreneurship as a causal mechanism in this way demands non-equilibrium bound methodologies (and according to McKelvey non-evolutionary (Kauffman, 2000; Rosenberg, 1994), grounded in an interpretative paradigm because the reflexive engagement between agent and structure – between agent and agent, between the entrepreneur and the firm, the firm and its networks and so on – is a social process, albeit that such processes include an economic dimension.

Complexity science informs us that initial conditions form part of the explanation for end-states. Our interpretation of this is that structure-breaking acts of entrepreneurship are informed by the structures they break. Despite its innovative and symmetry-breaking meaning, entrepreneurship is historically entangled within existing structures. This entanglement permits the human agent to have insights into pre-existing symmetries and the inefficiencies of such structures. Such entanglement enables entrepreneurial acts to be grounded in an understanding of salient structures and thus for symmetries to be broken and re-patterned in sustainable ways. This is an interpretative and socially negotiated process.

Our own contribution to this theoretical direction in this chapter is to offer a model of entrepreneurship operating within generalization of context. The model is one that includes: co-evolutionary or intersubjective small-scale activities, in the form of experiments; the continual shaping and reshaping of identity, giving rise to direction, meaning and motivation; patterns of re-patterning of everyday activity and the responsiveness to environmental change. This model is a contribution to knowledge, though none of the component concepts are new in themselves, and the body of literature supporting them is recorded elsewhere (Fuller et al., 2004). The model can only be understood in context, and the generalization of context in this chapter is: (1) one of emergent structures (emergent properties); and (2) negotiated through a mutable community of practice.

A theory of entrepreneurship from a complexity science perspective would, we suggest, assume that the production of sustained novelty (that is, as in entrepreneurial activities) has multiple (theoretically knowable) causes, is socially situated, is non-linear and generates unpredictable diversified patterns or symmetries. From this perspective, new ventures are emergent properties. This perspective informs methodological approaches to develop ontologically adequate explanations of the phenomenon in order to inform, as Aldrich and Martinez put it (Aldrich and Martinez, 2001, p. 52), how 'strategies are constructed, molded and adapted in processes of interaction with environments'. What we are suggesting is that the mechanisms for the emergence of such practices, and the negotiation and selection of the successful ones of these, is a deep social process that has multiple relational causes, and unpredictable outcomes; that is, they are complex but are not random nor uninformed.

In summary, through complexity science we have provided a coherent account of emergence that relates the dynamics of entrepreneurial activity to a hierarchy of structural elements, as depicted in the multi-layer model. A significant outcome of explaining entrepreneurial emergence this way is that the results of entrepreneurial activity are non-deterministic (that is, complex). The explanation is grounded in empirical analysis, the EROS model reflecting entrepreneurial processes at the level of the individual, the firm and interfirm connections – and the interactions between them. The discourse of the Community of Practice (CoP) is used to analyse further how the layers of the multilevel model are constituted through the entrepreneurial process over time.

We note that our explanation is based on two case studies in high-velocity industries; clearly, further studies are needed to support our conclusions, both in this type of industry and beyond. In doing so, we would hope to enhance the validity of our theoretical conclusions; in time, further understanding of the EROS model would develop its normative capabilities, supporting its use as a practical tool for entrepreneurial education.

NOTE

1. Space does not permit a detailed discussion of non-deterministic 'becoming' in the context of emergence, but this concept which is informed both by complexity science (Prigogine, 1980) and by postmodern thought (Deleuze, 1994; Grosz, 1999) and is seen as significant to this overall research.

REFERENCES

Aldrich, H.E. and Martinez, M.A. (2001). Many are called, but few are chosen: An evolutionary perspective for the study of entrepreneurship. *Entrepreneurship: Theory and Practice*, **25**(4): 41.

Brown, J.S. and Duguid, P. (1991). Organizational Learning and Communities-of-Practice: Toward a unified view of working, learning and innovation. *Organization Science*, **2**(1): 40–57.

Busenitz, L.W., West, I., Page, G., Shepherd, D., Nelson, T., Chandler, G.N. and Zacharakis, A. (2003). Entrepreneurship research in emergence: Past trends and future directions. *Journal of Management*, **29**(3): 285–308.

Bygrave, W.D. (1989). The Entrepreneurship Paradigm (I) A philosophical look at its research methodologies. *Entrepreneurship Theory and Practice*, **14**(1): 7–26.

Cilliers, P. (1998). *Complexity and Postmodernism: Understanding Complex Systems*. London and New York: Routledge.

Cox, A. (2004). What are communities of practice? A critical review of four seminal works. Paper presented at the OKLC04 Fifth European Conference on Organisational Knowledge, Learning and Capabilities, Innsbruck, April.

Davidsson, P. and Wiklund, J. (2001). Levels of analysis in entrepreneurship research: Current research practice and suggestions for the future. *Entrepreneurship: Theory and Practice*, **25**(4): 81.

Deleuze, G. (1994). *Difference and Repetition*. New York: Columbia University Press.

DiPrete, T.A. and Forristal, J.D. (1994). Multilevel models: Methods and substance. *Annual Review of Sociology*, **20**(1): 331–57.

Druilhe, C. and Garnsey, E. (2000). Emergence and growth of high-tech activity in Cambridge and Grenoble. *Entrepreneurship and Regional Development*, **12**: 163.

Fischer, E., Reuber, A.R., Hababou, M., Johnson, W. and Lee, S. (1997). The role of socially constructed temporal perspectives in the emergence of rapid growth firms. *Entrepreneurship: Theory and Practice*, **22**(2): 13.

Fox, S. (2000). Communities of Practice, Foucault and Actor-Network Theory. *Journal of Management Studies*, **37**(6): 856–67.

Fuller, T. and Lewis, J. (2003). Relationships mean everything. *British Journal of Management*, **13**(4): 317–36.

Fuller, T. and Moran, P. (2000). Moving beyond metaphor: Towards a methodology for grounding complexity in small business and entrepreneurship research. *Emergence: A Journal of Complexity Issues in Organizations and Management*, **2**(1): 50–71.

Fuller, T. and Moran, P. (2001). Small enterprises as complex adaptive systems: a methodological question? *Entrepreneurship and Regional Development*, **13**(1): 47–63, available at http://www.tandf.co.uk.

Fuller, T., Warren, L. and Argyle, P. (2004). Entrepreneurial foresight: A case study in reflexivity, experiments, sensitivity and reorganisation. In Tsoukas, H. and Shepherd, J. (eds). *Managing The Future: Foresight in the Knowledge Economy*. Oxford: Blackwell Publishing, pp. 171–8.

Garnsey, E. (1998). The genesis of the high technology milieu: A study in complexity. *International Journal of Urban and Regional Research*, **22**: 361.

Gartner, W.B. (1993). Words lead to deeds: Towards an organizational emergence vocabulary. *Journal of Business Venturing*, **8**(3): 231–9.

Giddens, A. (1984). *The Constitution of Society: Outline of the Theory of Structuration*. Oxford: Polity Press.

Grosz, E.A. (ed.). (1999). *Becomings: Explorations in Time, Memory and Futures*. Ithaca, NY: Cornell University Press.

Harvey, D.L. and Reed, M. (1996). Social science as the study of complex systems. In Kiel, L.D. and Elliot, E. (eds), *Chaos Theory in the Social Sciences*, Ann Arbor, MI: University of Michigan Press, pp. 295–323.

Holland, J.H. (1998). *Emergence*. Reading, MA: Addison-Wesley.

Kauffman, S. (2000). *Investigations*. New York: Oxford University Press.

Lave, J. and Wenger, E. (1991). *Situated Learning: Legitimate Peripheral Participation*. New York: Cambridge University Press.

Lichtenstein, B.M.B. (2000). Emergence as a process of self-organizing: New assumptions and insights from the study of non-linear dynamic systems. *Journal of Organizational Change Management*, **13**(6): 526–44.

Low, M.B. and MacMillan, I.C. (1988). Entrepreneurship: Past research and future challenges. *Journal of Management*, **14**(2): 139–61.

McKelvey, B. (2004). Towards a complexity science of entrepreneurship. *Journal of Business Venturing*, **19**(3): 313.

Miller, D. and Garnsey, E. (2000). Entrepreneurs and technology diffusion: How diffusion research can benefit from a greater understanding of entrepreneurship. *Technology in Society*, **22**(4): 445–65.

Moore, C.F. (1986). Understanding Entrepreneurial Behaviour. In Pearce (II), J.A. and Robinson, B. Jr (eds). *Academy of Management Best Papers Proceedings, Forty-sixth Annual Meeting of the Academy of Management*. Chicago, IL: Academy of Management.

Nicolaou, N. and Birley, S. (2003). Academic networks in a trichotomous categorisation of university spinouts. *Journal of Business Venturing*, **18**(3): 333–59.

Prigogine, I. (1980). *From Being to Becoming: Time and Complexity in the Physical Sciences*. San Francisco, CA: W.H. Freeman & Co.

Rosenberg, A. (1994). Does evolutionary theory give comfort or inspiration to economists. In P. Mirowski (ed.). *Natural Images in Economic Thought*, Cambridge: Cambridge University Press, pp. 384–407.

Sayer, A. (2000). *Realism and Social Science*. London: Sage.

Schumpeter, J.A. (1934). *The Theory of Economic Development: An inquiry into Profits, Capital, Credit, Interest and the Business Cycle*. Cambridge, MA: Harvard University Press.

Thornton, P.H. (1999). The sociology of entrepreneurship. *Annual Review of Sociology*, **25**: 19–46.

Warren, L. (2003). A systemic approach to entrepreneurial learning. *Systems Research and Behavioral Science*, **20**: 1–14.

Warren, L. (2004). Negotiating entrepreneurial identity: Communities of practice and changing discourses. *International Journal of Entrepreneurship and Innovation* (special issue edited by Patricia Lewis): 25–37.

Weick, K.E. (1995). *Sensemaking in Organizations*. Thousand Oaks, CA: Sage.

Wenger, E. (1998). *Communities of Practice: Learning, Meaning and Identity*. New York: Cambridge University Press.

Wenger, E., McDermott, R. and Snyder, W.H. (2002). *Cultivating Communities of Practice*. Boston, MA: Harvard Business School Press.

7. Extreme entrepreneurs: challenging the institutional framework

Bengt Johannisson and Caroline Wigren

ENTREPRENEURS AS OUTSIDERS AND CHALLENGERS IN SOCIETY

Adopting a constructionist view, the deconstruction of the subject in general and the male, paternalistic entrepreneurial hero in particular, appears as a major responsibility for entrepreneurship researchers with a concern for gender (see Ahl, 2001: Pettersson, 2002). Our ambition here is to construct an alternative image of the entrepreneurial subject with the help of institutional theory, itself originating in constructionist thinking. There are two related arguments for taking on this challenge. First, by definition institutions are expected to provide the 'rules of the game' for organizations in society, thereby defining what social phenomena are granted legitimacy (North, 1990). Introducing his seminal work Schumpeter (1911/1934) succinctly stated that the market, where in his mind the entrepreneur resides, is certainly an integral part of society. Second, the rules provided by the institutions will define whether or not entrepreneurship will appear and, if so, on what societal arenas (Baumol, 1990). Supplementing these views which suggest that entrepreneurship is defined and restricted by the institutional framework, we here want to present entrepreneurship as boundary-spanning activities which also encompass the institutional setting. We thus argue that as much as entrepreneurship thrives in a proper institutional setting, whether it entails a different Northian basic order or substantive support (Van de Ven, 1993; Brusco, 1992), entrepreneurship defies existing institutions.

Entrepreneurship is here conceptualized as creative organizing with the ultimate aim of constructing new worlds (Spinosa et al., 1997; Hjorth et al., 2003). This means that coincidences are made into opportunities which are subsequently enacted (Gartner et al., 2003). Such organizing may end up in the making of a new formal organizational (business) outfit, but the phenomenon remains processual, acknowledging an ontology of becoming (Tsoukas and Chia, 2002). Even as confined to the market alone, entrepreneurship may be associated with both the imaginative construction and the creative destruction of established structures (Schumpeter, 1943/1987). Viewing entrepreneurship as the management of ambiguity (Czarniawska-Joerges and Wolff, 1991; Johannisson, 1992, Gartner et al., 1992) suggests that entrepreneurial action both enforces and sabotages ongoing sense-making processes in society.

The adopted definition of entrepreneurship means that society at large and its institutions must be part of the conceptual framing when researching the entrepreneurial phenomenon. As indicated, any (innovative) entrepreneur on the market will upset existing standards and professional norms as codified by, for example, agreements between the members of trade associations. Putting their legitimacy at stake they, however, still remain law-abiding citizens. Yet, as pointed out by for example Rehn and Taalas (2004), this does not mean that a general definition of entrepreneurship should exclude those who use their ingenuity to cheat the legal system as a part of the institutional setting. Criminals as well as those who practise civil disobedience to promote a social cause may demonstrate a considerable social creativity and commitment to action. Therefore we here want to inquire into entrepreneurship that challenges not only the established order on the market, but also societal institutions of all kinds. We term the subjects that take such initiatives 'extreme entrepreneurs'.

The qualification 'extreme' on the part of the entrepreneurial phenomenon concerned here derives from four criteria. First, we address the innovative practice as extreme because it explicitly and publicly confronts an established institutional order, whether defined as collectively shared social practices or instituted as a formal structure. Second, whether primarily operating on the market or not, extreme entrepreneurs acknowledge financial resources primarily as a means to accomplish their mission. That is, wealth accumulation is not a goal *per se*. Third, while being socially constructed as outsiders both in their own domain and in society at large, extreme entrepreneurs are visible and influential far beyond their community of practice, typically thanks to rich exposure in the media. Fourth, extreme entrepreneurs like the Schumpeterian entrepreneur enjoy creating and fighting and, since they appear as charismatic persons on different social arenas, they are surrounded by an aura that causes emotional arousal in the general public.

Our inspiration originates in, and our potential contribution is to be found in, the intersection between theories on institutions and conceptualized images of entrepreneurship. However, we have no ambition to provide a comprehensive picture of either academic field. On the contrary, as regards institutional theory we will confine ourselves mainly to the text by Scott (2001). In his structuring of contemporary research into institutions, he (2001, p. 52, Figure 3.1) identifies three major pillars: regulative, normative and cultural-cognitive. Keeping different conceptual refinements in mind, the seminal work by Berger and Luckmann (1966/1979, p. 70) presents institutions as constituted of negotiations originating in mutual typifications of habitual behaviour by types of actors. This means that institutions appear as 'social structures that have attained a high degree of resilience' (Scott, 2001, p. 48), where the regulative pillar provides the formal, codified (legislative) order. The normative pillar infuses society with values and norms, that is, defining what is preferred or desirable and how – that is, through what behaviour – such ends should be reached, while the cultural-cognitive pillar carries the construction of shared frames for sense-making.

Submission to the rules that regulate an institutional arena renders the legitimacy (DiMaggio and Powell, 1983) that an organization needs for success in addition to efficiency. Yet, there are many reasons why entrepreneurs defy institutions. As much as organization members who are dissatisfied may remain silent and loyal, leave the organization or stay and give voice to their dissatisfaction (Hirschman 1974), entrepreneurs may silently accept the regulatory framework or engage in changing it. A complete denial of the authority of institutions would turn the entrepreneurs into outlaws. Their active involvement in institutional practices reflects an existential need to keep the illusion of freedom alive; that is, to escape the feeling of being locked up in a 'iron cage'. Furthermore, as pointed out by Schumpeter (1911/1934), it is difficult to imagine a path-breaking innovation that does not challenge existing norms in the organizational field concerned. Sensitiveness to institutional change may also be instrumental in the venturing career. Drucker (1985) vividly illustrates how entrepreneurship enforces and thrives on changes in the cultural and cognitive realm.

In some cases, such as national turmoil, established institutions have become obsolete and have therefore become obstacles to change and development. Often they have to be completely deconstructed and replaced in order to create space for market-oriented entrepreneurship, making it feasible and desirable. This calls for entrepreneurship that draws on knowledge that goes far beyond the market – for what we elsewhere have addressed as 'intellectual' entrepreneurship. Not surprisingly, this kind of entrepreneurship seems to have been especially needed and frequent in reformed Europe (Johannisson et al., 1999). Intellectual entrepreneurs use their own rich human and social resources to participate actively in the reformation of the institutional framework within which they themselves and their business are embedded. Extreme entrepreneurs, in contrast, are generally sceptical of regulation and use different tactics to oppose it, because rules and norms reduce their discretion. This means that extreme entrepreneurs are also different to 'institutional entrepreneurs' who institute formal structures to promote their own business. The institutionalization of these structures, though, is beyond the control of the entrepreneur, which makes the very notion of institutional entrepreneurship full of contradictions (cf. Czarniawska, 2004).

Social phenomena in general, as well as entrepreneurship, and institutions as negotiated collective practices in particular, are dependent on their cultural-historical context. Therefore we want briefly to introduce the reader to the Swedish setting (see Johannisson, 2004). Even in the late 1900s Sweden was a very homogenous country with a dense web of formal and informal institutions regulating private and public life. A corporatist regime emerged during the last century and its alliances between the state, the large corporations and the trade unions did not leave much space for individual initiatives. A strong wage-earner culture kept entrepreneurial initiatives at bay, on the market as well as in society at large. In spite of an ethnically more diverse population due to increased immigration, and a radically changed international context due to its entry into the European Union, Sweden's cultural legacy still hampers independent business creation. Entrepreneurship as an individual and a collective force is chiefly visible in Sweden in metropolitan and select local contexts. Financially strong and independent municipalities carry great responsibilities in the sparsely populated country.

This chapter is organized as follows. First we introduce the four extreme entrepreneurs who have enlightened and captivated us. Two are market entrepreneurs, while the other two operate as change agents on cultural arenas, usually assumed to be far away from commercial operations. The entrepreneurs all happen to be males. We then present them as challengers of institutions, and in the following section we discuss what additional themes emerge out of our initial interpretation and analysis of the interviews with the quartet. In the concluding section we propose some further steps to be taken in our ongoing research into extreme entrepreneurship.

PORTRAYING FOUR EXTREME ENTREPRENEURS

The four entrepreneurs we talked with at length were selected from very visible public change agents, whether considered mainly as villains or leaders with no further sampling rationale other than accessibility. As for Bengt Erlandsson, the first extreme entrepreneur encountered (August 2003), we had both met him before this research was launched and we carried out the interview together. In October 2003, Wigren met with

Jonnie Dahlström, while Johannisson had an informal conversation with him in March 2004. Both Lars Vilks and Sten Rentzhog were interviewed in May 2004, the former by the authors jointly and the latter by Johannisson alone. Three of our four meetings lasted for more or less a whole day, where time was not just used for conversations but also to get acquainted with the entrepreneurs' work. Besides the six-hour conversation with Bengt Erlandsson, the (formal) interviews lasted for about two hours. They were all audio-taped and transcribed.

The questions asked in the interviews were open-ended, enabling the entrepreneurs to choose what stories to tell and how. All interviewees were asked the same questions, but not necessarily in the same order. Follow-up questions were interposed when needed, typically phrased as, Could you develop your answer further? Why? Why not? and so on. In an ongoing dialogue the transcribed material was then analysed by the two authors: firstly, in general and according to the basic assumptions of institutional theory: and secondly, in the perspective of Scott's three pillars. Furthermore, emerging themes in our conversations, bridging between the four entrepreneurs, were identified in the empirical material.

Before turning to a thematic interpretation, the life stories of the four entrepreneurs are told. This is done in our own voices but with statements from the entrepreneurs integrated into the text. Obviously the material has a great potential for alternative narrative approaches. We also want to point out that our research venture has a 'political' dimension. All of the entrepreneurs, except for Sten Rentzhog, clearly expressed that they had been treated badly by society. Their participating in a research project probably provides some redress. It signals that their experiences and their deeds are taken seriously. How seriously they want to be taken is, however, difficult to know. Lars Vilks, for example, considers his art project to be a soap opera where we as researchers are considered to be co-actors.

Apart from conversations and interviews, secondary material like published articles, documents, TV programmes and so on have helped us to get to know the four extreme entrepreneurs.

Big Bengt: The Sheriff at High Chaparral

Bengt Erlandsson, alias Big Bengt, is a notorious Swedish entrepreneur. He was born in 1922 in the tiny village of Brännehylte in the Gnosjö industrial district in southern Sweden. As one of eight siblings he grew up on a forest farm that according to him was 'too small for making a living and too big to starve on'. While still very young he started his own business in engineering and trading machinery. However, it was as the founder and sheriff of the High Chaparral amusement park that he became well known to the general Swedish public. He had attended summer auctions dressed as a sheriff for several years. When making a bid he would shoot, not shout. This outfit has been his everyday attire ever since.

Big Bengt has always been fascinated by American culture. His first trip to the US in 1955 was made out of sheer curiosity. He became acquainted with a country that in his mind accommodated the true pioneering spirit. He was captivated by how the settlers managed to move all over the continent, how they appropriated their land, and how they pursued hands-on business venturing. The 'Big Bengt' epithet was given to him by a journalist who interviewed him about High Chaparral. The journalist wanted to give him a Western name, and since Bengt was talking a lot the journalist argued that the epithet 'big' was suitable (as a matter of fact Big Bengt is pretty short). Other journalists came to meet and talk with Big Bengt, and Bengt Erlandsson decided to make the nickname 'Big Bengt' public by printing it on his business card.

Tabloids published frequent reports on Big Bengt's dazzling behaviour and this provided High Chaparral with good publicity for free. There are also stories being told about Big Bengt's spectacular moves. For example, just to gain publicity he once entered Arlanda, Sweden's largest airport, on a horse, accompanied by a group of Indians from High Chaparral. Stories like these, often invented by Big Bengt himself, make him and his Wild West town stand out as odd and different. Not surprisingly, the local opinion of High Chaparral varies considerably. Some locals argue that it is a hotbed of sin, while others are proud of the amusement park and acknowledge its benefits as one of the region's major tourist attractions.

When Big Bengt founded High Chaparral in 1966 it was, predictably, difficult to obtain a building licence for a Wild West town in the middle of the Swedish woods. A way out appeared when he was told about the plans to make a Swedish Western movie. He immediately invited the producer to build the needed scenery on his land. The film-shooting attracted a great many people and Big Bengt charged an entrance fee. Soon after the making of the movie, the film company went bankrupt. Big Bengt bought the scenery for the symbolic amount of one Swedish crown. The town of High Chaparral was then created just by expanding the scenery into complete buildings (thereby avoiding an intervention by the building authorities). To Big Bengt the procedure was logical since, he argues, when the pioneers built America they drew their houses and factories in the sand with a stick before building them. Pragmatically he states: 'How could you ever know what you want before you have seen it?' There is a rumour that he had a competent architect to reconstruct appropriate drawings once the buildings were erected. Once the town was established, Big Bengt got in touch with people who wanted to become actors, trained them, and himself staged shooting incidents (without film in the camera) that soon attracted a huge paying audience. Over time the shooting turned into fully-fledged Western shows. Today High Chaparral still offers shows performed by professional stuntmen.

Big Bengt obviously opposes the norms in the rural small-business region where humbleness is a major cultural feature. He has his own knowledge centre that accommodates a museum, overloaded with curios and named BBC: Big Bengt Centre. He once advanced plans to erect a 120-metre high statue of himself, but since a construction of that size would have caused problems for the Swedish Board of Civil Aviation, no permit was granted. Instead a bust was created. In these days it has become a bit rusty, but Big Bengt declines renovation because its patina reminds him of how he feels about himself and how he is treated by society. In 1996 Big Bengt was jailed for allegedly taking part in illegal trading, but due to his age and illness he was pardoned after six months. He handed in a petition for a new trial in June 2000, but there is still (in 2006) no settlement. He claims to be innocent, but this experience is probably his major failure in life.

JD, King of Hudik

Jonas Martin Dahlström, or Jonnie Dahlström, a well-known businessman and collector, was born in 1921 in Bjuråker in Northern Sweden. He has a number of nicknames; the most frequently used are 'JD' and 'Jonne'. He grew up on a farm as the eldest among four siblings in a family that belonged to the Swedish Missionary Society, and his childhood and adolescence were pretty conventional. His mother thought that it would be good for him to leave the farm for some time and encouraged him to go to Forsa, a nearby folk high school. Convinced that he would never become a farmer he committed himself to the evolving (auto-) mobile society that had emerged in Sweden after WW2. He owned his first truck even before he was of legal age. Soon enough his fleet included six trucks and two excavators. He also started to trade with used cars. His business operated both in Bjuråker and in Stockholm, where he had a garage and spent about two days a week. Buying a Morris Minor for personal use, he considered becoming the distributor of the brand in the northern part of Sweden. In those days, JD's problem was not finding customers for the cars but convincing the Swedish agent that he was the right person to represent the brand. He successfully acquired the Morris Minor agency but his dream was actually to obtain a contract with GM or Ford. In the middle of the 1950s he got a contract with Ford and was also invited to America. He had read a lot about the US and even during his first trip there all of his great expectations were met. Since then he has crossed the Atlantic well over 100 times and, still, he gets the same strong feeling when he enters the country where 'only the sky is the limit'.

JD wanted to master the English language and in the early 1960s he realized that this called for a longer stay in the US. He therefore went to Chicago, rented an office and asked his wife Anna to join him. His idea was to sell tyre studs in order to get in touch with people and refine his homemade English. The business venture was not successful, but he and his wife became established in their second home country. She enjoyed the US as much as JD did. Their downtown apartment was decorated in blue and yellow and furnished with products of Swedish design. In 1968 he bought some land in the US, in Florida (whether that was a good deal or not is unknown). In 1971 Jonnie and Anna became American citizens.

JD has always been a collector of artefacts but not of money. He considers financial assets to be just the means to reach urgent non-economic goals. When needing money he will sell off something, for example a piece of art, an antiquity or a car. Conversing with us he says: 'When I have managed to access money, borrowed or my own, I have invested or spent it; it has been like that all my life. I have never owned a share in a public company. I never had a bank book, I have never been on a pension plan.'

While running his car dealership and investing in property in Hudiksvall (a town close to Bjuråker) he had a dream that contrasted his view as a young man: to run an intact farm in Hälsingland, his home county. When Hillsta, an old farm and building complex, was for sale he realized that he wanted it for himself. 'In my mind this was the most genuine farm in Northern Sweden.' However, both the county agricultural authorities and the National Board of Agriculture rejected his request to acquire Hillsta. He approached the Swedish government, but again he was turned down. JD still remained convinced that one day he would be able to get hold of Hillsta, even if that would mean the fall of the Swedish government. The authorities promoted large-scale farming, while JD wanted to preserve the cultural and historical value of Hillsta. 'I never gave up and then I found a solution which "touched upon the law", if I use a carefully chosen expression.' With help from a surveyor he managed to secure a legal confirmation of the acquisition of the property in spite of the fact that it was located in a prohibited area. The surveyor should actually not have signed the agreement. But he did, and therefore the deal was formally confirmed and enacted, an experience that turned into Lex Hillsta. 'Later, people have realized how grateful they should be that Hillsta remained; I was dedicated to keep the inventories, the buildings, and the environment.' JD invested 14 million SEK in Hillsta, and he certainly managed to get his way (even without changing the Swedish government).

During the real estate crisis, or bank crisis as Jonnie calls it, at the beginning of the 1990s, JD's empire was shattered. He left Sweden and stayed for a long period in the US, in what he regarded as exile. Then he returned to Sweden and stood up for his deeds. Once the 'King of Hudik' (short for the town of Hudiksvall where he still lives), he was now accused of having built castles in the air. People argued that everything he had acquired was through borrowed money. Jonnie Dahlström's comment to this accusation is straightforward: 'Of course it was borrowed money. All things you have got are lent to you, even your own life.'

Sten Rentzhog: The Greatest among Equals in the World of Museums

In his formative years in the 1940s and 1950s, Sten Rentzhog's two main interests were horses and history. When going south from Jämtland in Northern Sweden to Uppsala University with a political career in mind, he started to study cultural geography. His problem was that there was no political party that he could sympathize with. Pursuing his academic training, he studied history which taught him the importance of not only taking the spatial but also the temporal dimension into consideration when making society comprehensible. Quite by accident he then got interested in archaeology, and the associated fieldwork among ordinary people brought him close to everyday life in Sweden. His diligence granted him a scholarship that brought him to America, where he spent one year in Oregon studying economics and sociology. While travelling in the US, Rentzhog visited Charleston in South Carolina where he experienced how carefully kept the old town was. This concern for the cultural heritage was certainly in contrast to contemporary Sweden where, in the name of progress, the old town centres were systematically torn down and replaced with modern buildings. Back in Uppsala he started a movement for the preservation of the town that attracted 1000 sympathizers. When the organizing effort was institutionalized he left: 'I was too radical; most of the people on the board were there for social reasons.'

When Sten Rentzhog realized that he had become an expert on historical buildings, he decided to launch a career as a museum curator. Still in his early thirties, he got his first position as the director of a regional museum. Energetically he started with a group of like-minded young colleagues to reform an ageing structure, and soon enough he became the spokesman for the Swedish county museums. He says: 'Not officially, but it was I who decided when we should talk to the politicians, when we should write petitions. I wrote the most important pieces. I was also the one who kept all the contending parties away from each other – they are all independent and wilful individuals with their own opinions. It was about keeping the group of stakeholders in harmony and getting everybody to pull in the same direction.' The older generation of curators listened to him since they were not used to colleagues who could deal professionally with administrative and financial issues. He introduced a more efficient organization in his own regional museum, for example by administering the smaller local museums jointly, thereby considerably improving their financial situation. Early on he expanded the realm of the museum by organizing special activities for children and by collaborating with the (national) Nordic Museum in Stockholm he enlarged the regional resource base.

After some years as a county curator in southern Sweden, Sten Rentzhog was offered the same position in his native county. The museum in Jämtland then had a minute staff, few activities and a very weak financial base. To create space for renewal he had to carry through an extensive and controversial reorganisation of the museum administration; 'blood was shed in those days' is the way he puts it. He invited the county council and the local municipalities in the county on board, thereby giving them the opportunity to influence – and finance – the development of the museum including its open-air section, Jamtli. He had learned the lesson earlier: the important thing was to get as much money as possible in addition to the regular state grants. His regional financial strategy worked out well and this, according to the allocation model that was practised in those days, opened the way for additional state money. In the world of museums Sten Rentzhog enforced his position as a role model and in 1973, together with two colleagues, both senior to him, he launched a venture aimed at organizing the Swedish cultural-historical museums into a network (SAMDOK). When completed after eight years, that collaboration meant, for example, that the museums collectively saved money by each taking charge of one special field.

In 1988 there was a big crisis at the Nordic Museum in Stockholm. Sten Rentzhog was invited to become the director and asked to restructure its operations. He held this influential position for three years while commuting from Jämtland. In 1991, he was the curator at both the national and the regional museum.

Sten Rentzhog argues that it is important never to take anything for granted and to be focused when realizing ideas. In a bureaucratic context, things could always be done in a different way, for example because instructions are vague. His strategy for implementing changes has been to always give feedback to the different stakeholders concerned: 'Then they might change at last.' He considers himself to be pragmatic, a view that considerably facilitated his work at the Nordic Museum with its national responsibilities, and he linked this formal position to the informal leadership on the national stage that the SAMDOK initiative had brought him.

In 1992 Sten Rentzhog left the Nordic Museum and returned to Jämtland. Soon enough he started to enact his image of a museum where the visitors would experience historical times through all their senses. The museum in its new building was inaugurated in 1995. Its first years were very successful with a great number of visitors, but gradually the public interest declined. According to Sten Rentzhog only continued renewal will keep the number of visitors up. In 2001, close to his retirement, Sten Rentzhog was honoured by the Association of Swedish Museums and given the ultimate award because ‘Sten Rentzhog is simply the one from his generation who has had the greatest influence on Swedish museums’. After retirement he has begun a study of the entrepreneurs behind open-air museums around the world, and he has also resumed his academic career – he is qualified as an associate professor – by initiating and running a national doctoral programme in his field.

Lars Vilks: An Anarchist and State Founder

Lars Vilks is known to the general Swedish public as the artist who in 1996 founded his own nation of Ladonia on the sea shore in a nature reserve on the Kullaberg peninsula in Southern Sweden. Today Lars Vilks is considered to be a conceptual artist of great influence in Sweden. However, he was never trained to become a creative artist. Instead of qualifying for the senior high school he dedicated his youth to chess. Later he resumed his school studies as a distance student and with excellent grades he enrolled at Lund University. Undergraduate and graduate studies in the history of art and literature were completed in 1987 by a doctoral dissertation that dealt with the question: what is art?

At the beginning of the 1970s Lars Vilks was, in his own opinion, a romantic and conventional painter who produced art that attracted the general public. However, in the art community itself, conceptual art was then the major issue. Currently practising constructionist and postmodern reasoning, Lars argues that it is only at the end of the eighteenth century that art appeared as relational aesthetics, which means that in his mind earlier work cannot be classified as art. His theoretical views and academic background at the turn of the millennium gained him the temporary position as a visiting art professor in Norway.

Ladonia is an enclave on private property that Lars Vilks has high-handedly annexed. There he has erected three sculptures: Nimis, Arx and Omfalos. They materialize his conceptual art, which besides the sculptures as such encompass the processes and relationships that their creation has set free. As indicated, Vilks argues that his conceptual art could be considered as a soap opera, since it includes the same dramaturgy, and everyone who engages in it takes on different roles. In 1980 he began the construction of Nimis, a wooden structure that is (now) about 10 metres tall, but the soap opera only emerged in 1982. Then the authorities realized what Vilks was up to and launched a legal process against him. He himself cannot understand how the authorities could let this happen. In his mind they should just have had the illegally erected work destroyed and that would have been the end of the story. Now the legal fight has instead become the starting point for what seems to be a never-ending story with the authorities as major contributors and actors. Between 1991 and 1998 he built a stone sculpture named Arx. It was during its creation that he in 1996 'nationalized' the seashore on which the two sculptures stand as Ladonia. In 1999 Lars Vilks added a third piece of artwork to Ladonia – Omfalos (meaning navel, or the centre of the world). While Nimis and Arx because of their size are immobile structures, Omfalos is made out of stone and reinforced concrete and is possible to move because it is only 1.61 metres high.

To make the conceptualization of the constructs even more intriguing, Lars in 1984 sold Nimis to the well-known artist Joseph Beuys. After his death in 1986, Jeanne-Claude and Javacheff Christo bought the sculpture. Arx is owned by the Swedish people. When Lars was sentenced to pay a fine because of his legal offences, he raised the money needed by 'selling' the fine to the general public. The well-known Swedish artist Ernst Billgren bought Omfalos in 2001. Like Nimis and Arx, Omfalos was supposed to be removed from Ladonia. Vilks made Ernst Billgren the proposition that they themselves should destroy Omfalos. That event was planned for 10 December 2001 in order to celebrate the 100th anniversary of the Nobel Prize. Since they planned to use 100 kilos of dynamite, Lars Vilks applied for a blast permission at the County Administrative Board. The application was declined and instead the board decided to organize the removal of Omfalos. The decision was enacted by way of a sea-borne crane and Omfalos was brought to a neighbouring harbour during the night between 9 and 10 December. Vilks was not informed about the action but invoiced for its costs. He in his turn sued the government for having caused damage to Omfalos when moving the work. Even if he denied being the creator – and no one could prove it – he was considered to be the artist. In 2002, Vilks asked the County Administrative Board for permission to erect a memorial monument to Omfalos. His request was granted.

Lars Vilks sees himself as an outsider who has a passion for being provocative. He is driven by the paradoxical urge to get recognition for being a challenger of societal norms. He also wants recognition as an artist, but this desire puts him in a dilemma as well. Public appreciation in his mind seduces people into certain positions where it is hard to stay creative. Either you become an institution or you stay innovative. Therefore no artist wants to become an institution. Striving for being recognized means that you want to embody the creative institution, which, unfortunately, does not exist. Thus, according to Vilks, once recognized as an artist you will soon be forgotten.

On 27 March 2003 Omfalos was moved to Stockholm from its temporary domicile. Ernst Billgren then donated Omfalos to the public Museum of Modern Art in Stockholm. This means that the very same Swedish government that condemned Lars Vilks for breaking the law and took action accordingly now owns the art work that caused the turmoil. In May 2004 the Museum of Modern Art exhibited Lars Vilks's conceptual art. He admits that this meant some kind of recognition, though not enough to tame him. Vilks is trying to have part of the nature reserve embedding Ladonia revoked in order to secure a territory for his own state. Then there would be an authorized border demarcating the land of Ladonia. Revoking part of a nature reserve has so far never happened in Sweden.

THE ENTREPRENEURIAL HERCULES AS A CHALLENGER OF INSTITUTIONS

Our cases demonstrate that the non-market entrepreneurs, Sten Rentzhog the museum curator and Lars Vilks the artist also use market forces as a means to achieve ends in each of their domains. Rentzhog, even in his first position as a county curator, bought expensive exhibitions that had been set up by the Nordic Museum in Stockholm. Once having presented them in his own museum, he offered other regional museums the opportunity to rent them, raising money for further activities of his own. Later he commercialized the services his museum could offer on a broad basis, approaching both consumers and corporate and public customers. Lars Vilks's creative financing of his fine reflects his awareness of the market as an instrument in his artistry. Entrepreneurship as creative social organizing uses the market as a servant, not as a master.

In Table 7.1 some of the tactics used by the extreme entrepreneurs to undermine the institutions concerned are summarized. These efforts have had more or less the intended effects, which means either that the institution is questioned, or even denied, or that it is reformed to serve the entrepreneur's own interests. Extreme entrepreneurs may even initiate the creation of a new institution, as in the Rentzhog case, but then only as a means towards a greater cause. Interestingly enough, all our entrepreneurs reported, for instance, ways to deal with the detailed building regulations in Sweden. Big Bengt persistently asked for building permits retrospectively when creating his Wild West town of High Chaparral. Finally, the municipal architect gave up and declared High Chaparral a free town where Big Bengt got a general permit to build. Jonnie Dahlström managed to change

Table 7.1 Entrepreneurs shaking the institutional pillars

Institutional Pillar	Bengt Erlandsson	Jonnie Dahlström	Sten Rentzhog	Lars Vilks
Regulative	Trespassing building regulation; alleged fraud	Initiating the enactment of Lex Hillsta	Systematic lobbying on the local, regional and national levels	Trespassing property rights, and building regulation
Normative	Uncovering the boundaries of appropriateness	Challenging the 'Jante Law'	Creating a number of professional bodies	Personalizing civic disobedience
Cognitive-cultural	Epitomizing the local (business) culture	Introducing car driving as a way of life	Redefining collective memory-conscientization	Demonstrating art as rupture

the legislation so that he could acquire Hillsta, which he turned into a private home and museum. Sten Rentzhog used his negotiation skills to change a municipal decision to reduce the area of the open-air activities that constituted part of his regional museum. Then he turned both the indoor and outdoor exhibition areas into arenas for living history which served as models for other Swedish museums. Lars Vilks makes the erection of unauthorized constructions part of his conceptual and performing art, and he certainly cheated the authorities when he proclaimed Ladonia as an independent nation state.

Big Bengt contributes indirectly to the enforcement of dominating norms in the region. Stories that are told about Big Bengt are used to inform strangers and tourists as to what is *not* appropriate according to the local norms. According to one of these stories Big Bengt sells a lot of canned herring to a colleague in the region. The buyer opens a can to feed his cat. The cat gets sick and dies. The disappointed master calls Big Bengt and complains. Big Bengt exclaims: 'Why didn't you tell me that you were going to give it to the cat? I thought that you were going to trade the lot to somebody else!' Jonnie Dahlström devoted himself to 'conspicuous' investments in houses, factories and historical buildings, mainly for nostalgic reasons. This behaviour opposed the 'Jante law' that rules in Sweden (and other Scandinavian countries). The first paragraph of this cultural norm, originally stated by the Danish-Norwegian novelist Aksel Sandemose and thus a common characteristic of Scandinavian culture, says: 'You should not think that you are somebody.' The fact that JD accepted the epithet of

'King of Hudik' reveals his view on false modesty. Sten Rentzhog reformed the institutional setting of Swedish museums from below by changing a fragmented structure of regional units into a nexus of multiple national networks. The Nordic Museum was then redefined as a support structure that certainly changed the practices in the museum community. Once in charge of the national museum, he used his position to enact several networked nationwide structures from above. Lars Vilks uses his identity as an artist for subversive action, for generally challenging the existing norms in society, rationalizing it as the enactment of a soap opera.

As much as Big Bengt Erlandsson represents a forbidden world, he is admired – including by fellow owner-managers in the business community – for his courage to stand out with his behaviour and stand up for his opinions. He is also given credit for having supported many new-starters in his region with equipment from the machinery trade that he runs parallel to High Chaparral (see Johannisson and Wigren 2006). The region where High Chaparral is located is well known for its prosperous small-business structure (making it into a fully-fledged industrial district) and high free-church membership. Not only does Big Bengt believe in God, but his commitment to traditional family values and to the place is as strong as that of anybody else in the region. Jonnie Dahlström in the 1950s and 1960s added considerably to an emerging lifestyle by being a very aggressive car dealer. As much as Henry Ford made America mobile, (see Spinosa et al., 1997), Dahlström 'put his region on wheels'. Sten Rentzhog – to use Freire's vocabulary – 'conscientized' not only people in his own region but in Sweden nationwide of the collective memory that history contains. Lars Vilks dramatically redefines not only what art is but also how it may be enacted and where it may be located.

Whether challenging, destructing, reforming or constructing institutions, our four entrepreneurs alone provide a whole range of tactics. Some of these tactics may be considered part of intended strategies associated with concrete venturing, as in the case of Sten Rentzhog. Lars Vilks, in contrast, enacts an anarchic ideology, while Big Bengt Erlandsson stages Wild West shows as intensively as business deals. Jonnie Dahlström seems to have been more driven by nostalgia, possibly to balance his active part in the making of modern Sweden.

ENTREPRENEURSHIP BEYOND THE MARKET: EMERGING THEMES

Since extreme entrepreneurs are supposed not only to keep institutional forces at bay but to master such forces as well, they supposedly epitomize the constant oscillation between agency and structure, or what Giddens (1984) addresses as ongoing 'structuration' processes in society. Only if entrepreneurship is constructed as spanning across both the market and institutions will that image be sustained. In search of what may constitute extreme entrepreneurs as constructors of new social orders and reconstructors of old ones, some themes can be dimly seen across the life stories being told by the extreme entrepreneurs:

- treating words as deeds;
- sharing experiences with the public;
- playing games with institutions;
- constructing a glocal identity;
- keeping the family out;
- making entrepreneurship a way of life.

Treating Words as Deeds

The American Heritage Dictionary (1994) states: 'Deeds, not words, matter most'. We have learnt that entrepreneurs, not just in order to avoid being accused of being hypocrites, as initiators and enactors of change processes work hands-on to enact their ideas. However, as much as our academic jargon constructs what we define as entrepreneurship, the vocabulary entrepreneurs use in their practice defines what coincidences are seen as embryos of opportunities to enact (cf. Gartner, 1993). The identity of the extreme entrepreneur is certainly not just constructed out of their words and (other) deeds in everyday venturing. As a public person they are also formed by ongoing discourses and existing institutions in the contexts where they sojourn. It is a two-way process, since those who feed these discourses, such as the media, take an interest in extreme entrepreneurs as individuals – they are visible and outspoken. The entrepreneurs themselves actively search public arenas where they can communicate their ideas and enact them accordingly. This concern for publicity and contributions to the making of contemporary society by no means excludes them as business persons, nor as intellectuals or artisans.

Sharing Experiences with the Public

Operating on the large public arena where they navigate between the Scylla of narcissism and the Charybdis of marginality, the extreme entrepreneurs seem to be obsessed by their own identity construction. Public visibility gives the extreme entrepreneurs many reasons and opportunities to imagine how others may experience what they say and what they do. We thus propose that it is no coincidence that all the four extreme entrepreneurs that we have met operate in what is nowadays addressed as the 'experience economy' (Pine and Gilmore, 1999). Their 'official' occupations as a trader in machinery, a car dealer, a museum curator and a conceptual artist seem to be secondary to their mission to make life into an adventure for Swedes. Big Bengt Erlandsson as a sheriff certainly runs his High Chaparral, Jonnie Dahlström made the public experience his private life at historical Hillsta, Sten Rentzhog and his Jamtli pioneered the Swedish experience economy, and experiencing Ladonia with its monumental constructs is an extraordinary physical exercise indeed (it is only accessible by a spectacular walk down the coastal mountain) as well as an aesthetic one. This passion for making other people experience, whether triggered by spectacular and radicalizing art, as in the Vilks case, or by way of immersion into the collective memory in Jamtli, appears as a personal commitment that the extreme entrepreneurs cannot escape.

Playing Games with Institutions

The four extreme entrepreneurs all interact with society and in this interplay they have reconstructed established institutions or created new ones. According to Sten Rentzhog, a clear vision is the most important thing when embarking on building new structures. A reflected image of a future state in his mind makes the venturing process gain momentum. Accordingly, Sten Rentzhog has always deliberately tried to be ahead of others. Yet he has used an 'emergent strategy' view to enact his ideas, always being prepared to be surprised at what might hide around the corner. In his domains this has called for keen awareness of political processes and concern for dialogue. Jonnie Dahlström, in contrast, enacted his vision by proactive behaviour, presumably originating in his American experience.

Lars Vilks and Bengt Erlandsson have acted differently. They consider the institutional actors neither as partners to mesmerize, nor as barriers to overcome by force. Instead the very interaction with the representatives of authorities, relationships that are saturated with tensions, seems to trigger the putative sheriff and the artist. Big Bengt says: 'Thank God that the local authorities opposed me, since that gave me inspiration to do what I have done. If the local authorities had not done what they did, what you see here would never have existed. If you think that the fact that this exists is good, then you should say thank you to the local authorities.' According to Lars Vilks, intractable authorities have made significant contributions to the enactment of the soap opera and to his artistry. It is thanks to the recalcitrant authorities that his art survives.

Constructing a Glocal Identity

All four extreme entrepreneurs strongly identify with their local communities as historical-cultural contexts for everyday life: Brännehylte (Småland), Bjuråker (Hälsingland), Östersund (Jämtland) and Kullen (Scania). Big Bengt lives on the premises of High Chaparral, JD has returned to more or less his place of birth from urban America, Sten Rentzhog has returned to his roots and Lars Vilks runs his soap opera from a house within commuting distance from the place where he was raised. All of the extreme entrepreneurs have put their home towns on the map – Big Bengt with his High Chaparral amusement park, Jonnie Dahlström with Hillsta, his historical setting, Sten Rentzhog with his Jamtli museum and Lars Vilks with his own nation state of Ladonia. The extreme entrepreneurs seem to need the belonging that a spatial habitat offers to build and to maintain a strong public image of being different (cf. Jenkins, 1996, p. 22).

Being outsiders in both their local and national Swedish context, the extreme entrepreneurs all seem to search for contexts where their deeds and way of life are considered as 'normal'. It looks as if they have all found it in the US, where entrepreneurship is certainly more integrated into the culture as a web of meaning than in Scandinavia. Bengt Erlandsson and Jonnie Dahlström consider the US as their second home country. Their public nicknames – Big Bengt and JD – signify that their association with American culture goes far beyond their personal identification. Sten Rentzhog while still a student was inspired by the US action orientation as regards the preservation of historical milieux. His way of organizing the Jamtli open-air museum parallels the many pioneer villages in North America. Lars Vilks, too, has the US as a point of reference, mainly because of the recognized arenas for artists that New York offers. His website has visitors from all over the world, and they are all invited to become members of the state of Ladonia.

Keeping the Family Out

As indicated, Schumpeter (1911/1934) proposed that entrepreneurs build dynasties. The literature on family businesses, an organizational form that accommodates most entrepreneurs on the market, frequently reports how family and business 'systems' intertwine and how succession issues are, or should be dealt with (cf. for example Brunåker 1996). Our extreme entrepreneurs, however, separate their private and public life spheres. Big Bengt Erlandsson states his position quite bluntly: 'A really wise woman does not interfere with her husband and his business as long as he manages to run it.' Lars Vilks's private house literally hides behind a tall hedge that seems to have never been cut, keeping everybody, including relatives, out. While the extreme entrepreneurs all indicate that their wives play an important role in their emotional and social lives, neither of the two business entrepreneurs comments explicitly on the role of their children during or after their own venturing career. This may reflect their awareness of the fact that what they have achieved is intimately associated with them as embodied relations constructs in a special societal setting. When they are gone, literally or just out of business and public life, their legacy will not be transferable to anybody in the family. The extreme entrepreneurs will leave the stories and institutions with the very same public that co-constructed them.

Entrepreneuring as a Way of Life

All four extreme entrepreneurs are involved in processes that appear as never-ending to both themselves and outsiders. They all do their very best to immortalize themselves both by way of physical memorials – High Chaparral, Hillsta, Jamtli, Nimis and Arx – and through building a strong public image. However, none of the entrepreneurs seems to be concerned with legal ownership. Bengt does not own High Chaparral – the amusement park has been formally transferred to his sons. Today Jonnie owns no property apart from the house where he and Anna live. Sten Rentzhog as a public Swedish servant never literally owned any of his works – throughout his life he has managed to make others finance his ventures. Lars is selling off his works – if he is not giving them away.

The four extreme entrepreneurs thus seem to be more concerned about leaving symbolic impressions rather than economic wealth behind. Yet they are all fascinated by artefacts. Bengt Erlandsson, Jonnie Dahlström, and Sten Rentzhog all collect things for the future. Big Bengt keeps his museum with the argument that people throw away many things that have great stories to tell. Jonnie Dahlström is a genuine collector who never managed to throw away anything during his long life. He devotes his present time (in 2005) to ordering all the artefacts that have furnished his rich life: 'I have four, five hundred cartons full of collections of curios, I have never thrown anything away . . . it is never ending, short writings, brochures about cars . . .' Hillsta became a place for many, yet still a minor part, of his collected items. Sten Rentzhog as a professional collector has been very much concerned with dramatizing the messages that historical artefacts and persons carry. Sten Rentzhog was also one of the first Swedish museum curators to document our contemporary society (for example by asking regional firms to bring a copy of every product being manufactured). Lars Vilks practices hands-on collecting when looking for construction material for his Nimis and Arx on the beach, in the woods and in junk shops. The maintenance of the sculptures is a never-ending endeavour, especially considering that they have been sabotaged (Nimis, for example, has been set on fire). To Lars Vilks this Sisyfos fate is an inseparable part of venturing as an artist and entrepreneur.

CONTINUED TRAVELLING INTO THEORY AND PRACTICE

The narrated life stories do not just trigger reflections concerning the extreme entrepreneurship *per se*, but they also suggest alternative images of 'conventional' entrepreneurship and of institutional frameworks.

The ambitions and practices of the extreme entrepreneurs seem to have triggered them to cross multiple boundaries in society throughout their lives, making market forces an instrument for challenging institutions whenever possible. If compared with the market-focused entrepreneurs the extreme entrepreneurs stand out because of their childlike curiosity and unrest, a need to not just experience and learn new things but to make such experiencing itself a way of life. As much as children do not take the norms of adults for granted, extreme entrepreneurs do not accept the social restrictions carried by institutions. The life stories of the four extreme entrepreneurs, as summarized by us, tell about a need for 'self-actualization' that has accompanied the subjects throughout their lives. Obviously that urge is not triggered by simplistic hedonistic motives. Neither does their self-actualization appear as a 'peak' experience that can only be accomplished by the chosen few, as a conservative reading of Maslow (1968) suggests. Kostera (2005) proposes that self-actualization should not be associated with the ultimate state of a chosen few but rather with a basic human attribute that we may acknowledge as a guide in becoming social selves. 'Self actualization is a state of mind and a way of life that makes it as a habit to experience fully the reality the subject is immersed in and to express the experience in a way that is unique for the subject. It is about living in the present and not taking it for granted, as well as a creative way of being in the world' (Kostera, 2005, p. 15). This view suggests that as much as all human beings are enterprising as children, they may remain self-actualizing throughout life.

Alternative (comparative) ways of analyzing the stories told by the extreme entrepreneurs may be used to inquire deeper into how human agency appears as both a subject and an object in social construction processes. The institutionalization of the extreme entrepreneurs themselves and their deeds certainly inspires to such a venture. Concluding her reflections on the notion of 'institutional entrepreneurs', Czarniawska

(2004, p. 35) sees them as 'narrative characters: attributes of a genre, required to comply with the narrative coherence'. As much as this interpretation is in line with a linguistic-narrative turn in the constructionist or institutional tradition, the lessons from our research into extreme entrepreneurship suggest that narratives are as much a means in the making of embodied individual identities. Further conceptual and empirical inquiries, though, are needed to substantiate such an argument. Here we restrict ourselves to some comments on what contributions the emerging themes outlined above suggest for our understanding of institutions. Referring to the first theme, extreme entrepreneurs are recognized as able to master not just the concrete enactment of business ventures but also symbolic action, which makes them able to manage a dialogue with institutions. Obviously, research into extreme entrepreneurship offers an appropriate empirical arena to contrast bodily and linguistic turns in constructionist research. Much of the research into the experience economy is biased towards normative marketing models which hide the potential contributions of the proposed new economy. The lessons from these cases suggest that the ability to offer individuals unique experiences calls for special capabilities on the part of those providing the individualized services. The third theme proposes a different role for institutions in addition to those that concern bringing order and reducing uncertainty, namely that of being a sounding-board for individual initiatives. The proposition that extreme entrepreneurs simultaneously acknowledge a local and a global outlook brings alive the debate on the differences between the 'old' and the 'new' institutionalism (see Powell and DiMaggio, 1991). The words and deeds of our subjects seem to reflect analytical features of both images of institutionalism. Extreme entrepreneurs have a concern for both informal structure and the symbolic role of formal structure, for both organizing in a community context and in a field setting, for both commitment and habit as a basis for order. The way extreme entrepreneurs deal with the family institution brings interesting lessons both to family-business research and to research into the role of basic institutions in a fragmented, 'post-modernist' society. The last theme, reporting on the need of the extreme entrepreneurs to immortalize themselves, reveals another general challenge to the ambition of the constructionist and institutional frameworks to deconstruct the subject as anything but a relational self. On what and whose terms is that relational self constructed?

Our rudimentary institutional analysis of the life stories is based on the assumptions that the three proposed pillars of institutions are independent constructs. However, presumably there are both conceptual and empirical bridges – Scott's structuring of the institutional phenomenon is but one to organize academic insight in the field. Further exploration of the messages that the narratives hide will especially concern itself with the interdependencies between the institutional pillars in the (Swedish) institutional setting and how such bridging influences entrepreneurship. Researching extreme entrepreneurs may make us better understand the alleged lack of entrepreneurship (in the market) in Sweden. While Swedish culture disclaims heroes, especially in business, Swedes seem to follow the adventures of the extreme entrepreneurs with both enthusiasm and fear. The extreme entrepreneurs may arouse strong feelings in the Swedish context because they travel between different societal arenas, not confining their action to the market alone. In Sweden, initiative, creative organizing and success are appreciated in many fields, but not on the market. As much as both emotions (Fineman, 2000) and entrepreneurship are socially constructed phenomena (Goss, 2005), studying extreme entrepreneurship may bring both academic lessons and insights into what constitutes a Swedish entrepreneurial identity.

REFERENCES

Ahl, H. (2001). *The Making of the Female Entrepreneur*. Doctoral thesis, JIBS Dissertation Series, No. 015. Jönköping: Jönköping University.

American Heritage Dictionary (1994). 3rd edn. New York: Dell Publishing.

Baumol, W.J. (1990). Entrepreneurship: Productive, unproductive, and destructive. *Journal of Political Economy*, **98**(5): 893–921.

Berger, P.L. and Luckmann, T. (1966/1979). *The Social Construction of Reality*. Swedish version. New York, NY: Doubleday.

Brunåker, S. (1996). *Introducing Second Generation Family Members into the Family Operated Business: A Constructionist Approach*. Doctoral dissertation. Uppsala: SLU.

Brusco, S. (1992). Small firms and the provision of real services. In Pyke, F. and Sengenberger, W. (eds). *Industrial Districts and Local Economic Regeneration*. Geneva: ILO, pp. 177–96.

Czarniawska, B. (2004). Institutional entrepreneurs: An oxymoron in action. Paper presented at the Workshop in Institutional Entrepreneurship at the University of Melbourne, 15–18 December.

Czarniawska-Joerges, B. and Wolff, R. (1991). Leaders, managers, entrepreneurs on and off the organizational stage. *Organization Studies*, **12**(4): 529–46.

DiMaggio, P. and Powell, W. (1983). The iron cage revisited: Institutional isomorphism and collective rationality in organizational fields. *American Sociological Review*, **48**: 147–60.

Drucker, P. (1985). *Innovation and Entrepreneurship*. New York: Harper & Row.

Fineman, S. (ed.) (2000). *Emotions in Organizations*. 2nd edn. London: Sage.

Gartner, W.B. (1993). Words lead to deeds: Towards an organizational emergence vocabulary. *Journal of Business Venturing*, **8**: 231–9.

Gartner, W.B., Bird, B.J. and Starr, J.A. (1992). Acting 'as if': Differentiating entrepreneurial from organizational behavior. *Entrepreneurship Theory and Practice*, Spring: 13–31.

Gartner, W.B., Carter, N.M. and Hill, G. (2003). The language of opportunity. In Steyaert, C. and Hjorth, D. (eds). *New Movements in Entrepreneurship*. Cheltenham, UK and Northampton, MA, USA: Edward Elgar, pp. 103–24.
Giddens, A. (1984). *The Constitution of Society*. Cambridge: Polity Press.
Goss, D. (2005). Schumpeter's legacy? Interaction and emotions in the socioloy of entrepreneurship. *Entrepreneurship Theory and Practice*, **29**(2): 205–18.
Hirshman, A.O. (1974). *Exit, Voice and Loyalty. Responses to Decline in Firms, Organizations and States*. Cambridge, MA: Harvard University Press.
Hjorth, D., Johannisson, B. and Steyaert, C. (2003). Entrepreneurship as discourse and style of living. In Czarniawska, B. and Sevón, G. (eds). *The Northern Lights: Organization theory in Scandinavia*. Copenhagen: Liber/abstract forlag/ Copenhagen Business School Press, pp. 91–110.
Jenkins, R. (1996). *Social Identity*. London: Routledge.
Johannisson, B. (1992). Entrepreneurship: The management of ambiguity. In Polesie, T. and Johansson, I.-L. (eds). *Responsibility and Accounting: The Organizational Regulation of Boundary Conditions*. Lund: Studentlitteratur, pp. 155–79.
Johannisson, B. (2004). Entrepreneurship in Scandinavia: Bridging individualism and collectivism. In Corbetta, G., Huse, M. and Ravasi, D. (eds). *Crossroads of Entrepreneurship*. Dordrecht: Kluwer, pp. 225–41.
Johannisson, B., Kwiatkowski, S. and Dandridge, T.C. (1999). Intellectual entrepreneurship: Emerging identity in a learning perspective. In Kwiatkowski, S. and Edvinsson, L. (eds). *Knowledge Café for Intellectual Entrepreneurship*. Warsaw: Academy of Entrepreneurship and Management, pp. 29–46.
Johannisson, B. and Wigren, C. (2006). The dynamics of community identity making: The spirit of Gnosjö revisited. In Steyaert, C. and Hjorth, D. (eds). *Entrepreneurship as Social Change*. Cheltenham, UK and Northampton, MA: Edward Elgar.
Kostera, M. (2005). *The Quest for the Self-Actualizing Organization*. Malmö: Liber & Copenhagen Business School Press.
Maslow, A.M. (1968). *Toward a Psychology of Being*. 2nd edn. New York: Van Nostrand Renhold Company.
North, D.C. (1990). *Institutions, Institutional Change and Economic Performance*. Cambridge, MA: Cambridge University Press.
Pettersson, K. (2002). *Företagande män och osynliggjorda kvinnor: Diskursen om Gnosjö ur ett könsperspektiv* (*Enterprising Men and Women Made Invisible: the Discourse on Gnosjö in a Gender Perspective*). Doctoral thesis, Department of Geography. Uppsala: Uppsala University.
Pine II, B.J. and Gilmore, J.H. (1999). *The Experience Economy. Work is Theatre and Every Business a Stage*. Boston, MA: Harvard Business School Press.
Powell, W.W. and DiMaggio, P.J. (1991). Introduction. In Powell, W.W. and DiMaggio, P.J. (eds). *New Institutionalism in Organizational Analysis*. Chicago, IL: University of Chicago Press, pp. 1–41.
Rehn, A. and Taalas, S. (2004). Crime and assumptions in entrepreneurship. In Hjorth, D. and Steyaert, C. (eds). *Narrative and Discursive Approaches in Entrepreneurship*. Cheltenham, UK and Northampton, MA, USA: Edgar Elgar, pp. 144–59.
Schumpeter, J.A. (1911/1934). *The Theory of Economic Development*. Oxford: Oxford University Press.
Schumpeter, J.A. (1943/1987). *Capitalism, Socialism and Democracy*. 6th edn. London: Unwin.
Scott, W.R. (2001). *Institutions and Organizations*. 2nd edn. Thousand Oaks, CA: Sage.

Spinosa, C., Flores, F. and Dreyfus, H. (1997). *Disclosing New Worlds: Entrepreneurship, Democratic Action and Cultivation of Solidarity*. Cambridge, MA: MIT Press.
Tsoukas, H. and Chia, R. (2002). On organizational becoming: Rethinking organizatinal change. *Organization Science*, **13**(5): 567–82.
Van de Ven, A.H. (1993). The development of an infrastructure for entrepreneurship. *Journal of Business Venturing*, **8**: 211–30.

8. Debriefing and motivating knowledge workers in small IT firms: challenges to leadership

Mette Mønsted

INTRODUCTION

The perspective of this chapter is to illustrate the complexity of management and leadership as a negotiated relationship in complex small IT firms. The conditions are demanding and complex and the knowledge workers are determined to be self-managing. This creates a high level of complexity, which challenges existing management roles. Such extreme cases also illuminate the fundamental problems of innovation or research management in other types of organizations.

Management of knowledge workers is a delicate balance between motivation and coordination, between 'playfulness' and efficiency. It is also a perspective of leadership, where the manager is responsible for division of labour, but without the insight, as he is not highly competent on the content of the professional issues. The case is based on a small multimedia firm, which has been studied longitudinally for 2.5 years.

The perspective of asymmetric knowledge and the intangible knowledge in R&D open the need for managers to get close to the process of development for more efficient knowledge sharing and for the understanding of different layers and roles of leadership and management. The relationship between management and the knowledge workers represents a structure where the manager is dependent on the knowledge workers' insight, as the replicability and explicitation of knowledge is difficult.

The knowledge workers such as 'nerds' and 'stars' among programmers are the highly valued knowledge workers, and probably very efficient in solving certain tasks and creating commitment, but they are hard to control to make it economically feasible, when projects have to meet deadlines and be sold. Thus this type of relationships sharpens the attention to different leadership roles and the need for management and economic control (Yukl, 1989).

The chapter focuses on the management implications of asymmetric knowledge, or handling complex knowledge, and how to deal with knowledge sharing for constructing a platform for decision-making and management. The case of debriefing IT 'nerds' is a point of departure for laying out the arguments, and the special features of how turbulence and rapid technological changes constitute themselves in IT projects illustrate some of the management problems relative to motivated knowledge workers.

DEBRIEFING OF KNOWLEDGE FOR ACTION

Linear project management and detailed planning is not available to small high-tech firms. They have to survive and thrive on uncertainty and complexity as they lack control of the context, the customer and the progress of technology. A larger number of externalities have to be handled by the manager than is the case in more specialized functions in large firms. In IT firms the ability to persuade customers about expertise, to create credibility and to sell ideas is fundamental for the survival of advanced technology and service firms. The value of the solution is seen only if it works afterwards in the application. This is a dominant feature of all forms of service and immaterial production (Normann, 2000). The skills required to persuade customers are usually not those of the developers, and would demand skills from other fields in order to explain the applicability of a given solution.

The asymmetric knowledge *vis-à-vis* managers demands some learning spaces to try to communicate the content of the work, so as to be able to coordinate the consequences for other staff. The process of debriefing existing staff takes a lot of time, but is the foundation for generating knowledge about acting as manager of the other programmers. In this research project (Jensen and Mønsted, 2001; Jensen et al., 2004) we have used video registrations of some of these meetings to grasp the knowledge-sharing process.

Even at a stage without immediate crisis, the project manager has to make an effort at regular intervals to debrief the advanced developers to find out where they are and where they are heading. For example a video-scene shows the project manager trying to find out what the programmer has been doing. They start talking, leaning over a piece of paper. Then the project manager goes to the whiteboard, and starts explaining how he interprets what the programmer is saying (or mumbling). The project manager questions and interprets the answers. After a while they begin to 'think together' on possible solutions and interpretations (Jensen, 2001).

The scene illustrates some of the problems of the programmer in communicating and translating codes into explicit knowledge. He has difficulty formulating in words what he is doing, and especially the reflections behind the choices made. The whiteboard is used as a boundary object in Susan Leigh Star's (1989) version as a means to communicate and translate the part of tacit knowledge which is routine and self-evident knowledge to the programmer being debriefed. The project manager uses the drawings and codes to create a dialogue for understanding the codes developed and the reasoning behind them. The knowledge of knowledge workers is thus not in a form that can easily be explained, as is also seen in tacit knowledge in other scientific work (Collins, 1974).

The programmer is taking important knowledge as self-evident, and it is difficult to make it explicit and operational for others. The project manager needs knowledge, not only to give feedback to the programmer, but also to coordinate with other staff working on other parts of the programme. The need for division of labour demands that either the manager or the team knows the task, and they are able to create overlapping knowledge to handle boundaries between the different parts of the programme. The complexity of the tasks makes knowledge management very difficult, as knowledge is tied to the people and the actions involved as distributed knowledge (Tsoukas, 1996) and communication (Stacey, 2001).

Another debriefing scene is described in a video-clip. One of the 'talented' young programmers has a lot of difficulty in describing what he does. He is debriefed not only by the project manager in R&D, who is a programmer himself, but another strong programmer is aslo participating (he is one of the owners).

The problem in this scene is that the 'primadonna' cannot formulate in words what he is doing in a way which is understandable even for the competent project manager, who has programming skills. Also, he is into a logic of 'aesthetic codes' more than the codes in the assignment prescribed. The other 'star' has to participate in the debriefing, to help translate, and to follow up with supplementary questions to get into an interpretation of codes, and together they have to decide on the consequences of the choices made in the sections of the programme the young talent is working on.

The ability to put into words what the codes mean, and how they link to other programmers and application work, is rather limited. In this case it is a totally different language and culture, and translation to explain interpretations becomes important as a part of the joint development and interpretation of the project as organizational knowledge. Beautiful codes are not the purpose of the firm. Codes have to be used, and the young talent often has to be reminded about users. He puts a 'Post-It' note on the screen frame: 'Remember user'. The application is essential for a firm which is not a research lab, but has to sell the products and their applications. The dilemma between the need for programmers to play with innovations on the forefront of technology, and the need to do the necessary only to make price-competitive products, is evident.

The scenes illustrate some of the fundamental problems of what firms know, and who knows what in the firms. The importance is that division of labour presupposes that the work task is known, and can be delimitated and specified for all involved. Both in innovation and in most IT projects in the early stages, this is not the case, which makes management a very demanding task of coordination on the boundary of knowledge. Project managers need expertise in the field of programming to be able to communicate and lead.

The illustrating cases are from very small firms, but the boundaries between the groups of people are very similar to the boundaries between communities of practice or in tight networks (Mønsted, 2003; Wenger, 1998; Brown and Duguid, 2000). The problem is tied to individual learning, and has to be a social or organization-based knowledge. It is tempting to go into the discussion of transforming tacit to explicit knowledge (Nonaka and Takeuchi, 1995), or translating one form of explicit knowledge in the form of codes, to another form of explicit knowledge in the form of communication in words of what is achieved and the purpose of the codes. The translation is used in order to overcome communities of practice, and to communicate across professional groups. Such translation is not really the same as the perception of tacit knowledge in Nonaka and Takeuchi (1995), but is much more about communication and learning across communities of practice or across structural holes in networks for complementary knowledge (Burt 1992; Mønsted, 2003).

The debriefing in this case was seen as a communication of socially bound knowledge across cultural and professional barriers. The perception of knowledge is not just a translation, but is closer to Stacey's (2001) perception of creating knowledge not only as a mental individual map, but also as a social process constituted by communication. The debriefing is not only an effort to get knowledge as a ready formulated 'thing' out of the head of the programmers, but an effort to create a joint 'learning space' to get the codes into a perspective of creating knowledge about codes, their purpose and consequences for other parts of the system. Managers have to constitute meaning in the fragments of information, and this is a social communication process (Weick, 1995), but it also has to be communicated with the knowledge workers, who take decisions in action during the process.

PROJECT MANAGEMENT IN TIME DILEMMAS

In another project case the emphasis was on the study of the turbulence and time pressure in IT multimedia projects, which is extreme, and often changing and tightening during a project. Uncertainty on technology has to be dealt with, and raises the questions as to the needed overlap in skills, or the technical insight of the managers. The uncertainty is tied to technology, the time perspective for new development, and to the customer relations, where customers change projects and conditions especially in the first period of the project.

When crisis management becomes perceived as 'normal', a number of regular project management tools become obsolete, and a number of good management reflections and coordination are lost. The case presented is extreme, as everything is crisis management, but it raises a few questions on how knowledge workers handle responsibilities in coordination at many levels. It raises the question of what kind of management can cope with impossible situations. In the dotcom bubble, a number of firms managed to create projects with a very high and unrealistic level of ambition. Such ambitions and ideas actually inspired authors on project management (Kidder, 1981; Christensen and Kreiner, 1991), and created a special motivation of doing the impossible.

An example of this role is as follows. A newly recruited project manager manages a large project making a PC-based learning system. The firm had never before had such a large project. The sales manager has promised too much, yet they have decided in the firm and with the developer that they can do it, even if they have to develop the tool, and are forced not to use the existing tools normally used. It appears to be a totally impossible task. The new project manager starts building up a unit of production team, producing text and drawings. Most of these employees do not have much education and have to be trained on the job. The balance is to grow and get the right staff, but also to balance out the communication with the programmer responsible for the tool 'producer'. Using her tools from informatics and the business school, and a large Gantt scheme, she tried to get an overview of the complexity, but only for the application side of the project, as the tool development was dependent on the developer. The effort to mobilize motivation and energy among staff was one major aspect of the job, which they managed to finish, but not on time.

The complexity of the project is increased by the parallel development of tools and applications, which normally would be linear. The project manager is 'the helmet man' balancing between Scylla and Charybdis (Hampden-Turner, 1990). She is managing a project dependent on a tool which is not ready yet (A). Usually the 'producer tool' would be first, and the application for learning would follow (B) as shown in Figure 8.1.

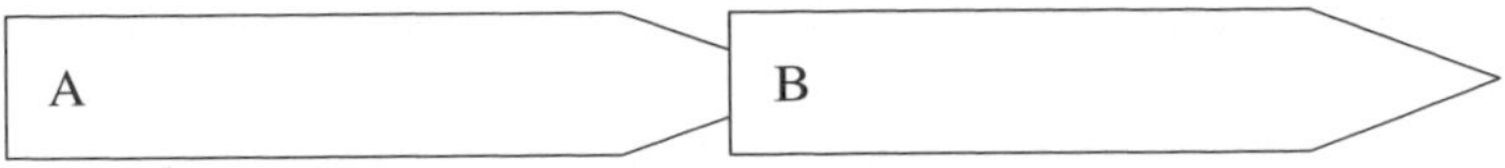

Figure 8.1a In a linear process, the flow should run from the development of the xml-tool (A) to the application (B)

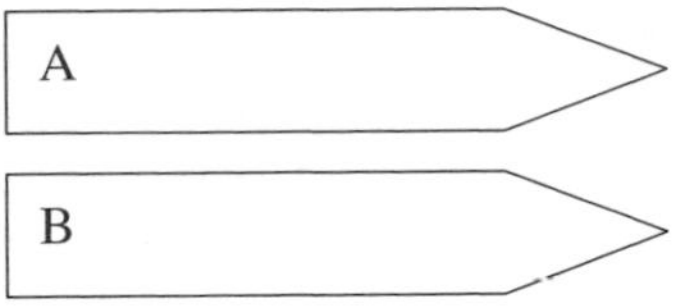

Source: Jensen et al., 2004, p. 174.

Figure 8.1b There is no time to wait for A to finish and B is cut from the end of the process and placed parallel to A

The project is organized in parallels, where the project manager is managing the application part, and getting an overview in an enormous Gantt scheme. She is recruiting and training new staff without much education; at the same time the tool development is for a long period only a 'one-man army', with talent and ability to correct and understand the application side, but very unstructured or rather inexplicit on the development process itself, where he is correcting at night and developing during the daytime. Applications are developed as a separate process on the basis of the 'black box'.

This organizing creates an extreme pressure on the programmer for the tool, a very high dependency of the application on the tool, and a need for frequent knowledge sharing and interaction, which disturbs the programmer. Managers at several levels should try to coordinate this process. As the timeline is 'folded' to a parallel process, there is a need for communication and coordination between the tool (A) and the application (B). The need for communication and coordination increases both at project management level, and also at other levels of management, but at the same time the means of control for project managers as well as top managers are meagre.

The pressure increased and it became necessary to employ a few more staff for the tool development and adjustment to the learning application. But the possibility of activating the two new programmers was not very easy. The two new recruits demanded a 'proper briefing'; if not, they were going to leave, as they could not get into the role they were supposed to do. A time-out for debriefing of the developer had to be accepted in order to allow new developers to work in the programme, as they could not read the mind of the original developer. There is a clash between the autodidact artist developer and the newly recruited, educated and structured developers. But it is interesting that the complexity of knowledge in IT makes several practitioners state that recruiting more people increases the time used on the programme (Brooks, 1995). The complexity of sharing knowledge within IT projects makes it difficult to make explicit what the firm knows. In complex tasks a lot of time is used on learning and exploring. The costs of introducing new staff are very high, and they need a long period of training and adaptation, making it extremely difficult when new staff are recruited to speed up the process, as it may demand more time to train than the new staff can create in value-added (Brogren, 2001; Brooks, 1995).

Strangely enough, the firm managed to deliver the product – not on time, but still to the satisfaction of the customer.

TECHNOLOGICAL CONDITIONS FOR LEADERSHIP

The coordination and management of 'black boxes of the unknown' appears in other cases of these firms as well. The barriers of communication and learning over communities of practice are a problem when knowledge is asymmetric and mutual dependency is still a dominant feature in the organization. The challenges and thrill of an R&D project are motivating factors, which may motivate programmers to elaborate and change standard tasks to more R&D. Even if the parallel development is not efficient, and is creating both errors and stress, it is also creating a 'gut feeling' and motivation for the project. Such motivation is harder to feel if jobs are more standardized, especially with an emphasis on timing and deadlines.

Within IT, however, turbulence and rapid change in technology is a dominating feature, and creates a very special perception of time. Evaluating time in non-routine work is a risky business under the uncertainty of innovative projects. Strangely enough, it is seldom an exceptionally short time, which is the big surprise. When time pressure is so high and compressed as is normally the case, many tasks have to be done in parallel which would otherwise be linear, as the second part depends on the first. The lack of time for linearity is a new feature, which is putting pressure not only on production but also on R&D and, especially, on management coordination (Jensen et al., 2004).

In IT the time pressure creates cases of parallel development of tools and applications, not only making coordination extremely difficult, but stressing new management roles as coordination is not only between two separate tasks that have to be combined afterwards, but communication is an embedded part of avoiding redoing many aspects of the two tasks. If it is interpreted in a systemic innovation perspective, then the constant coordination of the boundaries is necessary, a translation between relatively independent productions, and with very different skills and competence in the two projects. The learning experience is to allow for more time, but then the price is too high for the offer.

The turbulence of IT projects provides new perspectives on time. The rapid development features of technology change every third month. Turbulence and renewal imply that certain aspects change rapidly, but a lot of features remain. The time perspective could maybe more be seen in a biological way of perceiving change, as a seasonal and age change, where the main structure is still the same, but many features change and have to adapt to seasons or ageing (Adams, 1990; Jensen and Mønsted, 2001). Such perspectives on time could be helpful when considering IT projects, living with the intense and drastic turbulence and pressure from new technology and new methods. New methods may change a lot in a project, but changes are mostly recognizable patterns for the community of practice working within the field. The turbulence and 'panic solutions' put pressure on managers and on the communication between developers and managers. Both parties are stressed and take chances, which are sometimes good decisions, but not necessarily reflecting efficiency.

The problem of time has more dimensions, as the engagement of developers as experts implies that they want to put too much time into the work, and spend a lot of time on the creative part of the solution. It is hard to manage, as the profitability is tied to the capacity to meet deadlines, and the necessary solution. The overtime used should be 'free research time at night', when it is not part of the deal, and this is often the case.

KNOWLEDGE-INTENSIVE FIRMS AND KNOWLEDGE WORKERS

In IT firms the ability to persuade customers about expertise, to create credibility and sell ideas, is fundamental for the survival of advanced technology and service firms. The value of the solution is seen only if it works afterwards in the application, which is a knowledge criteria in IT, and a dominant feature of all service production (Normann, 2000). This fits with the perception of knowledge-intensive firms as a 'system of persuasion' (Alvesson, 2001).

Knowledge workers could be defined as highly educated professionals, which is a quite normal way of defining them (Alvesson, 2001, p. 863;

Davenport and Prusak, 1998; Newell et al., 2002). The highly educated who work in non-standard settings and have to innovate or analyse and reflect independently form a special group, and demand autonomy and authority of their expert skills. Some professionals have more routinized work, and may act on the basis of existing knowledge, as would be the case with lawyers, some engineers and architects. Professionals also in these professions work on the basis of their expertise, the insight and skills needed, which demands professional minds rather than databases or robots. The group of knowledge workers who independently exploit and explore new knowledge are maybe essential for the understanding of new conditions for management. The innovativeness and unpredictability of knowledge workers in IT development demand a capacity to create meaning in dialogues, and thus create knowledge as learning in dialogue (Stacey, 2001).

The skills of knowledge workers for such projects include the capacity to evaluate the relevance and potential of knowledge. The ambitions of managers and knowledge workers may not be the same, as R&D projects or consultancy projects may 'slide away' and expand to 'interesting related issues', and thus take much more time.

Skills in many knowledge firms are hard to define in terms of educational competence, as with consultancy and IT programmers, experienced-based learning plays an important role. The autonomy of knowledge workers to define what is relevant, interesting and necessary is hard to control and judge for people outside the profession or community of practice.

In IT firms, the skills of developers are hard to define, as mostly it is a description of practice and knowledge of existing programmes, but the ability to solve new problems within a certain sphere of programming is essential. Within the community of practice of the highly skilled programmers, stories and metaphors of work and codes are closer to art than to science. Methods and solutions are described by their 'beauty' and elegance. Between programmers, they know that elegance has something to do with efficiency, shortcuts and new possibilities, as one of the managers in a small IT firm said: 'The difference in efficiency between a good programmer and the excellent talent is 1:20, and this is not found in many other types of skills or work.'

This difference adds to the perception of IT appearing to be more like art than science. The ability to imagine possibilities and to start creating them is very close to artists' work, and may be managed in the same way. If they are efficient there is no conflict with management. But conflicts arise from problems of time limits. What solution is possible within the deadline? This is a question of the necessary solution, rather than the best solution. Such compromise does not create much motivation or commitment.

The problem seems to be to exploit the talent of the super-expert, where the structure and people should stimulate talent, but also create a framework for communication of consequences for the dependent people. Leaders have to be engaged in these processes, and assist the creation of frameworks and direction. In the cases observed, the project managers did this, whereas top management lost track of what was going on in the projects, and became marginalized.

Skills in programming may be acquired as engineers, mathematicians, physicists, or in informatics, but some of the talented programmers are autodidacts. This is not seen in other professional knowledge firms or disciplines. The IT field in multimedia production also includes a large group of 'unskilled young production workers'. Some from such groups have talents for programming, and a high commitment to learn in practice. Generally, however, these unskilled people need very well-defined jobs and instructions. The way of organizing in the two groups is very different, and in many ways only the developer types are considered knowledge workers with decentralized responsibility. The unskilled group needs other types of instruction and management, some even in a very Tayloristic and task-specific manner.

The organization of work in knowledge work responds to the demand for dialogue, self-management and distributed knowledge. The organization as a system of distributed knowledge as developed by Tsoukas (1996) illustrates the way tacit knowledge and explicit knowledge is intertwined and mutually dependent. The tacit knowledge is hidden in routines and presumptions about the work, as illustrated by Latour and Wolgar (1979) and Gourlay (2004). This perspective stresses the importance of a community perspective on knowledge (Newell et al., 2002, p. 107), but also the complexity of sharing knowledge, which is dynamic and fluid, and socially embedded.

Management of knowledge in IT demands a certain understanding of the field, but not necessarily with know-how for actions. Understanding the principles and knowing how to act are not the same thing (Garud, 1997). The essence for management is an understanding of the implications of codes, so as to create conditions for a division of labour with other staff. Decisions have to be taken before knowledge is certain, often at a stage of ideas and ascribed potential meaning of new ideas (Garud, 1997). IT systems are based on a high level of complexity and system dependence, and the competence of the team, and the management has to have knowledge of more than the part they are working with just now (Kogut and Zander, 1996). The mutual dependency in systems demands much more coordination for integration and managing consequences for other people, than the multidisciplinary aggregation of solutions (Newell and Swan, 2000).

LEADERSHIP AND PROJECT MANAGEMENT OF KNOWLEDGE WORKERS

Asymmetric knowledge is a management problem, which directly affects the project management, but also affects the manager responsible for external relations and finances. The researchers or developers do not feel the same need for communicating beyond their group. As individuals with a specific responsibility, they can 'see' where they are going. The need for complex coordination in a larger perspective is not necessarily the agenda for experts or developers. Autonomy and self-management did not in this case-study lead to a feeling of responsibility for the organizational perspective.

Management and leadership under these circumstances demand a high level of communication and awareness of interpretations in other communities of practice. The way the debriefing functions is by providing a platform for the manager's credibility for coordinating and getting the economic framework accepted. If the manager cannot get through to an understanding of what is going on, personal credibility is at stake, and it is even more difficult the next time, where debriefing is necessary. The leader is challenged in his leadership skills all the time. Communication across professional boundaries is based on trust in the other person's competence. Respect for other epistemological capabilities could be seen as a negotiated process of creating legitimacy, trust and meaning (Newell and Swan, 2000). If the manager does not maintain his respect both at a general management level, and in relation to ongoing projects, then the framework for a joint sense-making cannot be created, and misunderstanding may occur, as we have seen at many instances in the case study.

The effort to understand the work of the programmer is a necessary foundation for creating the division of labour in the team, but it is also one of the ways to create communication and mutual credibility. If the manager is not involved in this way he may lose his own credibility, because he is not even making the effort to try to understand.

The self-management of knowledge workers and the loosely coupled organization increase the need for coordination and knowledge sharing. The recent high focus on knowledge sharing reflects the needs for knowing what the organization knows, and for creating occasions to share knowledge. The flat organization and high level of decentralized management has an embedded problem of coordination and overview, which is easier in hierarchical organizations. Loose couplings in organizations create a high level of flexibility, but at the same time lose knowledge and overview. Newell et al. (2002) argue that managers have a more narrow span of control, and that subordinates control their own activities, and continue: 'middle managers are no longer able to act as the communication conduits within an organization – they do not know in much detail what is happening within their particular sphere of responsibility nor do they necessarily have time to engage in such activities' (Newell et al., 2002, p. 101). This implies that 'the very same organizational forms that help to nurture knowledge creation also provide more opportunity for knowledge loss' (ibid.). In a management perspective, the problems for middle and top managers in getting close to technological knowledge also provide a structure with high emphasis on the first-line project managers. The knowledge workers own responsibility and the team-leaders and project managers are crucial during stages of high uncertainty, where 'the impossible is created'.

The knowledge sharing is not only tied to the individual and the internal relations in the firm. In IT systems, the network and contacts to other talents are an important part of the intellectual capacity. The talent of developers is not only individual, but as the scientific and technological human capital is dependent on the social context:

> Much of this capital, especially that aspect that is interpersonal and social, is embedded in social and professional networks, technological communities or knowledge value collectives. . . . none of these discounts the more traditional aspects of individual scientists' talent . . . Our concept simply recognizes that in modern science being brilliant is only necessary, not sufficient' (Bozeman et al., 2001, p. 724).

Management in knowledge-intensive firms is less a position than an action, stressing the ability to facilitate and create the context and motivations to create knowledge-intensive products. It becomes more like the network manager's role, who is only the manager by acting and by being accepted by the partners as a manager (Mønsted, 2003). The position and control aspects of the manager's role are loosened considerably. Yukl (1989, p. 252) stresses the increasing emphasis within leadership research on shared leadership. The profile of knowledge workers and their wish for autonomy creates a knowledge-sharing context, where leadership is tolerated as long as the manager is credible both in his actions and as a person, and does not set too many obstacles in the way of the part of work which is interesting and fun. The platform for management has to be defined in the context, and a power base is not positional, but has to be created by the leader of the game.

In the case studies the recruited MBA top management became more and more marginalized due to the lack of insight, and lack of interest in understanding the development work. The perspectives illustrate some of the problems of creating management as a social construction in firms. If a joint framework is not established, the 'play and art culture' may go undisturbed and programmers in the studied case disrespected the economically motivated deadlines.

It is important to keep the levels of management separated, as the roles of the project managers become more and more important, both to coordinate the project, but also as the bridge and translator to other parts of the firm. Even if project managers often have very changing and fluid conditions for their work, they are close to the R&D and production, and this is the foundation for their influence and leadership in the organization. The role of the top management was more to set the rules and the framework, but even this level has to be related to the understanding of the conditions and timing of development.

The case studies also reflect some of the dilemmas of coordinating between different communities of practice (Wenger, 1998), and between disciplines, which is quite fundamental for the understanding of professional leadership in knowledge-based firms. The manager coming from outside represent a different community of practice, and the IT developers usually form their own understanding of relevance, competence and organizing. When self-managed knowledge workers refuse to accept management, they continue as they had done before, and then even less is coordinated, as authority is not accepted. It is a very dangerous situation, and emphasizes the need for a capacity to communicate and create a human resource environment for knowledge sharing and a mutual need for coordination. In many ways such traits may be found in other institutions as well, such as in research institutions. The difference with the IT world is the 'self-identification' as artists, rather than accepting a role as highly educated people who communicate and organize their knowledge in an organization where the dependency on people with these special talents has created a permissive culture close to anarchy.

The reaction of the developers in many ways illustrates some of the problems of the 'playfulness' and ways of working in the dotcom bubble. It is a very irresponsible way of working in a firm, as it is not 'only a playground'. The lack of responsibility of the decentralized authority could not survive economically.

One of the problems seems to be that a joint communication platform does not exist, and that the leader has not managed to constitute an accepted social platform for power. If the managed staff do not accept the power of the manager, the manager becomes an extra layer and barrier in the organization, as others will take over decision-making. The power game is one of the dimensions of management and leadership, and knowledge workers who are self-managed to a high degree do not accept positional power alone – it has to be linked to some kind of personal power and credibility (Haugaard, 1997, p. 31; Yukl, 1989, p. 254).

The problems of decentralization, the need for deadlines and for generating economy in the projects, are fundamental, and methods to control this are partly the same as always, as recruitment and laying off people is still an option. More than ever, it is important to create a joint platform of understanding and a bridge between the communities of practice. It could be that the knowledge workers can decide on methods and more incremental issues, where other decisions involving other people, and other groups in the firm, have to be communicated and decided at management level as well. Communication is the foundation for such decisions.

MOTIVATION AND CONTROL

In a knowledge-intensive firm the dependency of managers' credibility and trust is serious. The positional power of managers is limited in small firms, and the personal power stemming from the person and their expertise is essential (Yukl, 1989, p. 254). The ability to persuade externally is based on internal knowledge, and internally the insight depends on ability to communicate and create credibility. When managers are recruited to complement skills, and supply insight on financial issues and contracts, their knowledge can only be used in action if they can relate to the subject matter and the real deadlines of both R&D and production. Credibility is more easily accessible within the same disciplines and communities of practice, but the demand for other skills in management creates diversity and boundaries. When communicating across disciplines, as many professional managers do, it is even more important to question and debrief to get a platform for decision-making which may be recognized as relevant by the knowledge workers. If credibility is lost, the non-explicit routines and knowledge are kept hidden from decision-makers in the firm, and the credibility of the efficiency measures may be at stake.

A small IT firm may have more than one owner, with different management functions, and some project leaders who also participate in most decisions. Such structures are part of the knowledge work, and its organization. Hidden knowledge is seen even in large corporations, where R&D workers may get a green light to start a programme, but deliberately keep top management in the dark in the stages where the project is very experimental. Only when a new project begins to look less chaotic and more organized may it be 'sold' internally in a political legitimization process (Staudt, 1997).

The project manager has to create legitimacy as manager, both internally in the group, and outside the group. The project managers are more like the developers and may more easily achieve internal credibility in their group, but also have to be able to communicate and get respect upwards.

The conditions within the IT market often imply that the time pressure and resources are under constant changes, and project managers are part of the stressful game of both creating innovative solutions for new conditions, and creating efficiency to limit the innovative and beautiful solution to produce the necessary solution. Project managers have to adapt to new and stricter conditions at regular intervals, and have to negotiate and motivate in their teams to keep up motivation and energy at the critical moments. Even if project managers are close to developers, we have seen problems of asymmetric information, and lack of insight in the system programming, and how such features have to be translated and caught early in the development.

The role of management in knowledge-intensive firms could be seen as a negotiation and social construction of power in communication with subordinates. Power is given by the employees, and constituted in the community. Motivation has to be constituted and motivations are not linked to 'efficient work on the necessary', but to the chance to elaborate on the best solutions, to explore and learn. Interviews with Christensen indicate the need to remain playful in response to the challenges of development: 'if not, they could just as well have a 40 hour job with one of the large firms' (Christensen and Mønsted, 1999).

The knowledge workers are doing more than they should do, and in this way they overdo solutions, and keep on the track of artisan work rather than industrialize and recycle solutions. The work is a part of their self-identification, and motivation is tied to being on the boundary of the new. Such conditions create creativity and research-like conditions, but also lead to overwork, which is not necessarily paid.

CONCLUSION

The empirical case in this chapter is used to raise questions on the roles of leadership in knowledge-intensive firms as well as to try to use and illustrate a method of video-interviewing. The knowledge-intensive firm is based on mobilizing knowledge workers in a 'system of persuasion' (Alvesson, 1991). In a development process, where new knowledge is created, the lack of shared knowledge is detrimental to the organizing of the firm, and new roles for managers have to be found.

The project manager's debriefing of developers in IT firms in order to get organizational knowledge for managing is used as the illustrating case. The debriefing is not only a translation of codes, but also an effort to understand the context of codes for managing the division of labour. The explicitation of knowledge in these interviews is a very complex task, and demands a high level of insight and ability to communicate across disciplines and communities of practice. The sharing of knowledge is especially difficult in some high-tech communities, where only the experts understand what is going on, and the manager belongs to another professional discipline and community of practice, but has to coordinate and decide.

The understanding of the necessity of management is very different in the various groups, and reflects differences not only in conditions of work, but also in education, interests and the level of 'playfulness' of the dotcom generation. The IT field is not dominated by the highly educated, as are other knowledge-intensive firms (Alvesson, 2001, p. 863), but it has a lot of the same features as other types of expertise. If the knowledge workers are motivated by factors which are related to 'artisan' production, rather than industrial standardization, then managers will have to balance out motivation and efficiency. The overdoing of work could be an interesting issue to study in other knowledge-intensive work as well. The motivation for developers is working on creative solutions, but, for the business, economic frameworks have to be created as a necessary condition.

Motivation and coordination are a delicate balance, and the chapter outlines some of the dilemmas, and in what kind of situations these becomes obvious. Such illustrations of different values indicate not only different communities of practice, but also the need for good management to develop only the necessary, rather than the 'Rolls Royce' model, which may only be sold for the price of the 'Volkswagen'. In the process, the legitimacy of the manager is at stake as economic arguments are not enough for motivation. Management of deadlines for delivery has been fundamental for all the IT firms, though some have overlooked this. In the dotcom period the experience socialized a number of employees to a relaxed attitude to economic management, as value of sales and profit did not reflect the value of the firm.

The role of leaders in knowledge-based organizations is tied to the social skills of forming bridges to use the complementary expertise. The more the researchers or developers are technical 'nerds', the more the manager has to work on creating knowledge sharing, and a platform for communication and negotiation. Individual talent has to be organized in a structure to be applied and exploited, and this is the role of the manager.

REFERENCES

Adams, B. (1990). *Time and Social Theory*. Cambridge: Polity Press.

Alvesson, M. (2001). Knowledge work: Ambiguity, image and identity. *Human Relations*, **54**(7): 863–86.

Bozeman, B., Dietz, J.S. and Gaughan, M. (2001). Scientific and technical human capital: An alternative model for research evaluation. *International Journal of Technology and Management*, **22**(7/8): 716–40.

Brogren, J. Waras (2001). Om materialiseringer af ideer. Et casestudie af samspil, videnprocesser og ledelse i den midlertidige IT-organisation. Master's dissertation Copenhagen Business School.

Brooks, F.B. (1995). *The Mythical Man-Month*. Boston, MA: Addison-Wesley. (1st edn 1975.)

Brown, J. Seely and Duguid, P. (2000). Mysteries of the region: Knowledge dynamics in Silicon Valley. In Lee, C.-M., Miller, W.F., Hancock, M.G. and Rowen, H.S. (eds). *The Silicon Valley Edge. A Habitat for Innovation and Entrepreneurship*. Stanford, CA: Stanford University Press, pp. 16–39.

Burt, R. (1992). *Structural Holes. The Social Structure of Competition*. Cambridge, MA: Harvard University Press.

Christensen, S. and Kreiner, K. (1991). *Projektledelse i løst koblede systemer: Ledelse og læring i en ufuldkommen verden*. København: Jurist- og Økonomforbundets Forlag.

Christensen, P. Holdt and Mønsted, M. (1999). Uncertainty as motivation or when nerds rush in: A counterculture to managing routines. In During, W., Oakey, R.P. and Mukhtar, S.M. (eds). *New Technology Based Firms in the 1990s*, Vol. 6, Oxford: Elsevier Science.

Collins, H.M. (1974). The TEA set: Tacit knowledge and scientific networks. *Science Studies*, **4**: 165–86.

Davenport, T.H. and Prusak, L. (1998). *Working Knowledge. How Organizations Manage what they Know*. Boston, MA: Harvard Business School Press.

Garud, R. (1997). On the distinction between know-how, know-what and know-why. *Les Cahiers du Management Technologique*, January–April:5–30

Gourlay, S.N. (2004), Knowing as semiosis: Steps towards a reconceptualiztion of 'tacit knowledge'. In Tsoukas, H. and Mylonopoulos, N. (eds). *Organizations as Knowledge Systems*. London: Palgrare Macmillan, pp. 86–105.

Hampden-Turner, C. (1990). *Charting the Corporate Mind: From Dilemma to Strategy*. Oxford: Blackwell Publishers.

Haugaard, M. (1997). *The Constitution of Power. A Theoretical Analysis of Power, Knowledge and Structure*. Manchester: Manchester University Press.

Jensen, S. Siggaard (2001). *De digitale delegater – tekst og tanke i netuddannelse*. Copenhagen: Multivers.

Jensen, S. Siggaard and Mønsted, M. (2001). Tidsparadokser og ledelsesdilemmaer i IT projekter. In Poulfelt, F. and Mønsted, M. (eds). *Det er et spørgsmål om tid*. Copenhagen: Samfundslitteratur CD-ROM publication.

Jensen, S. Siggaard, Mønsted, M. and Olsen, S. Fejfer (2004). *Viden, Ledelse og Kommunikation*. Copenhagen: Samfunds litteratur.

Kidder, Tracy (1981). *The Soul of a New Machine*. New York: Avon.

Kogut, Bruce and Zander, U. (1996). What Firms Do? Coordination, Identity, and Learning. *Organization Science*, **7**(5): 502–18.

Latour, B. and Wolgar, S. (1979). *Laboratory Life. The Social Construction of Scientific Facts*. Los Angeles, CA: Sage.

Mønsted, M. (2003). *Strategic Networking for Small High-Tech Firms*. Copenhagen: Samfundslitteratur.

Newell, Sue, Robertson, M., Scarbrough, H. and Swan, Jacky (2002). *Managing Knowledge Management*. New York: Palgrave.

Newell, S. and Swan, J. (2000). Trust and inter-organizational networking. *Human Relations*. **53**(10): 1287–328.
Nonaka, I. and Takeuchi, H. (1995). *The Knowledge Creating Company. How Japanese Companies Create the Dynamics of Innovation*. Oxford: Oxford University Press.
Normann, R. (2000). *Service management: Strategy and Leadership in Service Business*. Chichester: John Wiley.
Stacey, Ralph, D. (2001). *Complex Responsive Processes in Organizations. Learning and Knowledge Creation*. London: Routledge.
Star, Susan, L. (1989). The structure of ill-structured solutions: Boundary objects and heterogeneous distributed problem solving. In Gasser, L. and Huhns, M.N. (eds). *Distributed Artificial Intelligence,* Vol. II. London: Pitman, pp. 37–54.
Staudt, Hubert (1997). Initiating corporate renewal: A study of the process of fundamental innovation development. Copenhagen: Copenhagen Business School, PhD dissertation.
Tsoukas, H. (1996). The firm as a distributed knowledge system: A constructionist approach. *Strategic Management Journal*, **17**(9): 11–25.
Weick, Karl, E. (1995). *Sensemaking in Organizations*. Thousand Oaks, CA: Sage.
Wenger, E. (1998). *Communities of Practice. Learning in Doing. Social, Cognitive, and Computational Perspectives*. Cambridge: Cambridge University Press.
Yukl, Gary (1989). Managerial leadership: A review of theory and research. *Journal of Management*, **15**(2): 251–89.

9. Business angels investing at early stages: are they different?

Nils Månsson and Hans Landström

INTRODUCTION

The establishment of new firms is of vital importance for the development and growth of the economy (Storey, 1994; Freear et al., 1995; Reynolds et al., 2003). Therefore, it is crucial to stimulate the emergence of companies, and in this respect the availability of financial resources is one of many factors that can be of importance for the creation of new firms (Lumme et al., 1998; European Commission, 2002). However, in the seed and start-up phases of company development, financial resources are limited. Factors that may hamper investments in early-stage ventures are the uncertainty inherent in the process, at least in more innovative ventures, and the information asymmetry that may be present in the relationship between the entrepreneur and investor.

Earlier research (Mason and Harrison, 1995; Coveney and Moore, 1998) has shown that while institutionalized capital, such as venture capital funds and banks, has been turning its back on high-risk investments in seed and start-up stages of firm development, informal investors, that is, individuals investing capital in unquoted companies to which the investor has no family connection, have become increasingly important for young firms, and it has been argued that informal venture capital has the ability to fill the 'equity capital gap' in early phases of development (Mason and Harrison, 1992).

When studying the individuals making informal investments in more detail, it has repeatedly been shown that the informal venture capital market is heterogeneous (Mason and Harrison, 1992; Landström, 1993). To be able to cope with this some attempts have been made to divide this group of investors into different subgroups in order to find common characteristics (for example Gaston, 1989; Freear et al., 1994; Kelly and Hay, 1996; Sullivan and Miller, 1996; Coveney and Moore, 1998; Sørheim and Landström, 2001; Avdeitchikova, 2005). Sørheim and Landström's (2001) and Avdeitchikova's (2005) models are similar to each other in dividing the informal investors' market into four categories of investors depending on their degree of investment activity and investor involvement. Based on these two studies, the four types of informal investors are 'traders', 'micro-investors', 'mentors' and 'business angels'. In this chapter we will focus on one particular group of informal investors, namely the 'business angels', that is, investors who repeatedly make informal investments and, apart from being active from a financial point of view, also contribute to the management of the company in which they have invested. However, even within the category of business angels we find a high degree of heterogeneity among investors. This heterogeneity has made it difficult to analyse the business angel community and it has hence been argued that more research is required to identify angel typologies, as well as research focusing on specific types of investors (Mason and Harrison, 2000). The high degree of heterogeneity among business angels does, however, according to Mason and Harrison (2000), mean that studies attempting to identify typologies are in need of large and unbiased samples in order to succeed.

The creation of business angel typologies is thus desirable from a theoretical perspective and, as this study is based on a database that is both relatively large and relatively unbiased, it is likely that it will be possible to distinguish between different types of business angels.

In addition, it is known that business angels tend to invest in industries and technologies in which they have experience (MacDonald, 1991), and business angels' backgrounds can hence be said to influence their investment preferences. On the one hand, this implies that business angels would primarily be interested in well-tried technologies and existing industries, and not in innovations and changes in industrial structures. However, on the other hand, as many investors have an entrepreneurial background (Mason et al., 1991; Harrison and Mason, 1992; Landström, 1997; Lumme et al., 1998; Brettel, 2003), the entrepreneurial process in itself may be regarded by some business angels as their key area of competence. Thus, it may be appropriate to differentiate between business angels who prefer early-stage investments, as they believe that knowledge of the entrepreneurial process is most important, and business angels who prefer to invest at later stages, as they believe, for instance, personal experience of the industry or technology in question to be most important.

Due to the importance of stimulating new firms in an economy, and the equity capital gap that we can identify in the early stages of many firms' development, it would be of crucial importance to be able to identify the business angels who preferably invest in companies at early stages. In other words, if there are stage preferences among investors it would be useful from a theoretical as well as a policy-making perspective to know whether the two groups differ, and if it is possible to identify early-stage investors and discriminate them from late-stage investors.

In light of the usefulness of the ability to discriminate between early- and late-stage business angels, and the possibility offered by a large and relatively unbiased sample, the aim of this study is to analyse differences and similarities between early- and late-stage investors regarding their expectations and background.

The chapter begins with a frame of reference in which informal venture capital and business angels are described. The development of hypotheses is followed by a methodological discussion and presentation of the empirical results. Finally, the conclusions of the study are presented.

FRAME OF REFERENCE

Mason and Harrison (2000) have reviewed the research within the field of informal venture capital and business angels, and divided the research into first- and second-generation studies.

First-Generation Studies

Seminal work by Wetzel initiated the focus on business angels in the early 1980s (Wetzel, 1981, 1983). Since then, we have seen the diffusion of research into a number of countries around the world, among them Canada (Riding et al., 1993), the UK (Harrison and Mason, 1992; Coveney and Moore, 1998), Sweden (Landström, 1993), Finland (Lumme et al., 1998), Australia (Hindle and Wenban, 1999), Singapore (Hindle and Lee, 2002), the Netherlands (K+V organisatie adviesbureau bv, 1996), Japan (Tashiro, 1999) and Norway (Reitan and Sørheim, 2000). Thus, research on informal investors is rather young, and in order to get a picture of it the market researchers have considered it important to quantify and describe the business angel market. This means that a large proportion of the literature discusses matters such as the size of the market, investor characteristics, decision processes, information channels and the initiatives intended to stimulate the informal venture capital market.

Comparing demographical data from first-generation studies in the search for differences and similarities between different countries can be misleading for several reasons: (1) different sampling methods and different questions are used in different studies; (2) confusion between the definitions of business angels and informal venture capital may lead to incorrect conclusions; (3) studies have been carried out over different time periods during which significant changes have taken place in the macro-environment; and (4) business angels are a heterogeneous group and comparisons based on average values may not give a complete picture of the market.

Despite the above-mentioned difficulties in comparing different studies, some characteristics recur frequently. Earlier research has, for instance, shown that business angels are predominantly male and that they are middle-aged. The average business angel, furthermore, shows entrepreneurial experience as the majority of them have started at least one company. The business angels' informal network is of importance when identifying new investment opportunities, and information on new investment opportunities is often provided by business associates and friends. However, contacting entrepreneurs also seems to be becoming increasingly important, as seen in later studies. Business angels, furthermore, prefer to invest in relatively close proximity to their home.

First-generation studies have, however, also revealed significant differences between the business angels' market in different countries. Business angels usually play an active role in the management of the companies in which they have invested, but in the cases of Norway and the UK business angels are often passive in their ownership. A high degree of syndication can explain why business angels remain passive, as not all of the investors involved have to be active, but the degree of business angel passivity in the UK is further enhanced by the fact that the UK market is the only market in which less than half of the investors have experience of making syndicate investments. However, if business angels are active, it seems to be a general characteristic that they become involved in companies through taking a position on the board of directors or by functioning as a consultant. Another difference is that Japanese and, to some extent, American investors more often take the majority of votes when investing in a company, whereas business angels in other countries usually take a minority share of stocks. Other differences that can be observed are that Swedish business angels show little interest in early stages, while German and American investors, on the other hand, seem to prefer early stages. Furthermore, Japanese and Scandinavian business angels seem to be slightly older than their counterparts in other countries (Gaston, 1989, Mason et al., 1991; Harrison and Mason, 1992; Landström, 1993; Lumme et al., 1998; Reitan and Sørheim, 2000; Vaekstfonden, 2002; Hindle and Lee, 2002; Brettel, 2003).

Second-Generation Studies

Second-generation studies show increasing sophistication compared to first-generation studies and can be grouped into three different categories of studies (Masons and Harrison, 2000). The first category is concerned with studies introducing theoretical perspectives. The perspectives examined are related to several aspects of informal investments. The business angels' investment decisions have been studied in the light of decision theory, whereas economic approaches have been used to explain the investors' motives. The second category consists of studies focusing on policy issues, where a large part of research with policy implications has been related to Business Angel Networks (BANs) and the way they can contribute to a more efficient market for informal venture capital. Some research has also been related to government interventions – for instance, tax reforms aimed at making informal investments more attractive. The third group of studies covers some new topics of the informal investment phenomenon such as: (1) the complementarity of formal and informal venture capital; (2) the relationship between investor and entrepreneur; (3) investors' risk return and holding periods; and (4) investment decision-making.

One topic that has emerged in research over the past couple of years is the business angels' decision-making criteria. These criteria are often structured through dividing the screening process into four phases: (1) first impressions; (2) the initial assessment; (3) analysis; and (4) negotiation (Riding et al., 1993; Dal Cin et al., 1995; Riding et al., 1995). Most investment cases are rejected as early as in the first phase, in which the business angel lets his first impressions guide him regarding whether the proposition should be further investigated or rejected (Landström, 1998). The decision is often based on predetermined preferences, which in turn are based on the business angel's previous experience (MacDonald, 1991). This means that business angels to some extent let their own background influence their investment-making decision. The business angels' decision-making process and their demographics are hence interrelated, and literature focusing on the decision-making process is therefore relevant in this study, although the empirical data are primarily related to the business angels' demographics.

Hypothesis Development

A large proportion of business angels have entrepreneurial experience (Harrison and Mason, 1992; Landström, 1993; Landström, 1997), and one of the factors that has been identified as motivating business angels is being able to live their entrepreneurial life over again (Aram, 1989; Sullivan and Miller, 1996; Landström, 1997). Taking this further, it may be assumed that an investor investing at an early stage has a stronger urge to once again experience entrepreneurial processes than a late-stage investor. Since early-stage development must be regarded as more entrepreneurial and later stages more managerial, early-stage investors could be expected to have a more entrepreneurial background. Furthermore, informal investments are high-risk investments and the risk is regarded as being higher at the early stages. One method of managing this risk is through one's own experience from the specific market and the process of entrepreneurship itself (Kelly and Hay, 1996).

The importance of prior experience is also emphasized as business angels regard it to be important to have knowledge and an understanding of the technologies and the industries in which the company is working (MacDonald, 1991). This means that business angels can easily become conservative and prefer well-tried markets and technologies to untested technologies and new markets. However, as indicated by Kelly and Hay (1996), business angels with a high degree of entrepreneurial experience may regard their capacity to adapt to a changing environment of new markets and new technologies to be central, and therefore regard the entrepreneurial process to be their key area of competence. This means that early-stage investors not only ought to have greater experience of starting companies, as suggested in hypothesis 1a below, but also greater experience of fast-moving and entrepreneurial industries building on new technologies in which constant and rapid development is part of the environment, such as IT and telecommunications:

Hypothesis 1a: Early-stage investors have more often started at least one company than late-stage investors.

Hypothesis 1b: Early-stage investors more often have experience of fast-moving industries than late-stage investors.

As an early-stage investment is riskier than a late-stage investment, it is less suitable to place a large proportion of one's personal wealth in early-stage informal investments. Assuming financial rationality among business angels, this means that early-stage investors would have a smaller share of their portfolio in informal investments than late-stage investors, since early-stage investments are often smaller than late-stage investments (Mason and Harrison, 1994). Aram (1989) found some evidence for this reasoning when establishing that investors solely investing in start-ups invested fewer dollars than other investors. This means that it is also probable that early-stage investors have less capital invested in unquoted companies than late-stage investors. An alternative is that the amount invested is the same, but that early-stage investors have more unquoted companies in their portfolio than late-stage investors in order to achieve a larger degree of diversification.

Hypothesis 2a: Early-stage investors invest a smaller share of their portfolio in informal venture capital than late-stage investors.

Hypothesis 2b: Early-stage investors invest smaller amounts of informal venture capital than late-stage investors.

Hypothesis 2c: Early-stage investors have more unquoted companies in their portfolio than late-stage investors.

Since it is almost impossible to conduct systematic due diligence of an early-stage company, early-stage investments must be deemed more risky than late-stage investments (Mason and Harrison, 1992), and as a consequence early-stage investments more often lead to losses (Mason and Harrison, 2000). Hence the compensation for early-stage investments should be higher than for late-stage investments. In practice the risk premium on early-stage investments implies that the same amount invested should render a higher share of stocks in an early-stage investment than in a late-stage investment. Furthermore, business angels have a tendency to manage risk through managerial involvement. Early-stage investors, making risky investments, should strive to obtain a higher proportion of stocks in order to have a stronger controlling power in the company compared to late-stage investors. (Kelly and Hay, 2001; Freear et al., 2002; Mason and Harrison, 2002.)

Hypothesis 3: Early-stage investors take a larger share of stocks than late-stage investors when investing in a company.

Kelly and Hay (2001) give support for the fact assumed in many studies that business angels manage their risk through active involvement in the management of the company in which they have invested. This phenomenon has been explained in terms of agency theory and is associated with the business angel's ambition to avoid the entrepreneur giving way to opportunistic behaviour. It has also been suggested in the literature that early-stage companies have greater needs of additional management skills, leading to the assumption that early-stage investors are more involved in the companies they have invested in than are late-stage investors.

Hypothesis 4: Early-stage investors play a more active role in the company they have invested in than late-stage investors.

The market for informal venture capital is imperfect, with considerable information asymmetry. Sellers often have more information than buyers as public information about small unquoted companies is finite, creating a situation in which it is difficult to harvest an investment as potential buyers are deterred from investing due to a lack of information. It is known that early-stage investments more often lead to total loss (Mason and Harrison, 2000), but whether it takes longer to harvest an early-stage investment is not known. It does, however, seem reasonable to assume that early-stage investments require a longer holding period before having gained a sufficiently stable and strong position to sell the company, for instance, to an industrial buyer or to a formal venture capital company.

Hypothesis 5: Early-stage investors expect longer holding periods than late-stage investors.

METHODOLOGY

Sample

Trying to sample a business angel population is a process with inherent difficulties. There are no registers or public records of informal venture capitalists. Since it is expensive to identify sufficient numbers of investors through random selection among the public, Harrison and Mason (1992) suggest three different methods of identifying informal investors: (1) send questionnaires to a large number of individuals believed to be investors; (2) contact investors through the companies they have invested in; and (3) identify investors using the 'snowball' method in which identified investors are asked to identify their peers. Each of these methods has drawbacks that make the samples obtained non-representative and biased in one way or another. Often the method employed in different research projects is chosen for convenience; for example, investors are contacted through different BANs or through snowball methods.

One method of making the sample more representative is to combine several different methods of finding business angels with the hope of offsetting the bias (Sørheim and Landström, 2001). In this study, members of 12 different BANs with different geographical locations and different operational procedures were sent questionnaires. The fact that almost all of the BANs were newly created is an advantage when trying to avoid bias,

Table 9.1 Number of investors divided according to source of identification

Source	Questionnaires sent out		Questionnaires returned		Active informal investors		Respondents analysed	
BANs	547	61%	239	60%	173	62%	135	64%
SPRO register	83	9%	35	9%	11	4%	8	4%
Other sources	264	30%	126	32%	94	34%	69	33%
Total	894		400		278		212	

since the BAN will not yet have had time to affect its members in their investment procedures. The second method of finding investors was through the Swedish Patent and Registration Office's (SPRO) company register in order to search for members of boards whose first names and surnames in combination with 'Investment AB' also make up a company name. Thirdly, investors were identified through companies known to have received venture capital, through articles in newspapers and business magazines, as well as through the snowball method where bankers, entrepreneurs, solicitors and not least business angels themselves have identified informal investors. The number of investors identified from different sources is given in Table 9.1.

Survey Process

In total, 894 questionnaires were sent out during the winter of 2003–2004, 400 of which were returned (45 per cent). Some 122 of the respondents had not yet made any investments or did not want to take part in the study, leaving 278 respondents (31 per cent) who had invested in unquoted companies to which they had no family connection. After having processed the questionnaires in order to find early- and late-stage investors, as described below, 212 or 24 per cent of the respondents remained for further analysis within this study.

The ten-page questionnaire based on earlier studies by Harrison and Mason (1992) and Landström (1993), as well as a study of formal venture capital carried out by the Swedish Business Development Agency (NUTEK) and the Swedish Private Equity and Venture Capital Association (SVCA), consists of 47 questions of different length taking in total about 30 minutes to answer. The questions concern demographical data such as education, age and financial aspects, previous investment history including a section on the most recent investment, and sections regarding investments during the past year as well as preferences regarding future investments.

If the respondent had not answered within three weeks they were sent a new questionnaire and a letter reminder. This procedure was repeated again after a further three weeks if an answer had still not been received. The questionnaire was accompanied by a cover letter from the BAN if the respondent was a member of such an organization.

In order to evaluate the non-response bias, the three groups of respondents answering the first, second or third questionnaire sent to them were compared. The basis for this comparison was that late respondents are expected to show similar characteristics to non-respondents (Armstrong and Overton, 1977). It was found that the proportion of respondents not having made informal investments rose significantly with each reminder sent. It was also found that early respondents invested more often through a privately owned company or through a partly owned company, which can be related to Swedish tax regulations favouring informal investments being made through companies. This means that investors investing through companies ought to be viewed as more structured and professional than those not investing through companies. Other significant differences between early and late respondents also supported the assumption that respondents are more active than non-respondents since early respondents had invested in larger numbers of companies than late respondents. Taken together, this information indicates that more active investors are over-represented in the survey.

Identification of Early- and Late-Stage Investors

Early-stage and late-stage investors were identified by asking whether their most recent investment was made in a company that was in the seed stage, start-up stage, expansion stage, or if it was a buy-out. If the investment was made in a seed or start-up company the investor was categorized as an early-stage investor, if on the other hand the investment was made at the expansion stage or if the investment was a buy-out, the investor was categorized as a late-stage investor. In total 112 early-stage investors were identified and 100 late-stage investors. The large proportion of early-stage investors was surprising, as the Swedish business angel market has previously been characterized by a high degree of late-stage investments (Landström, 1993).

In order to verify that the most recent investment constituted an appropriate variable for categorizing investors into early- and late-stage investors, it was compared with stage preferences for future investments. It was found that early-stage investors were significantly more willing to invest at early stages than were late-stage investors ($p = 0.002$ Seed, $p = 0.000$ Start-up).

Late-stage investors are also significantly more likely than early-stage investors to make future investments in expansion-stage companies ($p = 0.000$) while the greater preference for future buy-outs was not significant ($p = 0.365$). In spite of this, buy-out investors have been characterized as late-stage investors since it can be argued that companies that are acquired through buy-outs have reached later stages. Furthermore, when testing what would happen if buy-out investors were excluded from the group of late-stage investors, an analysis showed that no significant differences were found when they were included. The trait of early-stage investors being positively inclined towards continuing to invest in early stages has also been established by Aram (1989). The statistical analysis software SPSS was used to analyse the collected data, mainly for chi-squared tests to test the significance of the difference between early- and late-stage investors.

Strengths and Weaknesses of the Study

Compared with earlier research, this study has three methodological aspects in its favour. The sample is a mixture of different sub-samples originating from different contexts, meaning a less biased sample, although the sample still cannot be regarded as strictly representative of the population. The sample is large compared with many other studies (Sørheim and Landström, 2001), and the response rate is quite good since most studies achieve an unprocessed response rate of about 20 per cent, mainly due to the fact that informal investors tend to value their privacy (Mason and Harrison, 2000).

Although the sample in this study is probably less biased than other samples, it is difficult to tell in what way the present sample is biased. It is probably not representative from a geographical point of view since most BANs used to sample the population are found in more densely populated areas rather than in rural areas. It is also probable, although not known, that high net income individuals are over-represented since they are more likely to appear in newspapers and magazines.

EMPIRICAL RESULTS

The Business Angel Market in Sweden

Small firms in Sweden have shown that they are reluctant to accept external equity finance as only 3 per cent of small firms receive financing from informal venture capital, and 5 per cent from formal venture capital. Instead, small firms in Sweden rely heavily on bank financing as an external source of funds, and as much as 86 per cent of companies rely primarily on capital received from banks (Landström and Winborg, 1995). This dependency on bank financing, compared with for instance small firms in the USA, is probably related to the fact that the two countries' financial systems are based on different traditions. The Swedish system is a credit-based financial system, in which bank lending holds a central position, a system also employed in continental European countries such as Germany, Austria and France, whereas the USA and UK, on the other hand, have a market-based system in which equity finance, through for instance stock exchanges and venture capital, holds a strong position (Gerschenkron, 1962). However, there are reasons to believe that the Swedish financial system is becoming more capital market based and hence more equity oriented (Black and Gilson, 1998).

Although increased attention to informal venture capital investments has attracted new investors, the Swedish business angel can, as in many other countries, still be described as a highly entrepreneurial, middle-aged man, who has started on average 3.5* companies. This, and the fact that the results also reveal that a large share, or 52 per cent, of business angels have made their wealth through selling a company, supports Politis and Landström's (2002) conclusion that making informal investments is part of an entrepreneurial journey.

In addition, results show that Swedish business angels have invested a median of 2 million SEK in an average of 4.1* portfolio companies. From an historical perspective, the portfolio has been built up through repetitive investments, and during the previous five years the average business angel has invested in 4.7* companies. As a high proportion of these investments consists of syndicate investments, in which more than one investor is participating (77 per cent), syndication partly explains why as many as 51 per cent of the investments being made result in less than 10 per cent ownership, and that as many as 24 per cent of business angels are passive in their most recent investment. However, with 30 per cent of business angels becoming involved as chairman of the board and 33 per cent as a member of the board, they generally play an active role in the management of companies in which they have invested. These roles are furthermore often combined with help given in the capacity of a consultant or as a mentor. However, despite the fact that active involvement in the portfolio companies has been seen as a way of reducing investment risk, making informal investments is a high-risk venture in which the amount invested is expected to be tied up for an average of 5.6 years, and it is therefore understandable that business angels only invest 12 per cent of their fortunes in informal investments.

Test of Hypotheses Stated

In hypothesis 1a it was suggested that early-stage investors have a more entrepreneurial background than late-stage investors. The results show that, just as expected, early-stage investors have, to a higher degree than late-stage investors, started at least one company (see Table 9.2). The difference is significant ($p = 0.019$) but at the same time it must be observed that in both groups the vast majority had started companies: 95 per cent of early-stage investors and 85 per cent of late-stage investors.

Another dimension when investigating to what extent investors have started companies is to study how many companies they have started. It was found that late-stage investors had started on average 3.4 companies, while early-stage investors had started 3.7 companies, showing signs that early-stage investors do start more companies than late-stage investors, but the difference was not significant ($p = 0.419$).

In hypothesis 1b it was stated that early-stage investors have experience of fast-moving industries, such as telecoms and electronics, to a greater extent than late-stage investors. Many respondents had experience of several different industries (see Table 9.3). This makes it difficult to identify any major differences between the two groups when comparing their industrial background. The only significant difference found is within telecoms and electronics, where early-stage investors are more experienced, 30 per cent, than late-stage investors, 18 per cent ($p = 0.037$). However, industries such as computer and biotechnology showed no significant differences between the investor groups. As other differences for other industries were not significant, the observed differences for telecoms and electronics only partly support the hypothesis that early-stage investors have more experience in fast-moving, entrepreneurial industries than late-stage investors.

Regarding the overall results of entrepreneurial experience, early-stage investors have experience of starting at least one company significantly more often than late-stage investors. The observed difference for serial entrepreneurs, that early-stage investors had started more companies, was however not significant. Concerning previous industrial experience, early-stage investors more frequently have experience of telecommunications and electronics, rendering only partial support for the hypothesis that early-stage investors have a more entrepreneurial industrial background than late-stage investors.

Whether early-stage investors have less capital invested in informal venture capital investments than late-stage investors is a question that can be investigated in both relative and absolute terms. Starting with relative terms, it is stated in hypothesis 2a that early-stage investors have a smaller proportion of their wealth invested in informal venture capital

Table 9.2 Entrepreneurial experience

	Early-stage investors		Late-stage investors	
Have started at least one company	106	95%	85	85%
Have not started a company	6	5%	15	15%
Total	112		100	

Note: Chi-squared = 5.504, $p = 0.019$.

Table 9.3 Industrial background

	Early-stage investors	Late-stage investors	Significance (p)
Telecom and electronics	30%	18%	0.037
Computers and IT	33%	36%	0.652
Biotech and pharmaceuticals	17%	18%	0.844
Industrial production	46%	42%	0.607
Financial services	27%	30%	0.606
Consumer goods and retail business	24%	21%	0.592
Other industries	54%	58%	0.607

Note: Number of respondents: Early-stage investors n = 112; Late-stage investors n = 112.

than late-stage investors. Results show that early-stage investors place 10 per cent of their wealth in to informal investments, while late-stage investors place a slighter higher proportion (13 per cent) of their investments in informal investments. However, the difference is not significant ($p = 0.458$).

In absolute terms it is stated in hypothesis 2b that early-stage investors invest smaller amounts of informal venture capital than late-stage investors. The investors were asked to state the amount they had invested in unquoted companies to which they lack family connections. Since a few investors had invested very large amounts they would influence any comparison of the average amount invested for early- and late-stage investors. Hence the amounts of money invested have been divided into six different intervals (see Table 9.4). The results reveal that, although early-stage investors have small amounts invested (up to 0.5 million SEK) to a greater degree than late-stage investors, the two groups of investors cannot be significantly separated from each other ($p = 0.611$), nor can the medians be used to differentiate the groups since both groups stated that they had

Table 9.4 Capital invested in unquoted companies

	Early-stage investors		Late-stage investors	
Up to 0.5 million SEK	29	28%	20	22%
0.5–1 million SEK	10	10%	13	14%
1–2 million SEK	17	17%	15	16%
2–5 million SEK	22	21%	22	24%
5–10 million SEK	12	12%	6	7%
Over 10 million SEK	13	13%	15	16%
Total	103	100%	100	100%

Note: Chi-squared = 3.584, $p = 0.611$.

invested 2 million SEK in informal investments. This means that late-stage investors do not invest more informal venture capital in absolute or in relative terms.

When testing hypothesis 2c which states that early-stage investors have more unquoted companies in their portfolio than late-stage investors, it was found that early-stage investors had 4 unquoted companies in their portfolio and late-stage investors 4.2. The difference is not significant ($p = 0.696$), but as early-stage investors have a smaller portfolio than late-stage investors this indicates that the opposite may be true to what was believed in the hypothesis.

To summarize the results regarding the amounts invested and diversification of the investors' portfolios, early- and late-stage investors not only invest roughly the same amounts in terms of their private wealth, but they also invest the same amounts in absolute terms. As early-stage investments are of higher risk than late-stage investments, and early-stage investors do not diversify to a greater extent than late-stage investors, early-stage investors must be deemed to be less averse to risk than late-stage investors, unless early-stage investors are compensated for their higher risk or can reduce their risk level in some other way.

Hypothesis 3 states that early-stage investors take a larger share of the stocks than late-stage investors when investing in a company. A comparison of the two groups of investors, with regard to the share taken, shows that early-stage investors more often take a larger share than late-stage investors (see Table 9.5). However, the difference between the two groups is not significant ($p = 0.434$) and the hypothesis has not been proven.

It was stated in hypothesis 4 that early-stage investors are more active in the management of their investments in order to offset the higher risk taken. As shown in Table 9.6, early-stage investors are passive investors in

Table 9.5 Share taken in the company invested in

	Early-stage investors		Late-stage investors	
Only debt capital	6	5%	5	5%
Less than 11%	51	46%	56	60%
11–25%	24	22%	15	16%
26–50%	20	18%	13	14%
More than 50%	9	8%	5	5%
Total	110	100%	94	100%

Note: Chi-squared = 3.798, $p = 0.434$.

Table 9.6 Role taken in invested company

	Early-stage investors	Late-stage investors	Significance (p)
CEO	4%	5%	0.885
Employed in management position	4%	3%	0.817
Chairman of the board	30%	29%	0.830
Member of the board	37%	28%	0.183
Active as consultant	25%	18%	0.219
Passive ownership	16%	32%	0.006

Note: Number of respondents: Early-stage investors n = 112; Late-stage investors n = 112.

16 per cent of cases compared with 32 per cent for late-stage investors, a significant difference ($p = 0.006$). However, as far as the different active roles played by the two groups are concerned, the differences are not significant, but early-stage investors show strong signs of being more active as they are active to larger extent as members of the board (37 per cent vs. 28 per cent, $p = 0.183$) and as consultants (25 per cent vs. 18 per cent, $p = 0.219$). Taking active and passive roles together, early-stage investors seem to be somewhat more active than late-stage investors.

Although not directly upholding the hypothesis, there are also other variables that can be used to analyse whether late-stage investors are less active than early-stage investors. Late-stage investors more often invest as part of a syndicate than early-stage investors (83 per cent vs. 72 per cent, $p = 0.074$), and as it is often the case that not all investors in a syndicate are active, this indicates that early-stage investors are more active in the management of portfolio companies than late-stage investors. Although not significant, the larger degree of syndication of late-stage investors hence partly explains why late-stage investors are more passive than early-stage investors. Early-stage investors also show significantly greater preference ($p = 0.033$) for making investments closer to home than late-stage investors, as 64 per cent of early-stage investors prefer to invest within 300 kilometres of their home, while the equivalent figure for late-stage investors is 38 per cent. As the investors who do not prefer to invest within 300 kilometres regard distance as unimportant, this indicates that early-stage investors prefer to be in closer contact with the companies they invest in.

To summarize the test of hypotheses 3 and 4, early-stage investors seem to take a larger proportion of shares in the companies they have invested in, but the difference is not significant. Early-stage investors are, however, less passive. The greater activity among early-stage investors may be an attempt to reduce the overall risk in the early-stage investors' portfolios, but at the same time it can be argued that early-stage investors should be rewarded for the extra time devoted to the company; however, as the difference in share taken was insignificant it is not possible to argue that this is the case.

Hypothesis 5 states that investors investing at early stages believe their investments to be tied for a longer time, but the difference is not significant ($p = 0.216$), with early-stage investors on average expecting a holding time of 6 years and late-stage investors expecting on average a holding time of 5.1 years. It is important to bear in mind that an experienced business angel will know that some companies invested in will go bankrupt, and that this is more likely in the case of early investments (Mason and Harrison, 2002). After being engaged in a company for a while, the business angel may expect a shorter holding period due to an unavoidable and foreseeable future bankruptcy. In this study, for instance, after an average of about one year from investment, 13 per cent of early-stage investments and 9 per cent of late-stage investment companies had already gone bankrupt.

CONCLUSIONS

In an attempt to go beyond what Mason and Harrison (2002) called the first-generation studies, and to establish a typology of business angels, the aim of this chapter was to study business angels who prefer to invest at early and late stages. We have succeeded in showing that business angels making early-stage investments will also continue to invest at early stages to a large extent, while late-stage investors, on the other hand, will probably continue to invest at late stages, that is, the categories of business angels seem to be stable over time. Although a theoretically valid typology has been established, as called for, for instance, by Mason and Harrison (2000), it was interesting to find that the differences between the two categories were less than we expected. This can probably be explained by business angels being a heterogeneous group of investors demanding a database even larger than the one available in order to find statistically significant differences through offsetting the effect of heterogeneity. However, we have found some interesting results when comparing the two groups of investors:

- Early-stage investors have, as expected, proven to be more entrepreneurial as they have started at least one company significantly more often than late-stage investors, and early-stage investors also show signs of more often being serial entrepreneurs. Early-stage investors also have previous experience of the fast-moving telecom and electronics industry to a larger extent than late-stage investors.
- As early-stage investments must be regarded as more high-risk than late-stage investments it was expected that early-stage investors would be more cautious in their investments and invest smaller amounts as well as diversifying to a greater extent. However, early-stage investors do not invest a significantly smaller proportion of their wealth in informal investments, and both groups of investors seem to invest roughly the same amounts. As early-stage investors do not diversify to a greater extent than late-stage investors, this means that early-stage investors take greater risks than late-stage investors, and they may therefore be less averse to risk than late-stage investors. In addition, there is no significant difference in the amount of stocks taken by early- and late-stage investors.
- Early-stage investors are less passive in the management of a company in which they have invested than late-stage investors, and early-stage investors also show several signs of being more active than late-stage investors. Early-stage investors, furthermore, prefer to invest closer to home than do late-stage investors.

Having established that both groups invest about the same amounts in about the same number of companies, it was unexpected to find that early-stage investors only showed signs of taking a larger share of the company than late-stage investors. Either early-stage investors are less averse to risk than late-stage investors, or the results should be interpreted as showing that the risk premium for investing at early and late stages is assessed by the investors to be about the same. The latter would be surprising since it is often assumed that early-stage investments are more high-risk than late-stage investments, but it may be that early-stage investors are able to compensate in some way for the greater risk taken. One way of doing this, which was observed, may be through being less passive than late-stage investors, thus reducing the risk through active involvement in the company invested in, that is, the lack of management involvement by late-stage investors may make late-stage investments as risky as early-stage investments. A higher degree of involvement ought to lead to greater compensation for the extra effort; however, it could not be proven that early-stage investors take a greater amount of shares than late-stage investors. This leads us to the conclusion that early-stage investors either reduce their risk through other measures than the ones observed in this study, for instance making greater use of resources in their personal networks, or they are less averse to risk. It could, however, also be that early-stage investors are compensated for their extra effort in some other way, for instance through the satisfaction derived from investing at early stages. If this is the case, it would probably be possible to find differences in the motives of the two groups. It may, for instance, be that early-stage investors are driven by the possibility of being part of an entrepreneurial journey to a greater extent than late-stage investors.

The primary theoretical contribution of this study has been to establish that there are two distinct groups of business angels: early- and late-stage investors. Empirical differences have been observed, such as early-stage investors being more entrepreneurial as well as less passive than late-stage investors. However, unexpected similarities also indicated differences in the two groups' perception of risk. It may be that there are differences in their motives for making investments in unquoted companies, but it may also be that there are differences in the groups' ways of handling risk, for instance the way in which business angels in the two groups use their personal networks in the investment process in order to reduce the risk. Both reasons, however, speak for future use of in-depth studies in order to clarify what drives business angels to prefer early-stage investments.

From the results of this study we can draw the conclusion that in order to support young ventures business angels, primarily interested in early-stage companies, should primarily be sought among entrepreneurs within new and fast-moving industries such as telecommunications and electronics. Furthermore, business angel networks trying to attract early-stage investors should have a local perspective rather than a national perspective in order to enable investors to take an active part in the management of portfolio companies.

ACKNOWLEDGEMENTS

The present research project was made possible by, and financed through, the Swedish Business Development Agency (NUTEK) and the Swedish Foundation for Small-Business Research (FSF).

NOTE

* Extreme values have been neglected.

REFERENCES

Aram, J.D. (1989). Attitudes and behaviours of informal investors toward early-stage investments, technology-based ventures, and co-investors. *Journal of Business Venturing*, **4**(5): 333–47.

Armstrong, J.S. and Overton, T.S. (1977). Estimating nonresponse bias in mail surveys. *Journal of Marketing Research*, **14**(3): 396–402.

Avdeitchikova, S. (2005). Typologies of informal venture capital investors in Sweden. Paper presented at the 50th World Conference of ICSB, Washington, DC.

Black, B.S. and Gilson, B. (1998). Venture capital and the structure of capital markets: Bank versus stock market. *Journal of Financial Economics*, **47**: 243–77.

Brettel, M. (2003). Business angels in Germany: A research note. *Venture Capital*, **5**: 251–68.

Coveney, P. and Moore, K. (1998). *Business Angels*. Somerset: Wiley.

Dal Cin, P., Haines, P. and Riding, A. (1995). Financing enterprise development: Factors in the decision-making process employed by Canadian angels. Working Paper, School of Business, Carleton University, Canada.

European Commission (2002). *Benchmarking Business Angels*. Enterprise Directorate-General, Brussels: European Commission.

Freear, J., Sohl, J.E. and Wetzel, W.E. (1994). Angels and non-angels: Are there differences? *Journal of Business Venturing*, **9**: 109–23.

Freear, J., Sohl, J.E. and Wetzel, W.E. (1995). Angels: Personal investors in the venture capital market. *Entrepreneurship and Regional Development*, **7**: 85–94.

Freear, J., Sohl, J.E. and Wetzel, W.E. (2002). Angels on angels: Financing technology-based ventures – a historical perspective. *Venture Capital*, **7**(4): 275–87.

Gaston, R.J. (1989). *Finding Private Venture Capital for Your Firm: A Complete Guide.* New York: Wiley.

Gerschenkron, A. (1962). *Economic Backwardness in Historical Perspective*. Cambridge, MA: Harvard University Press.

Harrison, R. and Mason, C. (1992). International perspectives on the supply of informal venture capital. *Journal of Business Venturing*, **7**: 459–75.

Hindle, K. and Lee, L. (2002). An exploratory investigation of informal venture capitalists in Singapore. *Venture Capital*, **4**(2): 169–81.

Hindle, K. and Wenban, R. (1999). Australia's informal venture capitalists: An exploratory profile. *Venture Capital*, **1**: 169–89.

K+V organisatie adviesbureau bv (1996). *The Role of Informal Investors in the Dutch Venture Capital Market*. Arnhem: K+V organisatie adviesbureau bv.

Kelly, P. and Hay, M. (1996). Serial investors: An exploratory study. Paper presented at the Babson Entrepreneurship Research Conference, Seattle Washington.

Kelly, P. and Hay, M. (2001). Serial investors: An exploratory study. *Frontiers of Entrepreneurship Research 2001*. Wellesley, MA: Babson College.

Landström, H. (1993). Informal risk capital in Sweden and some international comparisons. *Journal of Business Venturing*, **8**: 525–40.

Landström, H. (1997). Synen på affärsmöjligheter – informella riskkapitalisters beslutskriterier i samband med bedömningen av nya investeringsförslag. SIRE – Working Paper 1997:3, Halmstad, Sweden.

Landström, H. (1998). Informal investors as entrepreneurs. *Technovation*, **18**(5): 321–32.

Landström, H. and Winborg, J. (1995). Small business managers' attitudes towards and use of financial sources. *Frontiers of Entrepreneurship Research 2001*. Wellesley, MA: Babson College.

Lumme, A., Mason, C. and Suomi, M. (1998). *Informal Venture Capital: Investors, Investment and Policy in Finland*. Dordrescht: Kluwer Academic.

MacDonald, M. (1991). *Creating Threshold Technology Companies in Canada: The Tool for Venture Capital*. Ottawa, Canada: Science Council of Canada.

Mason, C. and Harrison, R. (1992). The supply of equity finance in the UK: A strategy for closing the equity gap. *Entrepreneurship and Regional Development*, **4**: 357–80.

Mason, C. and Harrison, R. (1994). The role of informal and formal sources of venture capital in the financing of technology-based SMEs in the United Kingdom. In Oakey, R. (ed.). *New Technology-Based Firms in the 1990s*. London: Paul Chapman Publishing, pp. 104–24.

Mason, C. and Harrison, R. (1995). Closing the regional equity capital gap: The role of informal venture capital. *Small Business Economics*, **7**: 153–72.

Mason, C. and Harrison, R. (2000). Informal venture capital and the financing of emergent growth businesses, In Sexton, D. and Landström, H. (eds), *Handbook of Entrepreneurship*. Oxford: Blackwell, pp. 221–39.

Mason, C. and Harrison, R. (2002). Is it worth it? The rates of return from informal venture capital investments. *Journal of Business Venturing*, **17**: 211–36.

Mason, C., Harrison, R. and Chaloner, J. (1991). Informal risk capital in the UK: A study of investor characteristics, investment preferences and investment decision making. Venture Finance Research Project, Working Paper No. 2, University of Southampton, and University of Ulster at Jordanstown.

Politis, D. and Landström, H. (2002). Informal investors as entrepreneurs: The development of an entrepreneurial career. *Venture Capital*, **4**: 78–101.

Reitan, B. and Sørheim, R. (2000). The informal venture capital market in Norway: Investor characteristics, behaviour and preferences. *Venture Capital*, **2**: 129–41.

Reynolds, P.D., Bygrave, W.D. and Erkko, A. (2003). *Global Entrepreneurship Report: Executive Report 2003*. London and Wellesley, MA: London Business School and Babson College.

Riding, A., Dal Cin, P., Duxbury, L., Haines, G. and Safrata, R. (1993). Informal

investors in Canada: Identification of silent characteristics. Working paper Carlton University, Ottawa, Canada.
Riding, A., Duxbury, L. and Haines, G. (1995). Financing enterprise development: decision-making by Canadian angels. Working Paper, Carlton University, Ottawa, Canada.
Sørheim, R. and Landström, H. (2001). Informal investors: A categorization, with policy implications, *Entrepreneurship and Regional Development*, **13**: 351–70.
Storey, D. (1994). *Understanding the Small Business Sector.* London: Routledge.
Sullivan, M.K. and Miller, A. (1996). Segmenting the informal venture capital market: Economic, hedonistic, and altruistic investors. *Journal of Business Research*, **36**: 25–35.
Tashiro, Y. (1999). Business angels in Japan. *Venture Capital*, **1**: 259–74.
Vaekstfonden (2002). Business Angels i Danmark. Copenhagen.
Wetzel, W. (1981). Informal risk capital in New England. In Vesper, K.H. (ed.). *Frontiers of Entrepreneurship Research.* Wellesley, MA: Babson College.
Wetzel, W. (1983). Angels and informal risk capital, *Sloan Management Review*, **24**: 23–34.

10. Internationalization of new ventures: mediating role of entrepreneur and top management team experience*

Johanna Pulkkinen

INTRODUCTION

The interest for this study has emerged from the increasing references made in reseach to the firms that internationalize very soon after establishment and consequently, from their emphasis on the importance of understanding these firms' behaviour. These firms have been termed for example 'international new ventures', 'born globals', 'global start-ups' and 'infant multinationals'. In many studies, the high-technology character of the phenomenon has been stressed, as reflected by the concepts such as high-technology start-ups. In this chapter no industrial-wise limitations are made and the term 'international new venture' (INV) is adopted. In many studies of INV phenomenon, criticism is raised against the traditional internationalization theories (such as stage models). The research conducted so far points out that an increasing amount of firms do not internationalize according to the stages and that the time lag between firm foundation and internationalization has diminished. Existing theories of internationalization have been claimed to fail in explaining these firms not only because they assume a slow gradual development of firms and thus emphasize larger mature firms, but also because they focus too much on the firm level, ignoring the individual level (McDougall et al., 1994). In these theories the focus of studying the role of experience has often been on the firm-level experience, researching the firm's previous experience and development of internationalization (for example subsequent entry mode choice), especially among manufacturing firms but also among service firms (for example Erramilli, 1991). At the same time the time lag between internationalization and previous international exposure of the entrepreneur and management of the firm has been rather ignored (see the discussion by Wickramasekera and Bamberry, 2001 and their emphasis on the length of the learning process by management). The so-called Uppsala model of firm internationalization (Johanson and Wiedersheim-Paul, 1975; Johanson and Vahlne, 1977) emphasizes experiential learning but it has been criticized for the fact that it does not specify whose experience is being focused on (Oviatt and McDougall, 1997).

However, the INV as a firm typically goes international before having gained (firm-level) business experience even in the domestic market. Due to their small size they often also lack financial resources to acquire external professional advice on international entry. In this respect, the experience perceived as a characteristic of the entrepreneur and top management team (TMT) of firms, not as a characteristic of the firm, could be of importance. The experience as such might not explain the speed of internationalization, but through capabilities based on experience the mediating factors such as commitment and implementation of needed strategies to internationalize successfully might be more rapidly put into use. As expressed by Reid (1981), the individual characteristics such as foreign nationality, language skills, extent of foreign travelling, and education seem to be associated (as antecedents) with the decision-maker's existing stock of knowledge, his or her attitudes, and effective preferences concerning export marketing. Consequently, in this chapter experience is perceived as a characteristic of the entrepreneur and management team of firms (see for example Reuber and Fischer, 1997), not as a characteristic of firms as viewed in some key early studies on internationalization (for example Johanson and Vahlne, 1977).

The aim of the chapter is to research the link between the international experience of the entrepreneur and the TMT and the internationalization of new ventures. The experience is approached as a possible mediator of INV development through influence on specific decisions and use of strategies that might explain these firms' development. From the possible strategies, the strategy followed by the new venture is expected to be filtered and largely selected by the decision-makers' experience. Finally, the experience is expected to be related to the degree of internationalization through the impact on the time lag of international entry and strategic decisions regarding entry modes and markets and their geographical breadth. The theoretical base of the chapter is built by combining approaches in international business, management and entrepreneurship fields, with special focus on SME research as INVs are here regarded as a special type of SMEs.

The chapter is structured into six main sections. After defining the key concepts of the study, I present previous literature followed by identification of the research gap and presentation of the hypotheses for the empirical study. The methodology is discussed in the next section, followed by the findings of the empirical study. The chapter finishes with a discussion of the findings and suggestions for the next steps in research. This chapter covers work in progress, presenting the first part of the intended full study. The contribution of the final study will be that it will link together the international experience and new venture internationalization by bridging together individual-level experience, the expertise acquired though experience, and consequences of internationalization decisions.

KEY CONCEPTS

In this study INVs are referred to as firms that have been confronted with fast internationalization soon after establishment. The concept of internationalization has many definitions, but in general it can be regarded as a process through which the firm's international level of operations increases. This increase may be identified in both the inward and the outward operations of the firm. According to Kutschker et al. (1997), there is no such thing as 'the' internationalization process of the firm, but there exist several parallel processes in different layers of the firm, one of which is at the individual level and others at group or department level, or the whole company. These processes may differ in the speed and duration of change as well as their relevance for the organization. This study attempts to take into account and address these many dimensions of internationalization.

To acknowledge the multidimensionality of internationalization, the definition by Oviatt and McDougall (1994) of international new venture as 'a business organization that, from inception, seeks to derive significant competitive advantage from the use of resources and the sale of outputs in multiple countries' is adopted in this chapter. This definition is also most cited in the literature and can thus be used to support comparability across studies. However, while internationalization refers to both inward and outward operations, the key defining dimension of INVs is in this study regarded to be related to foreign sales. Obtaining foreign sales is likely to be more challenging than for example obtaining foreign inputs, and most of the other international dimensions are somehow associated with the initiation of foreign sales (see Oviatt and McDougall, 1997). The limitation of concentrating on sales operations has been made in the majority of earlier INV studies as well as can be seen from the operational definitions of the INVs (the internationalization of sales has often been named as the minimum criterion). In addition to many names given to these firms, the empirical definitions of INV, however, still differ. The scale of operational definitions is large; criteria are based on for example share of exports, and time lag between establishment and initiation of exports (varying from two to six or even more years). Some researchers also exclusively focus on younger firms, thus including the criterion of timing of establishment (for example Burgel and Murray, 2000; Zahra et al., 2000; Shrader et al., 2000; Moen, 2002). Few definitions include criteria such as international orientation or vision (for example Luostarinen and Gabrielsson, 2002). Examples of different operational definitions are those by Knight in 1997 (establishment after 1976, and share of exports at least 25 per cent), Harveston et al. in 2000 (engaged in foreign activities accounting for 25 per cent of all sales within three years of founding), and Moen in 2002 (establishment after 1990 and share of exports at least 25 per cent). The more definite operational definition of this study is presented in the methodology section.

Two meanings could be given for the term 'experience': (1) 'direct observation of or participation in events: an encountering, undergoing, or living through things'; and (2) 'knowledge, skill or practice derived from direct observation of or participation in events: practical wisdom resulting from what one has encountered, undergone or lived through' (Gove, 1981, p. 800 in Reuber et al., 1990). While experience may be of both kinds, as in the second meaning the relevant experience is regarded as 'experiential expertise' (Reuber, 1997) that has been gained through participation in events. With events, this study specifically relates to those in the international context. The expertise (knowledge and skills) may be of various kinds, but in this context the most relevant is that related to foreign markets and internationalization of business operations. When researching the link between experience and new venture internationalization, of special interest here is the international experience that the managers have gained before managing the new venture or during the venture's domestic period. This experience may derive from earlier business assignments at the international level, studying abroad, or from other experience abroad. The experience may vary in duration as well as in regional breadth, and in the case of business experience it may be from a similar or different industry (see Siegel et al., 1993) and vary in terms of functional breadth.

LITERATURE REVIEW AND HYPOTHESES

In this section the previous studies on experience of the decision-makers (manager, founder, owner or TMT) and internationalization are discussed under two sub-sections. As the new venture is here regarded as a special type of SME, the section will first review the research done on the experience–internationalization link in the context of SMEs. After this the focus will be on the research that has been carried out especially in the INV context. Finally, the research gap and hypotheses are presented the third sub-section.

International Experience and SME Internationalization

Dichtl et al. (1990) studied the role of the manager's foreign orientation variables (manager's experience of psychic distance, manager's age, education level, proficiency in foreign languages, travelling, risk-averseness, willingness to change, expectations of overseas job experience on career and family, attitude towards exporting) as a precondition for exporting in industrial SMEs from five different countries (182 exporters vs. 171 non-exporters). The command of foreign languages, vacations spent abroad, longer stays abroad as well as number of previous employers were on average higher among managers of exporting firms (except in Japan the number of previous employers and in South Korea longer stays abroad were slightly higher among non-exporter managers). Even one-third of the non-exporters or occasional exporters had future export potential, but due to deficiencies in the manager's characteristics (low foreign market orientation), did not export. The major problem in initiating export activity seemed to relate to language proficiency and availability of qualified personnel.

In a study of 58 Indian-based exporting firms (27 firms with less than 500 employees and 28 larger firms from seven industries), three managerial characteristics – years in the current position, whether the manager had past exporting experience and whether they had lived or worked abroad – were found as discriminating factors between unsuccessful and successful exporters as classified by export share from total sales (Das, 1994). Other discriminating factors between the groups were product nature, firm's years in business, country of the buyer and nature of the industry. As compared to these latter factors, managerial characteristics had lower discriminant loadings, and surprisingly the export experience of the manager was lower in firms with a higher export share (20 per cent or more) and living or working abroad experience was almost similar in both groups of firms. Success classified as growth in export volume during the past five years yielded three discriminating factors: living or working abroad, years in current position and product nature. Of all the firms, nearly 70 per cent had over 20 years' business experience and 74 per cent over ten years of export experience. As with many other studies, this study did not differentiate between individual experience prior to the export operations of the current firm and the experience gained during the current firm's operations. The export managers in successful firms in fact had over nine years' experience in their current job.

Also many other SME studies have touched upon the relationship between exporting or internationalization and managers' other international skills in different parts of the world. In most of these associated studies, the managerial characteristics are age, education and language skills. Obben and Magagula (2003) tested the links between some managerial and firm-related variables and the export propensity of SMEs in Swaziland, a small developing country in Africa. When comparing 20 exporters and 20 non-exporters, foreign language skills and business-related foreign trips of the managers were very highly significant explanatory factors of export propensity. On the other hand, in a sample of 158 exporting and 105 non-exporting Maine manufacturing firms, Cavusgil and Naor (1987) found three decision-maker characteristics – age, education and language skills – to be poor or insignificant differentiating variables between exporters and non-exporters. Although slightly higher education and level or amount of foreign language skills were related to export marketers, the relationships between these characteristics and export marketing were weak. As compared to other studies, the firm size of the sample firms was larger (employing less than 1000 people).

Reuber and Fischer have studied experience and its relationship to SME internationalization (1997), firm performance (Dyke et al., 1992) and also analysed the dimensions affecting experience (such as time) (Reuber and Fischer, 1999) as well as the role of owner's export experience as a criteria when targeting export support (instead of for example the stage of internationalization) (Fischer and Reuber, 2003). In Reuber and Fischer's study in 1997, the focus was on the experience of both the CEO and the management team, with an empirical sample of 49 small Canadian software product firms. International experience was measured with two measures: whether, before joining or founding the firm, the CEO had ever worked outside Canada and whether any of the management team members had experience in selling outside Canada. In 55 per cent of all the firms, the management team had gained foreign experience. The average timelag from firm foundation to initiation of foreign sales was 5.10 years and over 70 per cent of the firms also sold their products outside North America. However, while 10 per cent had no foreign sales, 51 per cent had at most one foreign partner. According to the findings, the international experience affected positively on the use of partnerships and negatively on the delay from start-up to initiation of foreign sales. In addition, firm age was also found to have a negative effect on the delay of foreign sales and the firm's number of employees was found to affect negatively on the level of TMT's international selling experience. International experience was a significant predictor of the degree of firm internationalization. Both the use of partners and delay in foreign sales mediate the effect of international experience on the degree of firm internationalization.

International Experience and INVs

Pioneering authors Oviatt and McDougall (1995, 1997) and McDougall et al. (1994) have stressed the importance of founder characteristics in researching and explaining INVs. While much of their research has had significant theoretical value, the empirical manifestations of these are fewer, except for the author's own case studies. Based on case studies of 24 INVs, McDougall et al. (1994) state: 'founders of INVs are individuals who see opportunities for earning high returns for establishing businesses that operate across national borders. These entrepreneurs see opportunities that others do not see because of the competencies (networks, knowledge, and background) that are unique to them' (p. 483). Based on 12 case studies, Oviatt and McDougall (1995) identified seven characteristics associated with the survival and growth of new ventures, one of which was internationally experienced managers. In the follow-up study of the same companies, this characteristic (along with global vision and strong international business networks) was found in all the ventures, and it was concluded to be a critical characteristic at the founding phase of the ventures. An interesting finding was, however, that three of the companies had failed and one was in the process of ceasing operations at the time of the progress report.

Many studies in the INV context have studied different experience types as discriminators of internationalization propensity. In most of these studies, the experience has been studied as one of many other explaining variables such as firm or external variables. As an example, Knight (1997) found in a US-based sample that as compared to traditional firms (n = 168), a higher proportion of 'born-global' firms (n = 122) had managers that had lived overseas for a substantial period of time. According to findings by Harveston et al. (2000) on US-based high-technology firms, the managers of INVs (n = 60) reported significantly more extensive international experience (travelling, vacations and holidays, work and education) as compared to managers of gradually globalizing firms (n = 146). In the study of 106 Australia-based exporting wineries (Wickramasekera and Bamberry, 2001), significant differences between managers of firms could be found in that higher numbers of born-globals had export or marketing managers that had previously worked for an exporting company (62 per cent vs. 37 per cent). Whereas the mean values for overseas work experience were the same in both groups of firms, the mean values for training in export matters and fluency in languages were slightly higher in the non born-global firms. In the study by Kunda and Katz (2003) among new firms in the Indian software industry, the education of CEOs predicted higher export performance (export growth and export share) but international experience of CEOs in different regions was significantly higher in highly exporting firms only when measured by export share. The foreign expertise of employees was also tested as a firm-level resource but it gained only marginal support as a predictor of higher export performance (namely export growth). Unlike in many researches, this study used a more profound theory-based approach.

In qualitative studies similar relationships have been studied. In the study by Knight et al. (2001), 16 out of 24 firms in the New Zealand seafood industry were established to serve international markets with no prior domestic sales. Most of these INVs were either established or purchased by persons having international industry links built up through previous work. Based on a case study of 22 New Zealand exporting manufacturing and service firms (nine born-globals) from different industries, Chetty and Campbell-Hunt (2003) found that the founder's prior international and work experience is important in establishing a rapid development path of internationalization.

Another approach in the research has been the link between experience and strategic internationalization choices such as market selection and choice of entry mode. In the study of small, technology-based Swedish firms (Lindqvist, 1991), the findings of 15 pilot case studies indicated that in firms having experienced managers (for example in the same industry as the current firm), the internationalization was characterized by more rapid foreign entry and a less traditional market selection pattern. The experience also helped in identifying foreign representatives. In other cases, acting as a subcontractor to large original equipment manufacturer (OEM) customers had led to rapid indirect spread to many foreign markets. In the survey of 95 sample firms (Lindqvist, 1991), the firms with management having previous industry experience and established contacts with representatives were significantly younger at the time of first foreign entry. However, the number of years required to enter five foreign markets did not vary with previous experience. The author also found that many of the sample firms which had established a subsidiary in a certain market did not possess earlier, lower commitment experience in that market. Rather surprisingly, another finding was that firms that could benefit from the manager's established representative contacts were less successful in export than others.

Bloodgood et al. (1996) studied 61 US-based venture capital supported firms (21 INVs). The degree of internationalization at the time of initial public offering (IPO) was directly related to product differentiation, previous international work experience of the top management, and firm size at the point of IPO. The international education of the management was not significantly related to the extent of internationalization of the firms. The degree of internationalization was measured as whether the firm was engaged on a foreign continent in each of Porter's five primary activities: inbound and outbound logistics, operations, marketing and sales, and service. The management-related variables were not directly related to firm performance (sales growth and earnings before interest and taxes) two years after IPO, but the internationalization degree in total was positively related to later earnings.

In the study by Shrader et al. (2000) of 212 foreign market entries by 87 US-based new ventures, the level of management experience (international, marketing and prior new venture experience) was positively associated with politically and economically riskier countries and more committed entry modes. Also, the larger management team size was associated with higher entry mode commitment. Among 246 high-technology UK start-ups, managers who had lived abroad were more likely to sell abroad without middlemen whereas prior international work experience did not impact on export decisions (Burgel and Murray, 2000). The interpretation was that these managers simply do not need the assistance (market knowledge, commercial network) of distributors, but can rely on their own established networks and knowledge.

According to findings in another UK-based sample (82 biopharmaceutical INVs), the TMT members do not have a major affect on the initiation of international activities, but this decision is primarily driven by the structure of this particular industry (Gurau and Ranchhod, 2003). Using cross-tabulations, the findings suggest a significant relationship between the proportion of the TMT members with international experience and number of world regions of TMT's experience, and the internationalization level of the firm. The medium-sized firms had more TMT members with international experience as compared to small firms. Also, the more developed the firm was in terms of its development stage (from building competitive advantage to being fully operational), the higher proportion of managers there were with international experience. There was no significant relationship between listed or unlisted firms or type of firm activity (platform technology or product development) and the proportion of experienced managers. Furthermore, the experience of TMT in certain world regions was a statistically significant determinant of the presence of the firm in that same region. The relationship between the type of professional expertise (in entry modes) and predominant foreign entry mode was positive and significant in the case of licensing, distribution and strategic alliances, that is, TMT member expertise of for example licensing and use of licensing as the predominant mode.

Research Gap and Hypotheses Development

The literature review indicates that the majority of the research on entrepreneur and management experience has not been linked with firm internationalization but rather with firm performance, strategy, growth and so on in general (see for example Dyke et al., 1992; Reuber and Fischer, 1994, 1999; Eisenhardt and Schoonhoven, 1990). In these studies different experience types have been investigated (for example experience in previous firms, previous start-ups or firm establishments as well as educational, management, ownership, small and large business and industry experience), but often no internationality of experience or internationalization consequences have been included as a measure. Most studies focusing on the relationship between experience and SME internationalization have exclusively explored the experience of a single decision-maker (founder or managing director), while a smaller number of studies have included the whole management team (see the discussion in Reuber and Fischer, 1997). In the context of INV research, only a few researches with the main focus being this issue can be listed (for example Harveston et al., 2000). In both SME and INV research, many of the studies focus on decision-maker and top management-level experience, while some studies have also been made on 'lower-level' experience such as expatriate experiences or international experience of the employees (for example Kunda and Katz, 2003). In many of these studies, the gained experience has been measured at the time of investigation, whereas fewer researches have focused solely on the experience that the decision-maker has gained prior to the current firm's establishment or internationalization.

While research has shown some evidence suggesting a link between the experience and the INV type of development path of the SME, much is still to be evidenced. Conflicting results seem to remain strong as researchers have also found either negative or no relationship between different internationalization and international experience variables (Cavusgil and Naor, 1987; Lindqvist, 1991; Das, 1994; Oviatt and McDougall, 1995; Bloodgood et al., 1996; Burgel and Murray, 2000; Wickramasekera and Bamberry, 2001; Gurau and Ranchhod, 2003; Kunda and Katz, 2003). One reason for this may be related to conceptual ambiguity in the present research. In previous research on founder and manager experience and internationalization (or firm performance, growth) the term 'international experience' has received rather less conceptual attention. Often the experience has been defined through different empirical operationalizations (such as years of export-related work experience, foreign education, number of foreign trips) without more general theoretical definition. Also the concepts 'international orientation' and 'international experience' have sometimes been used as synonyms (Gurau and Ranchhod, 2003). For definitions, see Table 10.1.

Furthermore, as earlier research has tended to focus on analysing the direct link between experience and (international) firm performance, it remains unclear in what manner the experience impacts upon internationalization

Table 10.1 Experience-related measures of entrepreneur, CEO and management in SME internationalization and INV research

SME literature	Empirical data	Level	Experience-related measures
Cavusgil & Naor (1987)	Survey	Chief executive	Age, level/place of education, knowledge of Spanish and German. Perceived management expertise in marketing, finance, production, planning.
Dichtl, Koeglmayer & Mueller (1990)	Structured interviews	Manager	Experience of psychic distance, age, education level, proficiency in foreign languages, traveling, risk-averseness, willingness to change, expects of overseas job-experience on career and family, attitude towards exporting.
Das (1994)	Survey	Manager	Export-related training, past exporting experience, foreign living/working experience, foreign travel in present job; attitude towards exporting; educational level; knowledge of foreign languages; age, years of service in firm, years in current position.
Reuber & Fischer (1994)	Survey	Owner	Prior management, industry, small firm and large firm experience Evaluation of the current expertise areas relative to other CEOs in the industry.
Reuber & Fischer (1997)	Survey	CEO TMT	Prior working abroad Experience in foreign sales.
Obben & Magagula (2003)	Survey	Manager	Age, level of education, proficiency in foreign languages, business-related trips to foreign countries, and perception of exporting on the profitability, riskness and cost of the business.

INV literature	Empirical data	Level	Experience-related measures
Lindqvist (1991)	Case studies, survey	CEO	Whether the firm has been able to use previous industry experience (agent/distributor contacts and industry experience) or local experience (local market knowledge) during internationalization.
Bloodgood,Sapienza & Almeida (1996)	Survey	TMT	No.of directors with previous work experience and schooling abroad.
Knight (1997)	Case studies, survey	Top 3 executives	Living outside the USA and Canada for at least 6 months.
Harveston, Kedia & Davis (2000)	Survey	Manager	Evaluation of the extent of respondent's experience in international traveling, education with international component, international vacations and work.
Shrader, Oviatt & McDougall (2000)	Survey	TMT	Years of international, technical and marketing work experience; new venture experience (prior new ventures started by TMT); TMT size
Burgel & Murray (2000)	Case studies, survey	Founder	Adopted from Bloodgood et al. (1996): Whether the founders had lived abroad/had worked for internationally operating companies before starting the present business.
Wickramasekera & Bamberry (2001)	Survey	Manager	Education, foreign work, export training, worked for exporting company, fluency in foreign languages; country of birth.
Gurau & Ranchhod (2003)	Survey	TMT	International experience (foreign education, work, previous position with international responsibilities); the proportion of TMT with international experience; world regions of experience; areas of professional expertise.
Kunda & Katz (2003)	Survey	CEO	Technical education, international experience (years of experience in foreign regions), technological innovativeness, strategic orientation.
		Employees	Foreign expertise.

behaviour more specifically, such as strategies employed. Additionally, the kinds of international experience and experientially acquired capabilities that are discriminators of different internationalization paths of firms are yet to be researched. Most of the previous studies indeed have deficiencies regarding this matter as they have taken rather narrow and superficial measures of international experience. Most studies do not differentiate between the two sides of experience discussed earlier (experience as such, and expertise acquired through experience), which causes problems (for example assuming that knowledge acquisition is directly proportional to the length of prior participation is maybe not well argued) (Reuber et al., 1990). Reuber and Fischer (1997) emphasize the importance of exploring more specifically what kind of knowledge, skills and abilities are acquired experientially, and their consequences for firm behaviour. Following this discussion, two areas for further research are identified:

- The direct impact of international experience of the entrepreneur and TMT on the internationalization motive and degree (speed of internationalization, market selection, entry mode commitment) of new ventures.
- The indirect impact of international experience on the internationalization behaviour and degree of new ventures, that is, what kind of knowledge, skills or expertise are acquired experientially by internationally experienced entrepreneurs and TMT, and what kind of impact these have on the internationalization of new ventures.

At this point, the aim of the empirical research is to contribute to the first area, which is arguable also by the nature of experience–expertise link. Consequently, it is first important to know the types of experiences that are related to new venture internationalization in the first place, after which the experiential expertise may be added to the context to deepen the understanding of the consequences of experience on internationalization. Based on discussion presented above, the following hypotheses are set:

Hypothesis 1: New ventures with higher prior international experience of the entrepreneur and TMT will have a higher degree of internationalization.

Hypothesis 2: In new ventures with higher prior international experience of the entrepreneur and TMT this experience will be of higher importance as a motive for deciding to initiate international operations.

Hypothesis 3: New ventures whose prior international experience of the entrepreneur and TMT is of higher importance as a motive for deciding to initiate international operations will have a higher degree of internationalization.

Hypothesis 4: Higher prior international experience level of the entrepreneur and TMT and higher importance of this experience as a motive for deciding to initiate international operations discriminate the rapidly internationalized new ventures from the slowly internationalized new ventures.

METHODOLOGY

The empirical data are based on a survey study of exporting Finnish SMEs and a qualitative case study of eight Finnish small- and medium-sized INVs. While the survey data is used to test the hypotheses on international experience and internationalization motives and speed, the case data is aimed at providing further information about the impact of experience on internationalization degree with regard to decisions concerning market selection and entry mode commitment.

Survey

The questionnaire was targeted at Finnish-based industrial and service (software, engineering and advertising) SMEs that were employing 5–500 people and informed to have performed export operations. Including multiple industries is arguable in order to ensure a sufficient number of international new ventures in the sample. In identifying the target companies the Yritys Suomi 2000 database as well as earlier surveys and articles in Finnish business magazines were used. On the basis of these sources, the total target group consisted of 2856 companies. After excluding 48 bankrupted firms, 154 firms that did not fulfill the selection criteria and firms whose address could not be identified, the final target group decreased to 2654 firms.

Altogether 486 responses were received, from which 473 were usable (response rate 17.8 per cent). However, only companies founded in 1985 or after are included in this study, since knowledge of the early years of older firms and their decision-makers' prior experience is more difficult to gain, and the reliability of such data is likely to be lower. Thus, from a total of 473 companies 211 are analysed. Descriptive statistics of these firms are shown in Table 10.2. Based on the number of employees, annual turnover and field of industry, there seemed not to be any great differences between responding and non-responding companies.

The survey was conducted between November 2001 and March 2002. The survey was part of a larger survey and the questions covered foreign

Table 10.2 Descriptive statistics of survey firms (n = 211)

Variable	Mean	S.D.	Range		Median
			Min	Max	
Foundation	1991	3.99	1985	2001	1991
Number of personnel in 2001	49.5	72.63	3	500	23
Turnover in 2001	6.98	11.35	0.12	90.52	3.03
Starting year of export	1993	4.08	1985	2001	1993
Share of exports in 2000–2001	40.4%	31.84	0	100	30.0%
Company form			**Field of industry**		
Family-owned	45.3%		Manufacturing		83.9%
Independent limited liability	31.2%		Service		16.1%
Part of larger group	23.5%				

purchasing, foreign sales, firm strategy in international business, performance, future prospects, and key figures, as well as other background information of the firms. The respondents of the questionnaire were either the managing director (in small firms employing less than 50 people) or the manager responsible for international operations (in medium-sized firms). The international experience measure concerned the characteristics of the TMT and was measured through the following questions: (1) whether the management members (none/one of the managers/many of the managers) had gained (a) business experience in international assignments in a domestic firm, (b) business experience in international assignments in a foreign firm, (c) educational experience abroad, or (d) other experience abroad before the current firm started international operations. (2) The competitiveness level of the management's (a) international experience, (b) education and (c) language skills (Likert scale 1–5). A subjective measure of the impact of experience in internationalization-related decision-making was measured through the variable 'to what extent the manager evaluates the international experience of the management to have impacted on the firm's decision to start operating internationally' (Likert scale 1–5). Whereas the first question can be regarded as rather objective, the two latter ones are respondents' evaluations of the TMT characteristics and decision-making motives. Concerning the TMT as a focus of experience, the management team of the venture in the inception, survival and growth phases is generally concerned to involve the founders of the venture and to be more entrepreneurial. In later stages of development, that is, in the expansion stage of the venture, the management is likely to involve more professional managers whereas the founders may step aside from the TMT (see for example Scott and Bruce, 1987). As measured by the number of employees, the size of the sample firms is rather small and the majority of the firms are family-owned (only 23 per cent belong to a larger group) (Table 10.2). Reflecting these factors, the owner-entrepreneur is likely to be highly present in the management of these ventures and thus be an acting member of the TMT.

Concerning the operationalization of experience, the experience measures are aimed to provide information on the level and types of experience of both the entrepreneur and the whole management team. As can be seen in the summary Table 10.1, the experience of the whole TMT has been included as a measure only in three earlier INV studies and one SME study. In two of these studies the measures of experience have been rather general, with specifying only one (Reuber and Fisher, 1997: 'experience in selling to foreign markets') or two (Bloodgood et al., 1997: 'international schooling or work experience') types of experience. The study by Shrader et al. (2000) is focused on issues other than experience, which in itself has also been measured more superficially and without specifying whether the experience has been gained prior to or during the current venture's internationalization. Regarding the experience types included in this study, four objective measures were included in order to give more specified information than in earlier studies. In addition, international work experience in domestic firms is included as one separate type, unlike in many earlier studies which tend to focus on 'working experience abroad' or 'foreign experience'. However, experience in a domestic firm that operates internationally is likely to be similarly or even more important than experience in foreign companies. This is because it adds to the experience of how to go abroad and do international business from this particular country and thus may be utilized in the new venture founded in the same country (as is the case in this study). There may be great differences between countries with regard to international trade policies and practices. Finally, regarding the subjective measure of experience used in this study, it is informative and unique to previous studies in the sense that it specifies how the CEO or international sales manager evaluates the competitiveness of the TMT's experience based on his or her knowledge of their experiences and does not just focus on the years of experience or number of persons having experience.

In the survey study, the degree of internationalization is only measured through speed of internationalization. As mentioned earlier, the entry mode commitment and market selection pattern are analysed in the case study part of the chapter. The degree (later referred to as speed) of internationalization of the new venture was operationalized as: (1) the share of foreign sales in the firm's turnover three years after the firm's foundation (classified as no foreign sales, <10 per cent, 10–24 per cent, 25–49 per cent or >50 per cent); and (2) years required until three foreign countries were entered with sales (age at entry in the third foreign entry). For the purpose of analysing hypothesis 4, the new ventures were classified into four groups on the basis of two variables: (1) share of foreign sales three years after firm foundation (being more or less than 25 per cent): and (2) firm age at its third foreign market entry (being more or less than three years) (see Figure 10.1). The 25 per cent has been used as the minimum share of foreign sales in INV criteria in studies for example by Knight (1997), Harveston et al. (2000) and Moen (2002). Three years has been used as a cut year between INVs and local new ventures for example by Harveston et al. (2000), Rasmussen et al. (2001) and Gurau and Ranchhod (2003). Most of the earlier studies only include export share soon after establishment as criteria of INVs, and thus neglect the actual international dispersion of activities. This latter factor is, however, an essential part of defining INVs and of discriminating them from very locally geographically focused new ventures. Thus, in this study years required to enter three foreign countries was used as another criterion to define the internationalization speed of new ventures.

To test the relationships in the first three hypotheses, two-tailed correlational analysis was used. This way the relationships between different types of experience and internationalization decision-making motives and speed can be analysed, and the relative strength of the relations between experience and internationalization versus decision-making motives and internationalization can be reported. To test the differences in four types of new ventures in hypothesis 4, one-way analysis of variance was employed together with the Bonferroni test to further investigate the differences found.

Case Study

The case studies were identified from 486 exporting Finnish SMEs that had participated in the mail survey as well as using other sources (earlier surveys and Finnish business magazines). Selection criteria included the following items: international sales three years after establishment at least 25 per cent of total sales; international sales at least 50 per cent of total sales in 2001; at least six foreign countries in which the company had sales in 2001; company establishment in 1985 or later (see argument above); the majority of the company not owned by any single larger Finnish or foreign group (to ensure the independence of early operations and decision-making). The basic information of the selected eight companies is presented in Table 10.3. The firms represent different industries and six of the companies are categorized as high-tech (R&D costs at least three per cent of turnover)

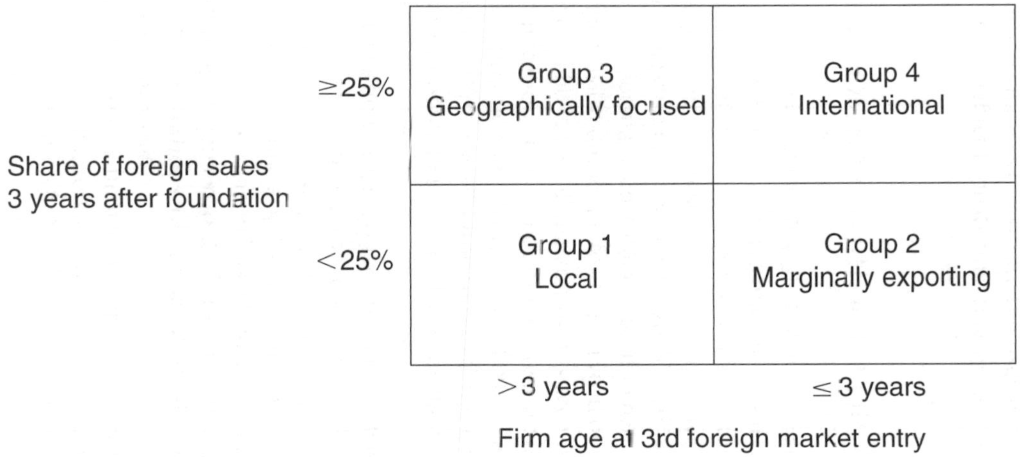

Figure 10.1 Classification of new ventures into four groups

Table 10.3 Basic information of the case companies

Company	Founded	Main products	Number of personnel[1]	Turnover[1]	Starting year of export	Share of exports[1]
A	1996	Laminated log houses	76	12.9 Meur	1996	60%[3]
B	1992	Light forest machines	50	12.0 Meur	1992	75%
C	1997	Fibre reinforcements	15	0.4 Meur[2]	1999	58%[3]
D	1993	Frequency converters	426	97.5 Meur	1995	82%[3]
E	1988	Liquid handling, diagnostic tests	303	25.4 Meur	1990	97%
F	1992	Public space furniture	28	4.1 Meur	1992	50%
G	1994	Square bale wrapping systems	13	1.4 Meur	1994	95%
H	1994	Machinery for textile industry	13	2.4 Meur	1996	98%

Notes: [1] in 2002, [2] in 2001, [3] in 2001–2002.

and two as low-tech. Accordingly with the research focus of the study, case firms vary in terms of experience and internationalization degree.

The data of the case firms was collected through the above survey questionnaire, personal contacts (using a semi-structured questionnaire) and firm reports (annual and other reports), newspaper and journal articles. More profound information has been gained from one case company by in-depth interview. In addition to international experience variables (included in the survey), the managers of eight INVs in the case study were also asked to specify whether one or several of the founders and/or early management team members had gained previous industry experience and whether this experience was short- or longer-term (less or more than three years). Also the background of the establishment was identified (another company, bankruptcy of another company, MBO – management buy art, research project and so on). The semi-structured questionnaire also included questions of international operations (operation modes used, countries entered and so on) in the beginning phase of firm existence (first six years) and currently.

RESULTS

Survey: International Experience and Speed of Internationalization

The analysis of survey data is focused on the link between international experience and speed of internationalization variables as well as the motives behind the internationalization initiation. The distribution of firms with regard to experience of different types is shown in Table 10.4. All these experiences were gained before the current firm had started international operations. As can be seen from the table, in a large proportion of the firms there is actually no international studying experience or work experience in foreign companies, a fact that weakens the usability of these variables in further analysis. With the subjective measures, on average the respondents rated the level of management's international experience in the firm as 3.45, of education 3.66 and of language skills 3.67 (on a scale of 1 = extremely low to 5 = extremely high).

The mean values, standard deviations, range and medians of the international experience, internationalization motive and speed of internationalization variables are shown in Table 10.5. The correlations between (hypothesis 1) seven experience measures and two internationalization speed measures and (hypothesis 2) seven experience measures and one measure of the impact of experience as a motive impacting upon the decision to initiate international operations are shown in Table 10.7.

Table 10.4 The distribution of previous international experience variables in sample firms (n = 211)

Variable	None of the managers	One of the managers	Many of the managers	Missing
Int'l living	55.90%	24.60%	12.30%	7.10%
Int'l studying	69.20%	15.20%	8.10%	7.60%
Int'l work in domestic firm	35.10%	28%	29.50%	7.60%
Int'l work in foreign firm	72.50%	10.40%	9.50%	7.60%

When measuring the link between (hypothesis 1) earlier international experience of managers and speed of internationalization, the following results were found. The higher share of foreign sales three years after foundation correlated significantly and positively with managers' experience in international work in a domestic company as well as the respondents' evaluation of their firm's managers' international experience level. This finding suggests that companies having management team members with prior experience of this type are likely to have a higher share of foreign sales soon after establishment. As expected, significant negative correlation could be found with international experience and years from firm establishment to three foreign entries. Specifically, the age at third foreign entry was lower among companies having managers with experience of studying abroad, and international work in a domestic company and a foreign company. Correlations with other experience measures and age at entry were negative but not at the significant level. The correlations with international experience of studying and living abroad and of working in a foreign firm must however be interpreted with the fact that the experience of these types were less evenly distributed as they were rather low in all the sample firms. Thus, overall partial support for hypothesis 1 was obtained.

In addition to the above measures, this study uses subjective measures of the impact of 13 different firm and environment-related factors on internationalization initiation motives. The means, standard deviations, range and medians of the measures are shown in Table 10.6 and correlations between the 13 measures of the motives behind the decision to initiate international operations and two internationalization speed measures in Table 10.8. The mean value for the impact of international experience of the management on the firm's decision to start operating internationally was 3.02 (on a scale of 1 = extremely minor impact to 5 = extremely major impact). The manager's own evaluation of the

Table 10.5 Means, standard deviations, range and medians of the experience and internationalization speed variables (n = 211)

Variable	Mean	S.D.	Range		Median
			Minimum	Maximum	
1. Mgm int'l living	0.5	0.72	0	2	0.0
2. Mgm int'l studying	0.3	0.63	0	2	0.0
3. Mgm int'l work in domestic firm	0.9	0.84	0	2	1.0
4. Mgm int'l work in foreign firm	0.3	0.65	0	2	0.0
5. Level of mgm int'l experience[1]	3.5	1.04	1	5	4.0
6. Level of mgm education[1]	3.7	0.89	1	5	4.0
7. Level of mgm language skills[1]	3.7	0.98	1	5	4.0
8. Impact of mgm int'l experience on int'lization initiation[1]	3.0	1.23	1	5	3.0
9. Share of foreign sales 3 years after foundation[2]	1.7	1.47	0	4	1.0
10. Firm age at 3rd foreign market entry (years)	4.2	3.87	0	15	3.0

Notes:
[1] The variables 5–8 are respondent's evaluations of the impact/level.
[2] Scale: 0 = no foreign sales, 1 = less than 10%, 2 = 10–24%, 3 = 25–50%, 4 = more than 50%.

Table 10.6 Means, standard deviations, range and medians of the internationalization motive variables ($n=211$)

Variable	Mean	S.D.	Range		Median
			Minimum	Maximum	
1. Int'lization of customer	2,6	1.45	1	5	2
2. Int'lization of competitors	2.4	1.28	1	5	2
3. Success of competitors in int'l markets	2.4	1.23	1	5	2
4. Mgm interest in int'lization	4.0	0.92	1	5	4
5. Mgm int'l experience	3.0	1.23	1	5	3
6. Competitive foreign sub-contractors	2.2	1.27	1	5	2
7. Inadequate demand in the home market	3.7	1.28	1	5	4
8. Increasing competition in the home market	2.9	1.30	1	5	3
9. Foreign enquiry	3.7	1.09	1	5	4
10. Lack of sub-contractors in the home market	1.7	0.99	1	5	1
11. The firm has never considered its home market as the only market	3.5	1.38	1	5	4
12. Export subsidies	2.1	1.09	1	5	2
13. Contact from the chamber of commerce or related organization	1.6	0.89	1	5	1

Table 10.7 Pearson correlations of the experience and internationalization speed variables

Variable	1	2	3	4	5	6	7	8	9	10
1. Mgm int'l living	1									
2. Mgm int'l studying	0.523(**)	1								
3. Mgm int'l work in domestic firm	0.249(**)	0.166(*)	1							
4. Mgm int'l work in foreign firm	0.523(**)	0.388(**)	0.273(**)	1						
5. Level of mgm int'l experience	0.240(**)	0.200(**)	0.409(**)	0.211(**)	1					
6. Level of mgm education	0.165(*)	0.104	0.194(**)	0.098	0.502(**)	1				
7. Level of mgm language skills	0.170(*)	0.193(**)	0.200(**)	0.088	0.513(**)	0.665(**)	1			
8. Impact of mgm int'l experience on int'lization initiation	0.244(**)	0.207(**)	0.482(**)	0.170(*)	0.539(**)	0.300(**)	0.351(**)	1		
9. Share of foreign sales 3 years after foundation	0.118	−0.009	0.229(**)	0.108	0.166(*)	0.120	0.078	0.218(**)	1	
10. Firm age at 3rd foreign market entry (years)	−0.104	−0.172(*)	−0.259(**)	−0.221(**)	−0 152	−0.051	−0.013	−0.160	−0.529(**)	1

Notes:
** Correlation is significant at the 0.01 level (2-tailed).
* Correlation is significant at the 0.05 level (2-tailed)

Table 10.8 Pearson correlations of the internationalization motive and internationalization speed variables

Variable	1	2	3	4	5
1. Int'lization of customer	1				
2. Int'lization of competitors	0.381(**)	1			
3. Success of competitors in int'l markets	0.181(*)	0.747(**)	1		
4. Mgm interest in int'lization	−0.034	0.13	0.189(*)	1	
5. Mgm int'l experience	0.098	0.134	0.115	0.238(**)	1
6. Competitive foreign sub-contractors	0.227(**)	0.268(**)	0.252(**)	0.1	0.122
7. Inadequate demand in the home market	−0.03	0.129	0.124	0.221(**)	0.205(**)
8. Increasing competition in the home market	0.084	0.259(**)	0.329(**)	0.181(*)	0.075
9. Foreign enquiry	0.002	0.099	0.106	0.147(*)	0.062
10. Lack of sub-contractors in the home market	0.236(**)	0.253(**)	0.214(**)	0.163(*)	0.062
11. The firm has never considered its home market as the only market	−0.033	0.088	0.056	0.190(**)	0.322(**)
12. Export subsidies	0.021	0.122	0.132	0.253(**)	0.031
13. Contact from the chamber of commerce or related organization	−0.004	0.285(**)	0.267(**)	0.266(**)	0.079
14. Share of foreign sales 3 years after foundation	−0.106	0.118	0.162(*)	−0.018	0.218(**)
15. Firm age 3rd foreign market entry	0.198(*)	−0.03	−0.118	−0.002	−0.16

Notes:
** Correlation is significant at the 0.01 level (2-tailed).
* Correlation is significant at the 0.05 level (2-tailed).

impact of management's international experience on the decision to start operating internationally correlated positively and significantly with all the variables measuring the amount of international experience of management (hypothesis 2). Thus, the findings give strong support for hypothesis 2. Three experience variables (studying experience, subjective evaluation of management international experience and language skills) correlated positively and significantly with the management international interest as a stimulus for internationalization. Five variables (living experience, international work in domestic firms, and subjective evaluation of management international experience, education level, and language skills) correlated positively and significantly with the internationalization stimulus of the management having never considered its home market as the only market.

6	7	8	9	10	11	12	13	14	15
1									
−0.083	1								
0.167(*)	0.302(**)	1							
0.096	−0.045	0.113	1						
0.557(**)	0.023	0.111	0.045	1					
−0.066	0.251(**)	−0.186(*)	0.119	0.005	1				
0.161(*)	0.165(*)	0.057	0.087	0.115	0.162(*)	1			
0.224(**)	0.133	0.254(**)	0.168(*)	0.236(**)	0.02	0.488(**)	1		
−0.071	0.242(**)	−0.079	−0.019	−0.084	0.429(**)	0.063	−0.034	1	
−0.023	−0.264(**)	−0.031	0.007	0.06	−.314(**)	−0.077	0.04	−0.529(**)	1

The evaluated impact also correlated positively with the actual share of foreign sales three years after foundation (hypothesis 3). The correlation with age at third entry was negative as expected, but weaker. This finding gives partial support for hypothesis 3. Other significant correlations could be found with the share of foreign sales three years after foundation and three other stimuli: success of competitors in international markets, inadequate demand in the home market, and the fact that firm had never considered its home market as the only market. The age at third foreign entry seemed to correlate negatively at a significant level with inadequate demand in the home market and firm never having considered its home market as the only market. Surprisingly, a significant positive correlation was found with the age at entry and internationalization of customers as a stimulus for internationalization.

Hypothesis 4 was employed to further research the role of individual-level experience in explaining the differences between the initial internationalization behaviour of new ventures. Thus, the possible differences in the mean

Table 10.9 Differences in experience variables between the groups

	Group 1 a<25% b> 3 years	Group 2 a<25% b≤3 years	Group 3 a≥25% b>3 years	Group 4 a≥25% b≤ 3 years	Total	Sig. level
N	**64**	**38**	**10**	**46**	**158**	
1. Mgm int'l living	0.43	0.59	0.78	0.63	0.55	0.377
2. Mgm int'l studying	0.22	0.41	0.22	0.36	0.31	0.423
3. Mgm int'l work in domestic firm	0.80	1.00	1.00	1.25	0.99	0.058*
4. Mgm int'l work in foreign firm	0.23	0.41	0.00	0.55	0.35	0.043**
5. Level of mgm int'l experience	3.45	3.37	3.89	3.84	3.57	0.079*
6. Level of mgm education	3.70	3.55	4.00	3.87	3.73	0.283
7. Level of mgm language skills	3.75	3.39	3.70	3.89	3.70	0.108*!
8. Impact of mgm int'l experience on int'lization initiation	2.85	2.94	3.13	3.33	3.03	0.248

Notes:
Analysis of variance, test of group means, *<0.1, **<0.05.
Grouping variables: (a) share of exports 3 years after foundation; and (b) firm age at 3rd foreign market entry.
! is included to note that the result is nearly significant.

values of decision-makers' prior experience between international, geographically-focused, marginally but geographically widely exporting and local types of new ventures (see classification in the methodology section) were tested using one-way analysis of variance. The results of the analyses are shown in the Table 10.9. In four of the experience measures – international work experience in domestic firm, international work experience in foreign firm, level of language skills, and impact of international experience on the decision to start operating internationally – the highest mean values were found in group 4, that is, the firms that had at least 25 per cent of initial export share and had sales operations in at least three foreign countries three years after foundation. Comparing the groups, the mean values in three of the variables – living experience abroad, the level of manager's international experience as evaluated by the CEO or international sales manager and level of education as evaluated by the CEO or international sales manager – were highest in the third group of new ventures, that is, those that had an initial export share over 25 per cent but were more than three years old when entering the third foreign market with sales. In one variable, the studying experience abroad, the highest mean value was found in group 2.

Significant group differences were found in three variables – international working experience of the entrepreneur and managers in a domestic firm, international working experience in foreign firms, and level of international experience as evaluated by the CEO or international sales manager – whereas in the variable measuring the level of language skills as evaluated by the CEO or international sales manager nearly significant differences between the group mean values were found (p = 0.108). Using the Bonferroni test to investigate further the group differences, only two significant results were found however. First, the international work experience in domestic firms of group 4 was significantly higher than in group 1. Second, the evaluated level of language skills of group 4 was significantly higher to that of group 2. In the variable of international work experience in a foreign firm, a nearly significant difference in the expected direction was found between groups 1 and 4 (p = 0.120). Thus, hypothesis 4 received partial support in the analysis. The uneven distribution of variables of studying experience and working in foreign firms, however, has to be noted when interpreting the results.

Case Study: International Experience and Internationalization Decisions

The function of the case studies is to give more information on the link between experience and internationalization decisions concerning entry mode commitment and market selection strategies. In the case study firms, variety with regard to prior international experience of focal actors could be identified. In all cases there existed earlier experience from working on international assignments at home or abroad, from studying abroad or in some cases from the research field at international level, but this experience varied significantly with regard to duration and number of persons having the experience. The case study results suggest a link between previous international experience of management and degree of internationalization, especially with entry mode commitment but also with market strategy of the current venture. Higher international coordination of operations (such as purchasing, sales, R&D cooperation, marketing cooperation and financing) soon after establishment was met with firms having decision-makers with higher previous international experience. Two of the most globalized companies – as determined by internationalization level of different business operations as well as number and breadth of countries with international operations – were characterized by extremely high previous international experience of the TMT. Three other companies characterized by high previous experience of the decision-makers were also coordinating the majority of operations internationally, but instead concentrating on fewer countries. Results on companies that were characterized by moderate or low international experience by the entrepreneur and TMT support this conclusion. Three companies had managers with less previous international experience as compared to other cases. The international operations of these three firms were mainly restricted to exporting, except for some R&D and marketing cooperation with customers and distributors and marginal purchasing from abroad by one company. Regarding market strategies in the beginning, one of the three companies gained 75 per cent of exports from three markets, while the two other companies were less geographically concentrated.

In terms of industry-related experience, the previous industry experience and the contacts of the founders and early management team established during this experience were high in three firms and extremely high in four of the firms. In the eighth case company the founder had worked in the same field, but only for a shorter period. In half of the cases, the background of foundation was linked to change in another company (such as bankruptcy or sell-off of a business unit).

Direct links between international experience and more specific internationalization behaviours and decisions are further illustrated with firm D (see Table 10.3). This firm is one of the two most globalized companies. Firm D is regarded as appropriate for further discussion, since it can in all respects most strongly be defined as an INV. First, the company is presented in terms of its international development, after which the impact of the international experience on market entry strategies is discussed.

Firm D is operating in the electrotechnical industry and manufacturing frequency converters. The first two years after establishment in 1993 were dedicated to product development. The first foreign distributor contract was already established before the product launch in 1994 at an international exhibition, followed by establishment of many more distributor contracts, subsidiaries (joint and wholly-owned) and a brand label contract in the next year. The share of exports reached 80 per cent three years after foundation. In 2002 the company's products were sold to over 100 countries. About 67 per cent of the sales are to Europe, 18 per cent to North America and 12 per cent to Australia and Asia. The main market is the USA, accounting for a quarter of exports. The company aims at increasing its presence in South-East Asia, the Middle East, Eastern Europe, South America and Africa. Also, supply and R&D have from the beginning been conducted with worldwide partners, and capital is raised from investors outside Finland. Since 2000, firm D has been a public company.

The company was established in 1993 by former managers and employees of a multinational corporation (MNC), which decided to move its division to another location. The core people wanted to continue in the old location and were encouraged by the positive prospects due to their advanced technological knowledge, international experience in doing business in the field, and the advantages of smaller organization. The success of firm D is strongly linked to the background of the foundation and management team having vast international-level industry experience and thereby contacts to customers, suppliers, financiers and other parties. In the beginning the TMT consisted of three experienced persons: the CEO had worked as a top manager and R&D manager of the frequency converter division of the MNC, the executive vice-president was experienced in many manager positions in different divisions of the MNC (being responsible for sales, purchasing and material operations), and the third person had worked as a business controller of the MNC, and also gained international education experience through an MBA degree. The persons joining the TMT in the following years added to the stock of international industry experience as well as experience in other internationally operating companies. The international dimension of business was also familiar to many of the firm's employees, having high experience of international assignments in domestic and foreign companies as well as of studying abroad.

Together with inadequate domestic demand and international orientation, the international experience of the founder managers was an important internationalization trigger for the firm. The TMT members' former assignment in the multinational company in the same field resulted in important knowledge and familiarity of the international business in the field. In later phases, in addition to TMT-level experience, the firm also benefited from the employees' earlier international experience and the company's own expatriates, especially in the form of foreign market and industry knowledge. The foreign sales were initiated in 1995 in Sweden, Germany, Austria, the UK and Spain. The first foreign markets were selected primarily on the basis of managers' established contacts and facilitated by the managers' reputation in the midst of the distributors and customers with whom they had become acquainted during former assignments. As a small company, it was crucial that the managers were known from the earlier assignments. The prior experience also impacted on the entry modes employed in the beginning. In the first country the sales were through the distributor, in the second country through the firm's own sales subsidiary and in the third country through brand label contract. All these entries were linked to a relationship that was established prior to the current venture and thus to previous assignments in the field. One of the main markets of firm D today is the USA. Originally the company had decided not to enter this market as it was regarded as too resource-demanding for a small company. However, following the local interest for the firm's technology, the company signed brand label contracts with large MNCs in the market. Through these arrangements the firm could lower the resource requirements and risk of doing business in this large, distant country. Going behind the contracts again raises the earlier experience of the decision-makers – the contracts were largely facilitated by the strong personal relationships that the managers had gained based on previous experience with persons in these MNCs.

In summary, these case studies suggest a relationship between international experience and decision-making concerning entry modes and market selection. Whether the international experience is from the same or another field of industry seems to be decisive.

CONCLUSIONS

The aim of this chapter was to research the link between the international experience of the entrepreneur and TMT, and the internationalization of new ventures. The experience was approached as a possible mediator of INV development through influence on specific decisions that might explain these firms' development and the consequent internationalization degree. After reviewing previous findings on this issue, the research gap was identified and two areas in need of further empirical research were presented. This chapter presents findings for the first area, that is, the direct impact of international experience of the entrepreneur and TMT on internationalization motives and degree (speed of internationalization, entry mode commitment and market selection). The empirical findings are based on survey data of 211 exporting Finnish SMEs established in 1985 or after, and a qualitative case study of eight Finnish-based INVs. Four hypotheses of the links were developed for the empirical research and tested with methods of correlational analysis and ANOVA (together with the Bonferroni test), followed by further elaboration of the results of the case study.

To test the three first hypotheses concerning the relationship between experience and internationalization, two-tailed correlations were made. Except for one of the seven variables, all the experience types were related to speed of internationalization in the expected direction and the results reveal many significant relationships between experience and internationalization. Especially, prior experience in international work in domestic firms is related to faster internationalization in the beginning phase of the new venture, that is, in terms of market entries and export share. The higher overall international experience level of the TMT is related to gaining a higher share of sales from foreign markets soon after establishment. Studying experience abroad as well as prior international work in foreign firms is significantly related to firms' faster entry into many countries. Thus, these results give partial support to hypothesis 1.

Hypothesis 2 was concerned with relationships between the level of prior international experience of the entrepreneur and TMT, and the importance of this experience as a motive in the decision to start international operations. In new ventures having the entrepreneur and TMT characterized by high experience as measured by all the seven variables, the decision to start internationalization also seems to be more strongly affected by this experience. Thus, the results support hypothesis 2. Finally, in hypothesis 3 a positive relationship was expected between the importance of experience as a motive for initiating international operations and the actual internationalization degree of the new venture. The decision to start to internationalize with decision-maker experience as a strong motive indeed correlated positively with speed of internationalization and significantly with obtaining a higher share of foreign sales soon after establishment. Thus, partial support for the third hypothesis was obtained.

To test the discriminating role of experience between highly internationalized new ventures and their counterparts, one-way analysis of variance was performed. The highest experience values could be found in half of the variables in group 4, that is, firms that can most be characterized as international new ventures. Three experience types – living abroad, level of overall international experience and education – were highest in group 3, that is, firms that after three years of foundation gained over a quarter of total sales from a few foreign countries. As a surprising finding, international studying experience was highest in group 2. Further analyses, however, suggest that, as compared to marginally exporting new ventures, the international new ventures (group 4) have significantly higher scores only on two types of experience: language skill level of the TMT and international working experience in domestic firms. Thus, only partial support for hypothesis 4 was found in the survey sample.

As in the above tests only speed of internationalization was used as a determinant of internationalization degree, the case studies were used to give more information about the possible links between experience and international market and entry strategies. In the case study firms different management-related attributes were found to be important explanatory factors for internationalization behaviour. International experience was highest in firms especially characterized by the employment of several different foreign operation modes soon after establishment, whereas in firms with less experienced managers the international operating was mainly restricted to exporting. In addition, industry experience gained through prior assignments was important when looking at the international development of the companies. This finding is in line with Siegel et al. (1993) who found that the experience in a similar industry is a key discriminator of high- and low-growth ventures. Thus, the case results support the survey findings concerning the mediating role of experience in decision-making, and furthermore, they deepen the understanding of the link of decision-maker experience to specific foreign market entry operations and related decisions.

When reflecting upon the findings with regard to their theoretical implications, the following conclusions can be made. Overall the survey findings would suggest certain consequences of experience on decision-making motives concerning internationalization as well as on the actual degree of internationalization. The survey results indicate that the experience level in itself is directly related to the degree of internationalization of the ventures. They also reveal that in firms where the management has gained prior international experience, this capital has been used in decision-making concerning the initiation of international operations of the current venture, thus being an important motive behind internationalization. Going further, the use of experience in decision-making is related to the higher degree of internationalization of the venture. As compared to other factors in the decision-making, from 11 factors only inadequate domestic demand and the fact that the firm had never considered its home market as the only market had stronger correlations than experience with the speed of internationalization. The latter motive (view of the market) may indeed be a consequence of the international experience and thus more internationally oriented managers running the firm, as is reflected by the significant positive correlation between five experience-level measures and this particular internationalization motive measure.

The link between experience level and internationalization speed is also supported by some previous studies. However, as compared to previous studies, the findings of this study on the impact of experience on internationalization through internationalization motives and operational decisions provide important new information for the theory and certainly also call for more research about the indirect impacts of experience. In the INV context Madsen and Servais (1997) for example emphasize the consequences of past experience of new venture founders, for example on the lower perceived uncertainty, increased market knowledge and thereby increased market commitment of the firm's operations. However, empirical researches on the links between these issues published so far are few, and thus the case study findings reported here are also important for theory building.

The findings also have managerial value, especially in the case of new ventures with narrow globally spread markets. These types of cases are growing in number in many high-tech or highly specialized low-tech industries. As an example, the findings are of use from the point of view of the managers preparing financing applications for the ventures and of financiers evaluating them. It is general that in financing decisions of new ventures the financiers emphasize the skills and background of the management (for example McKinsey & Company, 1999). This study shows that when evaluating the success and growth possibilities of new ventures whose product markets are spread globally over country borders, the critical management experience is that related to international business and other international activities. The financiers should pay special attention to both the entrepreneur's and TMT's international experience level and its nature (especially prior work experience, but also other experience types seem consequential). As the findings of this study indicate, international experience of different types does have an effect on the decision-making of the new venture as well as on its actual international growth. Following this, the findings of this study may be of use when recruiting the management team of a new venture. The different types of experience backgrounds of the possible managers are to be appreciated if the new venture seeks rapid international growth.

Future Research

Although this study revealed many relationships between experience and new venture behaviour, it also calls for deepening this knowledge: A rather unexplored area is the mechanism behind experience influences, that is, how experience impacts behaviour before leading to a higher degree of internationalization. This study revealed the indirect link of experience through decision-making motives used in behaviour, but more knowledge on the influence mechanisms of experience is needed. An important area of future research will also be to seek understanding of the question as to why the decision-maker's experience does not always lead to certain consequences in the firm behaviour. This is reflected by the many conflicting results in research. The previous research has usually been based on the assumption that people having international experience have also been able to learn from their experience with a similar intensity. However, the knowledge, skills and expertise of people with similar types (and durations) of experience are likely to vary and thus indicate different consequences on the new ventures that these people manage later. Possibly, the experience may not lead to an increase in relevant knowledge in the context of INV that the person is managing, the experience and related expertise may not be utilized or the experience may lead to a decrease in interest towards internationalization. In the context of new ventures, focusing on the level of expertise that the entrepreneurs and TMT have gained through experience could reveal more consistent relationships between experience and internationalization than has been achieved so far (see Reuber and Fischer, 1994). Related to this indirect link of experience to internationalization (through knowledge, skills and expertise), the areas of expertise relevant for internationalization of a (new) venture need to be identified (see Athanassiou and Nigh, 2002) as well as the factors that impact upon the expertise that one gains through experiences and the utilization of this expertise when managing the new venture.

The issue of experience is also closely linked to relationships and networks and their social capital. Firstly, the networks that are spread over country borders increase the international experience of the decision-makers involved in the network. Second, the networks are important means of diffusion of the experience-based knowledge across persons and companies. Third, the experience is often in the form of business networks, that is, business contacts formed in the previous assignments which may be significant factors in explaining for example the market and entry mode choices and the rapid establishment of regular sales abroad. According to Riddle and Gillespie (2003), the founders of new ventures in the Turkish clothing export industry 'seem to be aware of the importance of employing all of the social contact resources (such as friends and relatives) they have at their disposal, particularly when seeking information about technological innovations and buyers' (p. 112). Likewise, the business contacts held by the founder and TMT may have a crucial affect. The personal relations may act as an impulse and first contact to new international business, and also strengthen and broaden it (Halinen-Kaila and Salmi, 2001). Going further, in several studies it is also mentioned that the managers of INVs can be characterized by strong international orientation or global mindset. Earlier findings suggest that the managers of INVs or born-global firms typically are growth-oriented, tend to have strong international vision, emphasize a proactive approach and high commitment to international markets, are responsive to customers' needs, and possess high competence in conducting international marketing activities (for example Rennie, 1993; Oviatt and McDougall, 1995; Knight, 1997; Nummela et al., 2002). Researching the link between experience and international orientation could produce important results (more specifically, whether there exists a positive impact of international experience on the level of international orientation).

This study revealed the role of many internal and external motives in initiating international operations and also revealed that, except for inadequate demand, the external motives were less important than the internal (decision-maker experience and interest) motives. However, the industry nature as well as situational factors in venture internationalization (such as internationalization of the customer) deserve more attention in the future. The small sample size, and especially the small number of INVs in this study, did not allow differentiation between service and manufacturing firms or limiting the research to one industry.

Finally, as was noted in this study, experience has been measured differently in previous research, and more comprehensive measures and multidimensional research of the relationships are needed.

ACKNOWLEDGEMENTS

This study was part of a national LIIKE programme. The author wishes to thank the University of Vaasa, the Academy of Finland and the National Technology Agency of Finland for the financial support for this research. The author is also thankful for the valuable comments by Professors Jorma Larimo and Kjell Gronhaug as well as the reviewers and commentators of the RENT XVIII and EFMD 35th EISB Conferences. For statistical advice the author thanks Professor Esko Leskinen and Project Manager Mikael Hallbäck.

NOTE

* This chapter is based on the article by Johanna Pulkkinen (2005), Die Internationalisierung von Jungunternehmen: Die Mittlerrolle der Erfahrung von Unternehmern und Top-Management Teams, *Zeitschrift für KMU und Entrepreneurship*, **53**(3): 208–38.

An early version of this study received the Award for the Best Paper of the RENT (Research in Entrepreneurship and Small Business) XVIII Conference.

REFERENCES

Athanassiou, Nicholas and Nigh, Douglas (2002). The impact of the top management team's international business experience on the firm's internationalization: Social networks at work. *Management International Review*, **42**(2): 157–81.

Bloodgood, James M., Sapienza, Harry J. and Almeida, James G. (1996). The internationalization of new high-potential US ventures: Antecedents and outcomes. *Entrepreneurship: Theory and Practice*, **20**(4): 61–76.

Burgel, Oliver and Murray, Gordon C. (2000). The international market entry choices of start-up companies in high-technology industries. *Journal of International Marketing*, **8**(2): 33–62.

Cavusgil, Tamer S. and Naor, Jacob (1987). Firm and management characteristics as discriminators of export marketing activity. *Journal of Business Research*, **15**: 221–35.

Chetty, Sylvie and Campbell-Hunt, Colin (2003). The internationalization process of regional, global and born global firms. Presented at the EMAC Conference.

Das, Mallika (1994). Successful and unsuccessful exporters from developing countries: Some preliminary findings. *European Journal of Marketing*, **28**(12): 19–32.

Dichtl, Erwin, Koeglmayr, Hans-Georg and Mueller, Stefan (1990). International orientation as a precondition for export success. *Journal of International Business Studies*, **21**(1): 23–40.

Dyke, Lorraine, Fischer, Eileen M. and Reuber, Rebecca A. (1992). An inter-industry examination of the impact of owner experience on firm performance. *Journal of Small Business Management*, **30**(4): 72–87.

Eisenhardt, Kathleen M. and Bird Schoonhoven, Claudia (1990). Organizational growth: Linking founding team, strategy, environment and growth among US semiconductor ventures, 1978–1988. *Administrative Science Quarterly*, **35**(3): 504–29.

Erramilli, Krishna M. (1991). The experience factor in foreign market entry behavior of service firms. *Journal of International Business Studies*, **22**(3): 479–501.

Fischer, Eileen and Reuber, Rebecca A. (2003). Targeting export support to SMEs: Owners' international experience as a segmentation basis. *Small Business Economics*, **20**(1): 69–82.

Gove, P. (ed.) (1981). *Webster's Third New International Dictionary of the English Language*. Springfield, MA: Merriam-Webster Inc.

Gurau, Calin and Ranchhod, Ashok (2003). Managing the international expansion of UK biopharmaceutical SMEs. Paper presented in the 3rd EURAM Annual Conference, in Milan, Italy, 3–5 April.

Halinen-Kaila, Aino and Salmi, Asta (2001). The role of personal contacts in the development of business relationships. Paper presented in the 30th EMAC Conference, Bergen.

Harveston, Paula D., Kedia, Ben L. and Davis, Peter S. (2000). Internationalization of born global and gradual globalizing firms: The impact of the manager. Advances in Competitiveness Research, **8**(1): 92–9.

Johanson, Jan and Vahlne, Jan-Erik (1977). The internationalization process of the firm: A mode of knowledge development and increasing foreign market commitments. *Journal of International Business Studies*, **8**(1): 23–32.

Johanson, Jan and Wiedersheim-Paul, Finn (1975). The internationalization of the firm: Four Swedish cases. *Journal of Management Studies*, October: 305–22.

Knight, Gary A. (1997). *Emerging Paradigm for International Marketing: The Born Global Firm*. Doctoral dissertation, Michigan State University, East Lansing, MI: UMI Dissertation Services, A Bell & Howell Company.

Knight, John, Bell, Jim and McNaughton, Rod (2001). 'Born globals': Old wine in new bottles? Presented at the ANZMAC Conference in Auckland, New Zealand.

Kunda, Sumit K. and A. Katz, Jerome (2003). Born-international SMEs: BI-level impacts of resources and intentions. *Small Business Economics*, **20**(1): 25–47.

Kutschker, Michael, Bäurle, Iris and Schmid, Stefan (1997). International evolution, international episodes, and international epochs: Implications for managing internationalization. *Management International Review*, **37**(2): 101–24.

Lindqvist, Maria (1991). *Infant Multinationals. The Internationalization of Young, Technology-Based Swedish Firms*. Doctoral dissertation. Stockholm: Institute of International Business (IBB), Stockholm School of Economics.

Luostarinen, Reijo and Gabrielsson, Mika (2002). Globalization and global marketing strategies of born globals in SMOPECs. Presented at the 28th EIBA Conference in Athens.

Madsen, Tage Koed and Servais, Per (1997). The internationalization of born globals: An evolutionary process? *International Business Review*, **6**(6): 561–83.

McDougall, Patricia P., Shane, Scott and Oviatt, Benjamin M. (1994). Explaining the formation of international new ventures: The limits of theories from international business research. *Journal of Business Venturing*, **9**: 469–87.

McKinsey & Company (1999). *Starting Up – Achieving Success with Professional Business Planning*. McKinsey & Company.

Moen, Oystein (2002). The born globals: A new generation of small European exporters. *International Marketing Review*, **19**(2): 156–175.

Nummela, Niina, Saarenketo, Sami and Puumalainen, Kaisu (2002). Global mindset: A prerequisite for successful internationalization? Presented at the 5th McGill Conference on International Entrepreneurship in Montreal, Canada.

Obben, James and Magagula, Phumzile (2003). Firm and managerial determinants of the export propensity of small and medium-sized enterprises in Swaziland. *International Small Business Journal*, **21**(1): 73–91.

Oviatt, Benjamin M. and McDougall, Patricia P. (1994). Toward a theory of international new ventures. *Journal of International Business Studies*, **25**(1): 45–64.

Oviatt, Benjamin M. and McDougall, Patricia P. (1995). Global start-ups: Entrepreneurs on a worldwide stage. *Academy of Management Journal*, **9**(2): 30–43.

Oviatt, Benjamin M. and McDougall, Patricia P. (1997). Challenges for internationalization process theory: The case of international new ventures *Management International Review*, **37**(2): 85–99.

Rasmussen, E.S., Madsen, T.K. and Evangelista, F. (2001). The founding of the born global company in Denmark and Australia: Sensemaking and networking. *Asia Pacific Journal of Marketing and Logistics*, **13**: 75–107.

Reid, Stan D. (1981). The decision-maker and export entry and expansion. *Journal of International Business Studies*, **12**(2): 101–11.

Rennie, Michael W. (1993). Global competitiveness: Born global. *McKinsey Quarterly*, **4**: 45–52.

Reuber, Rebecca (1997). Management experience and management expertise. *Decision Support Systems*, **21**: 51–60.

Reuber, Rebecca A., Dyke, Lorraine S. and Fischer, Eileen M. (1990). Experientially acquired knowledge and entrepreneurial venture success. *Academy of Management Best Paper Proceedings*, pp. 69–73.

Reuber, Rebecca A. and Fischer, Eileen M. (1994). Entrepreneurs' experience, expertise, and the performance of technology-based firms. *IEEE Transactions on Engineering Management*, **41**(4): 365–74.

Reuber, Rebecca A. and Fischer, Eileen (1997). The influence of the management team's international experience on the internationalization behaviors of SMEs. *Journal of International Business Studies*, **28**(4): 807–25.

Reuber, Rebecca A. and Fischer, Eileen (1999). Understanding the consequences of founder's experience. *Journal of Small Business Management*, **37**(2): 30–45.

Riddle, Liesl A. and Gillespie, Kate (2003). Information sources for new ventures in the Turkish clothing export industry. *Small Business Economics*, **20**: 105–20.

Scott, M. and Bruce, R. (1987). Five stages of growth in small business, *Long Range Planning*, **20**(3): 45–52.

Shrader, Rodney C., Oviatt, Benjamin M. and McDougall, Patricia P. (2000). How new ventures exploit trade-offs among international risk factors: Lessons for the accelerated internationalization of the 21st century. *Academy of Management Journal*, **43**(6): 1227–47.

Siegel, Robin, Siegel, Eric and MacMillan, Ian C. (1993). Characteristics distinguishing high-growth ventures. *Journal of Business Venturing*, **8**: 169–80.

Wickramasekera, R. and Bamberry, G. (2001). Born globals within the Australian wine industry: An exploratory study. CSU – Faculty of Commerce, Working Paper No. 1/01.

Zahra, Shaker A., Ireland, R. Duane and Hitt, Michael A. (2000). International expansion by new venture firms: International diversity, mode of market entry, technological learning, and performance. *Academy of Management Journal*, **43**(5): 925–50.

Index

absorptive capacity thesis 106–7
Acs, Z.J. 69, 71, 96
Adams, B. 187
Adizes, I. 12, 13, 14
Ahl, H. 156
Alänge, S. 94
Aldrich, H. 12, 37, 51, 70, 73, 138, 152
Allison, P.D. 62
Almeida, P. 69
Alsos, G.A. 36, 37
Alvesson, M. 187, 194, 195
Ancona, D.G. 18
Anderson, J.C. 50, 52
Angel, D. 121
angels, *see* business angels
Aram, J.D. 202, 203, 208
Armstrong, J.S. 207
asymmetric knowledge 180, 181, 190
Athanassiou, N. 254
Audretsch, D. 63, 70, 73, 78, 85, 86, 90, 106
Avdeitchikova, S. 198

Bamberry, G. 220, 226, 229
Baptista, R. 103
Barnett, W.P. 73
Barney, J.B. 59
Barth, H. 10
Baum, J.A. 88
Baum, J.R. 10
Baumol, W.J. 69, 72, 95, 97, 156
Bayona, C. 104, 105, 107, 108, 109, 110, 123, 129
Becattini, G. 126
Beesley, M. 108, 126
Benavides-Velasco, C. 103, 110, 127
Bengtsson, M. 110
Berger, P.L. 158
Berte Qvarn 26, 28
Besam 28
Bianchi, G. 126
Birch, D.L. 85
Birley, S. 38, 50, 51, 52, 57, 144
Bloodgood, J.M. 227, 229, 235
Blorn, Peter 26
Borgatti, S.P. 52
Bottazzi, G. 73, 78
Bougrain, F. 103
Bourdieu, P. 53
Bozeman, B. 191
Brass, D. 58
Brettel, M. 201
Brogren, J.W. 186
Brooks, F.B. 186
Brown, J.S. 145, 183
Bruce, R. 12, 235
Brüderl, J. 88
Brunåker, S. 173
Brusco, S. 126, 156
Brush, C.G. 37
Bullock, A. 112
Burgel, O. 223, 228, 229
Burt, R.S. 51, 58, 59, 64, 183
Busenitz, L.W. 138
business angels 198–200, 214–16
- empirical results 208–14
  - Swedish market 208–9
  - test of hypotheses 210–14
- first-generation studies 200–201
- hypothesis development 202–5
- methodology of study 205–8
  - identification of early and late stage investors 207–8
  - sample 205–6
  - strengths and weaknesses of study 208
  - survey process 206–7
- second-generation studies 201–2

Bygrave, W.D. 138
Byrk, A.S. 62

Caldwell, D.F. 18
Camagni, R. 126
Cameron, K.S. 12, 13, 30

Campbell-Hunt, C. 227
Canada, internationalization of new ventures in 225
capital
  human capital 108
  investment, *see* business angels
  social, *see* social capital
Carlsson, B. 69
Carroll, G.R. 72, 73, 78, 79
Carter, S. 36, 37, 48
Casson, M. 86
Caves, R.E. 72, 73, 88, 91, 95
Cavusgil, T.S. 225, 229
Chaganti, R. 37
Chandler, G.N. 14, 15, 17
Chetty, S. 227
Chia, R. 156
Christensen, S. 184, 194
Churchill, N.C. 12, 13, 14, 30, 57
Cilliers, P. 140
Coase, R.H. 52
Cohen, W.M. 55, 106, 108, 111
Coleman, James S. 53, 59
collaborative relationships 50–51, 63–4
  hypotheses on 54–6
    test and results 60–63
  implication of study 64–5
  innovation and 103–5, 129–31
    characteristics of cooperative innovators 105–11
    data for study 112–14
    descriptive analysis 114–21
    multivariate analysis 121–9
  method of study 56–60
    analysis 59–60
    measures 57–9
    sample and data 56–7
  theoretical background 51–4
Collins, H.M. 182
communities of practice, entrepreneurship and 144–7, 153
complexity science, entrepreneurship and 136, 137, 140, 151–3
  communities of practice 144–7, 153
  emergence 138–9, 142–7, 152
  EROS model 136, 143–4, 146, 149, 153
  Flight Directors Ltd case 142–4
  HotAir case 147–51
  multilevel models 138–9, 141–2
  order creation 140–41
  socially constructed entrepreneurship 139–40, 144–7, 156
configuration models of firm growth 14–16
constructionism, *see* social construction
Cooke, P. 103
Cooper, A.C. 37, 52
corridor principle 39
Cosh, A. 112
Coveney, P. 198, 200
Covin, J.G. 50, 57
creative destruction 137, 140, 157
crime, entrepreneurship and 157
crisis management 184
customers
  innovation and 127
  relationships with, *see* collaborative relationships
Czarniawska, B. 159, 175–6
Czarniawska-Joerges, B. 157

Dahlqvist, J. 86
Dahlström, Jonnie 160, 162–4, 168–9, 170, 172, 173, 174
Dal Cin, P. 202
Daloc 20, 22
Das, M. 224, 229
Davenport, T.H. 188
Davidsson, P. 79, 91, 93, 97, 138, 139
de la Mothe, J. 106
debriefing of knowledge for action 181–3
Deeds, D.L. 54
Delmar, F. 70, 75, 78, 79, 85, 91, 97
Demsetz, H. 103
Dichtl, E. 224
Diez, J.D. 123
DiMaggio, P. 158, 176
DiPrete, T.A. 138
Dodgson, M. 106, 107
Dollinger, M.J. 52
Drazin, R. 15, 30
Drucker, P. 158
Druilhe, C. 141
Duguid, P. 145, 183
Dunkleberg, W.C. 37
Dunne, P. 78, 79

Dunne, T. 73
Dupuy, R. 85
Dyer, J.H. 50, 55, 63, 65
Dyke, L. 225, 229

economic growth 69
endogenous growth theory 70–71, 94
neoclassical growth theory 70–71
Eisenhardt, K.M. 13, 56, 59, 106, 229
Eliasson, G. 69
embedded relationships 53
emergence 138–9, 142–7, 152
communities of practice 144–7, 153
endogenous growth theory 70–71, 94
entrepreneurship 35–7, 136–7
complexity science and 136, 137, 140, 151–3
communities of practice 144–7, 153
emergence 138–9, 142–7, 152
EROS model 136, 143–4, 146, 149, 153
Flight Directors Ltd case 142–4
HotAir case 147–51
multilevel models 138–9, 141–2
order creation 140–41
socially constructed entrepreneurship 139–40, 144–7, 156
discussion 46–8
extreme, *see* extreme entrepreneurs
internationalization of new ventures and 221, 224–5, 226–8, 239–50
investment, *see* business angels
literature review 37–9
method of study 39–41
results of study 42–6
Swedish science and technology labour force 69–70, 93–8
industrial organization and firm behaviour 72–3
method of study 74–9
new knowledge and entrepreneurship 70–72
practical implications 96–7
results of study 79–93
theoretical implications 94–6
theory 70–74
entry barriers 73
Erlandsson, Bengt 159, 160–62, 168, 169, 170, 172, 173, 174
EROS model 136, 143–4, 146, 149, 153
Erramilli, K.M. 220
extreme entrepreneurs
as challenger of institutions 168–70
emerging themes 170–75
constructing a glocal identity 173
entrepreneurship as way of life 174–5
keeping family out 173–4
playing games with institutions 172
sharing experiences with the public 171–2
treating words as deeds 171
entrepreneurs as outsiders and challengers in society 156–9
examples 159–68
Bengt Erlandsson 159, 160–62, 168, 169, 170, 172, 173, 174
Jonnie Dahlström 160, 162–4, 168–9, 170, 172, 173, 174
Lars Vilks 160, 166–8, 169, 170, 172, 173, 174–5
Sten Rentzhog 160, 164–6, 168, 169, 170, 172, 173, 174
theory and practice 175–7

Feldman, M. 63
Fichman, M. 88
Fidell, L. 121
financial constraints, innovation and 108, 109
Fineman, S. 177
Finland, internationalization of new ventures
case study 236–9
international experience and internationalization decision 247–50
international experience and speed of internationalization 239–47
survey 233–6
Fiol, M. 37
firm behaviour, industrial organization and 72–3
firm growth 10–11
configuration models 14–16
empirical study of Gröna Kvisten prize winners 16–28
'circulators' 24–6

discussion 28–31
identified patterns of growth 18–19
implications 31–2
method of study 18
'recession bloomers' 26–8
recessionists 28
'steady growers' 20–22
'steady un-growers' 22–4
life-cycle models 12–14, 17, 30
stage models 12–14, 17, 30
Swedish science and technology labour force and 69–70, 93–8
industrial organization and firm behaviour 72–3
method of study 74–9
new knowledge and entrepreneurship 70–72
practical implications 96–7
results of study 79–93
theoretical implications 94–6
theory 70–74
Fischer, E. 138, 221, 225, 229, 232, 235, 254
Flight Directors Ltd 142–4
Florida, R. 103
Folta, T.B. 95
Ford, D. 50, 52
Forristal, J.D. 138
Freear, J. 198, 204
Freel, M. 104, 106, 108, 114, 119, 127, 129
Freeman, M.T. 72
Friesen, P.H. 12, 15, 17
Fritsch, M. 103, 104, 105, 107, 109, 111, 123
Fuller, T. 137, 138, 141, 142, 152

Gabrielsson, M. 223
Galbraith, J. 12
Garnsey, E. 12, 24, 141
Gartner, W.B. 138, 156, 157, 171
Garud, R. 189
Gaston, R.J. 198, 201
Geroski, P.A. 72, 73, 83, 85, 88, 90, 91, 103
Ghoshal, S. 54, 55, 58, 59, 63, 64
Giddens, A. 142, 171
Gillespie, K. 254
Gilmore, J.H. 172
global markets
cooperation and 110
see also internationalization of new ventures
Goss, D. 177
Gourlay, S.N. 189
Gove, P. 223
Graddy, E. 79
Granovetter, M.S. 51, 52, 53
Granstrand, O. 94
Greiner, L.E. 12, 13, 14, 30
Gröna Kvisten prize, empirical study of winning firms 16–28
'circulators' 24–6
discussion 28–31
identified patterns of growth 18–19
implications 31–2
method of study 18
'recession bloomers' 26–8
recessionists 28
'steady growers' 20–22
'steady un-growers' 22–4
growth
economic, *see* economic growth
firms, *see* firm growth
Gulati, R. 50, 51, 53
Gurau, C. 228, 229, 236

Hagedoorn, J. 103, 111
Hair, J.F. 18
Håkansson, H. 50, 52, 103
Halinen-Kaila, A. 254
Hampden-Turner, C. 184
Hanks, S.H. 13, 15
Hannan, M.T. 72, 73, 78, 79
Hansen, M.H. 59
Harrison, R. 198, 199, 200, 201, 202, 203, 204, 205, 206, 208, 214, 215
Harveston, P.D. 226, 229, 236
Harvey, D.L. 139
Haudeville, B. 103
Haugaard, M. 192
Hay, M. 198, 203, 204
Hayek, F.A. 69, 71
Henrekson, M. 94, 96
Hindle, K. 200, 201
Hipp, C. 120
Hirschman, A.O. 158
Hitchens, D.M.W.N. 13, 14

Hjorth, D. 156
Hoffman, K. 126, 129
Holland, J.H. 138
Hommen, L. 120
HotAir 147–51
Huggins, R. 105
Hughes, A. 78, 79, 112
human capital, innovation and 108

Iacobucci, D. 48
India, internationalization of new ventures in 224
industrial organization 94, 95
  firm behaviour and 72–3
industrial policy 103
information, *see* knowledge and information
information technology firms
  knowledge workers, motivation and control 193–4
  knowledge workers in 180, 194–5
    debriefing of knowledge for action 181–3
    knowledge-intensive firms and 187–9
    leadership and project management of 190–93
    project management in time dilemmas 184–6
    technological conditions for leadership 186–7
innovation 94–5, 103
  cooperation and 103–5, 129–31
    characteristics of cooperative innovators 105–11
    data for study 112–14
    descriptive analysis 114–21
    multivariate analysis 121–9
  see also entrepreneurship
institutional theory, entrepreneurship and 157–8
intellectual entrepreneurs 158
internationalization of new ventures 220–22, 250–55
  future research 253–5
  key concepts 222–3
  literature review and hypotheses 223–33
    international experience and INVs 226–8
    international experience and SME internationalization 224–5
    research gap and hypotheses development 228–33
  methodology of study 233–9
    case study 236–9
    survey 233–6
  results of study 239–50
    international experience and internationalization decision 247–50
    international experience and speed of internationalization 239–47
investment, *see* business angels
Italy, study of collaborative relationships 56–60

Jacobs, J. 53
Jacobsson, S. 97
Jagger, N. 120
Jarillo, J.C. 36, 51
Jenkins, R. 173
Jensen, S.S. 181, 186, 187
Johannisson, B. 36, 37, 157, 158, 159, 170
Johanson, J. 221
Johansson, Inga-Lisa 20, 22, 31
Jonsson, Kjell 22
Jovanovic, B. 73, 95

Katz, J. 226, 229
Kauffman, S. 151
Kaufmann, A. 119
Kazanjian, R.K. 12, 15, 30
Keeble, D. 32
Kelly, P. 198, 203, 204
Kidder, T. 184
Kirat, T. 114
Kirzner, I.M. 71
Kleinknecht, A. 105, 106, 107, 110, 111, 114, 120, 121, 123, 129
Klepper, S. 79
Knight, J. 223, 226, 227, 236, 255
knowledge and information 95
  asymmetric 180, 181, 190
  collaborative relationships and 50
    hypotheses on 54, 55–6, 60–63
    implication of study 64–5

method of study 56–60
theoretical background 51–4
economic growth and 71
entrepreneurship and 38–9, 69, 70–72
see also innovation
knowledge workers 180, 194–5
debriefing of knowledge for action 181–3
knowledge-intensive firms and 187–9
leadership and project management of 190–93
motivation and control 193–4
project management in time dilemmas 184–6
technological conditions for leadership 186–7
Kogut, B. 54, 69, 189
Kolvereid, L. 36
Koschatzky, K. 107, 110, 111, 123, 129
Kostera, M. 175
Krackhardt, D. 58
Kreiner, K. 184
Kriss 24
Krugman, P. 103
Kunda, S.K. 226, 229
Kutschker, M. 222

Landström, H. 36, 37, 198, 199, 200, 201, 202, 205, 206, 207, 208, 209
Lane, P.J. 54, 55, 59
large firms, innovation and 111
Larson, A. 50, 55, 59
Larsson, A. 20
Latour, B. 189
Lave, J. 145
Le Bars, A. 111
Lee, L. 200, 201
Levinson, D. 13
Levinthal, D.A. 55, 88, 107, 108
Lewis, J. 141
Lewis, V.L. 12, 13, 14, 30
Lichtenstein, B.M.B. 137, 138
life-cycle models of growth 12–14, 17, 30
Lin, N. 51, 52, 54
Lindholm Dahlstrand, A. 97
Lindqvist, M. 227, 229
Love, J. 104, 105, 107
Low, M.B. 138
Lubatkin, M. 54, 55, 59
Luckmann, T. 158
Lukas, R. 103, 104, 105, 107, 109, 111, 123
Lumme, A. 198, 199, 200, 201
Lundvall, B.-Å. 103, 106, 109
Lung, Y. 114
Luostarinen, R. 223

MacDonald, M. 199, 202, 203
McDougall, P. 50, 220, 221, 222, 226, 229, 255
McEvily, B. 55, 64
McGrath, R.G. 38, 98
Machado, J.A. 73
McKelvey, B. 137, 140, 151
McKelvie, A. 14, 15, 17
McMahon, R.G.P. 13, 15
MacMillan, I.C. 35, 38, 52, 138
MacPherson, A. 104, 128
Madsen, T.K. 253
Magagula, P. 225
Mahmood, T. 70, 73, 78
Maillat, D. 103
Malmberg, A. 63, 129
management
crisis management 184
innovation and 108
internationalization of new ventures and 221, 224–5, 226–8, 239–50
project management
knowledge workers 190–93
time dilemmas 184–6
technological conditions for leadership 186–7
Martinez, M.A. 138, 152
Maskell, P. 63, 129
Maslow, A.M. 175
Mason, C. 198, 199, 200, 201, 202, 203, 204, 205, 206, 208, 214, 215
Mata, J.M. 73
Meeus, M. 107, 110, 123
Melin, L. 14
Miller, A. 198, 202
Miller, D. 12, 15, 17, 18, 141
Miner, J.B. 14
Miotti, L. 105, 109, 111, 123, 129
Moen, O. 223
Mønsted, M. 181, 183, 187, 191, 194
Moore, C.F. 138

Moore, K. 198, 200
Moran, P. 64, 137, 138
Morgan, K. 103
motivation, knowledge workers 193–4
Murray, G.C. 223, 228, 229

Nahapiet, J. 54, 55, 58, 63
Nählinder, J. 120
Naor, J. 225, 229
Nelson, R. 94
neoclassical growth theory 70–71
network approach 51–2, 53
  innovation and 103, 109, 110
Neumair, U. 13
New Zealand, internationalization of new ventures in 227
Newell, S. 188, 189, 190, 191
Nicolaou, N. 144
Nigh, D. 254
Nobeoka, K. 65
Nonaka, I. 53, 183
Nooteboom, B. 58, 59, 114
Normann, R. 181, 187
North, D. 129, 156
Norway, entrepreneurship study 39–40
  discussion 46–8
  measures 40–41
  results 42–6
Nummela, N. 255
Nunnally, J.C. 60

Oakey, R. 121
Obben, J. 225
O'Brien, J.P. 95
Oerlemans, L. 104, 107, 110, 114, 123
O'Farrell, P.N. 13, 14
order creation, entrepreneurship 140–41
Oughton, C. 103
Overton, T.S. 207
Oviatt, B.M. 221, 222, 226, 229, 255

Paquet, G. 106
partnerships, *see* collaborative relationships
Patel, P. 105
Pavitt, K. 105
Peak Performance 24, 26
Penrose, Edith T. 10, 14, 31, 54, 108
Perryman, S. 120
Pettersson, K. 156
Picot, G. 85
Pine, B.J. 172
Polarrenen 22
Politis, D. 209
Poole, M.S. 12, 30
Portugal, P. 73
Powell, W. 158, 176
project management
  leadership and project management of knowledge workers 190–93
  time dilemmas 184–6
Prusak, L. 188
public sector, cooperation in innovation and 128–9

Quinn, R.E. 12, 13, 30
Quintana-García, C. 103, 110, 127

Rabellotti, R. 126
Ramachandran, K. 52
Ramnarayan, S. 52
Ranchhod, A. 228, 229, 236
Rasmussen, E.S. 236
Raudenbush, S.W. 62
Reed, M. 139
Rehn, A. 157
Reid, S.D. 221
Reijnen, J. 105, 106, 107, 110, 111, 114, 120, 121, 123, 129
Reitan, B. 200, 201
Rennie, M.W. 255
Rentzhog, Sten 160, 164–6, 168, 169, 170, 172, 173, 174
research and development (R&D), cooperation and 105–7, 120, 127, 130
Reuber, R. 221, 223, 225, 229, 232, 235, 254
Reynolds, P.D. 73, 198
Riddle, L.A. 254
Riding, A. 200, 202
Ring, P.S. 55
Romer, P.M. 71
Ronstadt, R. 38, 39
Roper, S. 104, 106, 107
Rosa, P. 37, 47, 48

Rosenberg, A. 151
Rosenberg, N. 94, 96
Rothwell, R. 104, 106, 107, 108, 121, 126

Sachwald, F. 105, 109, 111, 123, 129
Sako, M. 109, 128
Salmi, A. 254
Sandemose, Aksel 169
Santarelli, E. 106
Saxon, John 147–51
Sayer, A. 140
Schoonhoven, C.B. 13, 56, 59, 106, 229
Schumpeter, J.A. 71, 136, 137, 156, 157, 158, 173
Schussler, R. 88
science and technology labour force (STLF) 69–70, 93–8
  innovation and 107–8, 129
  method of study 74–9
    data sources 74
    descriptor variables 78–9
    population 74–8
  practical implications 96–7
  results of study 79–93
    entry and exit from STLF firm population 83–8
    growth of *de novo* entries 91–3
    population of firms owned by STLF entrepreneurs 79–83
    survival of *de novo* entries 88–91
  theoretical implications 94–6
  theory 70–74
    industrial organization and firm behaviour 72–3
    new knowledge and entrepreneurship 70–72
Scott, M. 12, 37, 47, 235
Scott, W.R. 157, 158, 176
Servais, P. 253
Shane, S. 72, 86
Shrader, R.C. 223, 228, 235
Siegel, R. 223, 252
Simmie, J. 103
Singh, H. 50, 55, 63
Singh, R.P. 38
skills, innovation and 108
Slevin, D.P. 50, 57
Smith, N.R. 14
social capital 50–51, 52, 53–4, 64–5, 191
  hypotheses on 54–5
  measurement 58–9
social construction, entrepreneurship 139–40, 144–7, 156
Söderhjelm, T. 20
Sölvell, Ö. 110
Sorensen, O. 73
Sørheim, R. 198, 200, 201, 205, 208
specialization 103
Spender, J.C. 54
Spinosa, C. 156, 170
Stacey, R.D. 182, 183, 188
stage models of growth 12–14, 17, 30
standardization 128
Star, S.L. 182
Starr, J.E. 52
Staudt, H. 193
Sterlacchini, A. 105, 106
Sternberg, R. 104, 107, 110, 111, 123, 129
Stevenson, H.H. 36
Storey, D.J. 73, 79, 91, 198
Stubbart, C. 14
Sullivan, M.K. 198, 202
suppliers, relationships with, *see* collaborative relationships
Swan, J. 189, 190
Swann, G.M.P. 109, 126
Swann, P. 103
Sweden
  business angels in 208–9
  empirical study of Gröna Kvisten prize winners 16–28
    'circulators' 24–6
    discussion 28–31
    identified patterns of growth 18–19
    implications 31–2
    method of study 18
    'recession bloomers' 26–8
    recessionists 28
    'steady growers' 20–22
    'steady un-growers' 22–4
  extreme entrepreneurs in 159–68
  internationalization of new ventures in 227